WITHDRAWN

DATE DUE

DEC 1 0 1998			
GAYLORD			PRINTED IN U.S.A.

NO-FAULT POLITICS:

Modern Presidents, the Press, and Reformers

Eugene McCarthy

Edited and with an Introduction by
Keith C. Burris

TIMES BOOKS

RANDOM HOUSE

Library of Congress Cataloging-in-Publication Data

McCarthy, Eugene J.
No-fault politics: modern presidents, the press, and reformers / by Eugene McCarthy; edited and with an introduction by Keith C. Burris — 1st ed.
    p.   cm.
Includes index.
ISBN 0-8129-3016-9 (acid-free paper)
1. United States—Politics and government—1993–   I. Burris, Keith C.   II. Title.
E885.M39   1998
320.973'09'045—dc21   97-37297
                                                                    CIP

Random House website address: www.randomhouse.com
Printed in the United States of America on acid-free paper
9 8 7 6 5 4 3 2

First Edition

Book design by Interrobang Design Studio

For Mary McCarthy, my daughter who played a central role in my 1968 campaign for the presidency, and Jerome Eller, my longtime Senate and campaign aid, in memoriam

Acknowledgments

The author would like to gratefully acknowledge the assistance and dedication of Kathryn Dowling.

The editor wishes to gratefully acknowledge the patience and assistance of Kathy Tofflemire, Sam Vaughan, and Amy McConnell Burris, who helped bring this book to fruition.

Contents

Introduction

By Keith C. Burris

*Politics is like football. You have to be smart enough
to understand the game but not smart enough to lose interest.*
—E. McC.

*I*t might surprise both his friends and his enemies to know that
Eugene J. McCarthy began his public life as Democratic Party
chairman of Ramsey County, St. Paul, Minnesota. One does
not think of McCarthy as a party animal.

That was in the spring of 1948. Later that year he became a candidate for the U.S. House of Representatives. McCarthy ran with Harry
Truman in the hopeless campaign of '48. The president was not supposed to have even gotten close to challenger Thomas E. Dewey, of
course. Tom Dewey had been anointed; Truman was "a loser." But
Truman won. And McCarthy won too.

McCarthy has been what his friend the poet Robert Lowell called a
"lost cause man" ever since.

Sometimes the lost causes panned out. Truman and a Democratic
Party that then stood for civil rights, national health insurance, and rebuilding Europe were such causes. So was the antiwar movement of
1968.

McCarthy was elected to the House five times. In 1952 his opponent campaigned against him by calling him a communist. Gene
McCarthy responded by debating Joe McCarthy on national radio.

McCarthy was elected to the Senate in 1958, again winning primary and general election races that were supposed to be near impossible. He was re-elected to the Senate in 1964 by a record plurality.

In 1968 he took the matter of the Vietnam War from the Senate to the streets, and after that the political professionals never let McCarthy back into the club—even as an outsider within the club (Republican Richard Nixon is the only president who ever offered him a cabinet post). But McCarthy never really was of Washington. He came from a very different tradition than, say, the Kennedy brothers. He was what is today referred to as a "conviction politician." And his convictions ran deep, in part because they were not simply his.

McCarthy's worldview is rooted in Catholicism—in Thomism, personalism, the Rule of St. Benedict, and Catholic literature. It is the product not of an ideology of the day or decade but of the Christian interpretation of history. McCarthy sees almost everything in historical terms. And his Christian view combines skepticism about human nature and the uses of power with a desire for justice. History is mostly a tale of folly, but it is also the story of man's continuing attempt to civilize himself. So history is tragic and ironic, but it is sometimes enlightened by the exceptional acts of heroic and noble persons, such as Thomas More, a conviction politician whose heroism and stoicism McCarthy admired.

McCarthy's concept of the political life (so foreign to us in a time when Bill Clinton and Newt Gingrich are as deep thinking as most politicians get) made his politics seem more quirky—quixotic was often the word applied—than it really was. In McCarthy's world, a vocation is not just what you do but who you are. As one friend said of him, "He lives his values."

II

In 1948 Gene McCarthy was a young sociology professor at St. Thomas College in St. Paul. He was a product of another Catholic college. At St. John's in St. Cloud, Minnesota, he had been a novice Benedictine monk for a year. Next he had taught public school, worked for the Office of Strategic Services (OSS) during the war, and married Abigail Quigley, a young woman who wanted to write "Catholic" fiction, in the tradition of Graham Greene and J. F. Powers. Together, they had started a family on a small Minnesota farm. At the time of his election to the House, McCarthy was active in the Catholic Rural Life Movement.

McCarthy's 1948 platform was "full employment." The candidate spoke often about a papal encyclical on the dignity of work. And in the years since, McCarthy has continued to make full employment the centerpiece of his economic plank and what he hoped would be the Democratic Party's.

Eventually, the professor became a pol—a savvy one. In both the House and Senate, McCarthy was known as a pragmatic idealist and as a hard man when crossed. Lyndon Johnson told Russell Baker, when the former was running the Senate and the latter was covering it for *The New York Times,* that he dared not deny McCarthy a commit-tee assignment he had asked for. "McCarthy is tough," LBJ suppos-edly said. "He'll cut my heart out." But even then he was Mr. Outside on the Inside.

McCarthy was always both poet and politician, with the pol domi-nant for most of his public life and the poet stronger in the years since 1968.

From the start, McCarthy was also both rebel and traditionalist. He was the kind of young congressman who organized fellow liberal firebrands in the 1950s House. The group was called McCarthy's Mavericks, and it issued a document called "McCarthy's Manifesto," which became the basis of LBJ's 1964 landmark civil rights legislation. The group itself eventually became the Democratic Study Group, the progressive arm of Democrats in the House to this day.

Yet McCarthy, ironically, was also a personal favorite of some of the Old Guard in the House, especially of Speaker Sam Rayburn, to whom McCarthy dedicated one of his early books. McCarthy wanted a progressive Democratic Party, but he respected the traditions and folkways of Washington, and even as a young congressman, he had a sense of the limits of reform. He knew that the tendency of modern politics, especially modern liberal politics, was to overreach. In his early House speeches, McCarthy lacked the usual penchant for overstatement. He tended to put his proposals in modest, relative, even negative terms. McCarthy's liberalism, or progressivism, was never of the standard issue. As *The New York Times*'s E. W. Kenworthy, McCarthy's Boswell in the campaign of 1968, wrote: "There runs through the senator's speeches a sense of history and continuity. And this is because he is basically a conservative, though his legislative record is liberal."

This book demonstrates that basic conservatism—McCarthy's sense of history and continuity, his respect for learning and tradition, his sense of the necessary limits of politics, and the irrationality, often absurdity, of politics. This is *not* the same as thinking politics beneath one or unworthy of one's talents. McCarthy loves politics and has given his life to it. But he has seen it as a humble craft, not the master science. And, like the Founders, he was wary of power and the uses of power.

Now in his ninth decade of life, McCarthy remains a rebel and something of an apostate within the Democratic Party: a Catholic committed to social justice but a skeptic about reform, about do-gooders, about the power of the state and the competence of government, and about the liberal reliance upon material cures for social problems. One might call him the first neoliberal, in that his liberalism was never rooted in materialism or statism. But he really is something more complicated: a liberal Catholic and a conservative human being.

McCarthy's liberalism, as Kenworthy noted, is humane and pragmatic. His view of human nature and the uses of power is deeply conservative. He is a man of limits: the limited potential of government, the limited possibilities of the craft of politics (though honorable and important), and the limits of the state's capacity for social engineering and political reform.

It is the conservative McCarthy whom we mostly find in these pages, for this is a book about the political process—the rules of the game—and the subculture it entails. McCarthy applauds the political will to seek the good but warns of the folly of seeking a political process that is all clean and well lighted.

This is a book about the craft of politics as practiced in the United States today and the near ruination of politics, as McCarthy sees it, by attempts to simplify and purify it.

III

McCarthy's instinctive conservatism, deepened with age and experience, is based on the notion that tradition is a more reliable guide than progress. Tradition tells us what is a tolerable degree of injustice (or justice), evil (or good). Schemes to improve mankind usually backfire because reformers usually wind up shooting the rest of us in the foot.

McCarthy's sense of limits derives from the poet's eye for flaws and foibles, his twenty-two years in Congress, and his long experience in national politics, dating back to Hubert Humphrey's pursuit of a vice presidential nomination in 1956.

Man's thirst for "enough justice" (Reinhold Niebuhr's phrase) makes positive government necessary. But his capacity for wisdom, and therefore successful reform, is limited. Man's tendency toward injustice should make us skeptical of all reform—but especially reform of the political process itself.

McCarthy thinks government has lost its commitment to justice *and* its capacity to limit itself. Politicians have lost their capacity to be skeptical about how much they can accomplish while still trying to achieve a minimum of good-enough justice.

This is a nuanced and complex worldview, and thirty years of political experience only make it harder for McCarthy to boil himself down to a sound bite or to condense his views to the bumper-sticker attention span.

As a liberal Catholic and a conservative thinker, McCarthy is equally bound to distrust political power and conventional wisdom, to challenge the claims of secular authority, *and* to seek to limit economic power and the extent of economic maldistribution in America.

McCarthy's is a fundamentally religious outlook—one based on vocation, duty, the search for wisdom, and finally what he calls "the mystery and dignity of the individual person."

And maybe the religious temperament is the same thing as the poetic temperament, for the young monk was eventually to become the old poet.

•

Poetry is essential to McCarthy. Two of his poems seem to summarize his personal credo. In "Lament of an Aging Politician" he says: "I have left Act I, for involution/and Act II. There mired in/complexity/I cannot write Act III."

In "Courage at 60" he writes: "Now it is certain./There is no magic stone,/No secret to be found./One must go/With the mind's winnowed learning."

His poetic practicality has meant that McCarthy distrusted abstract solutions—ideology, heroes, royal families, quotas. He trusts the specific, the concrete, the personal. He is the most internally consistent of politicians but the least dogmatic of liberal leaders since Franklin Delano Roosevelt. (This is one reason why he was not the leader of liberal Democrats for long. By 1972 Democrats on the Left had moved to George McGovern.)

McCarthy is distrustful of "wars" on poverty, ignorance, or disease and of great crusades, schemes, and grand diagnoses. In fact he is so counterideological that his "big message" sometimes seems to be: Let's stop the foolishness. Or, failing that, let's laugh at it.

McCarthy speaks of postmodern politics and postmodern presidents. This is his terminology for the triumph of form over substance, of abstraction and ideology over experience, of negative ads over rhetoric and wit, and of plasticity over rootedness.

McCarthy does not believe in "problems" and "solutions" in government. He sees politics as the philosopher Michael Oakeshott does—as "an ocean voyage." Politics, as understood by McCarthy, is a discipline of mind and a learned tradition of conduct. It is not, for him, a means of social reconstruction or a way of getting more people more stuff. Sometimes the most important work of politics is stopping something: resistance to folly. Like Joe McCarthy. Like the Vietnam War. Like legal racism. Like what is, in Gene McCarthy's view, the increasing bureaucratization of American life and politics.

In this book McCarthy is critic, not advocate; commentator, not political leader. The skeptic is dominant. He considers what he calls the great foolishness of modern American politics—the failure of contemporary political reform.

IV

In 1968 Gene McCarthy led the way to driving LBJ from the White House and inspired the youth of America with the sort of hope and idealism that was supposed to have died with John Kennedy. McCarthy and Robert Kennedy fought each other for the Democratic presidential nomination, though they agreed on winding down the war in Vietnam. Then Robert Kennedy was killed. At the start of the Chicago convention in 1968, McCarthy led Richard Nixon by nine points in the polls. McCarthy might have beaten Nixon. But the Democrats nominated Hubert Humphrey, who trailed Nixon in the polls and never caught up.

The Democratic Party did not recover quickly from the thuggishness of the Chicago convention, and politically neither did McCarthy. The outsider was no longer working inside. McCarthy was further marginalized and too proud to beg forgiveness for a campaign he felt should have made all Democrats proud. He was mostly ignored by the national press and his party.

In 1972 and 1992 McCarthy's campaigns for the Democratic nomination never got off the ground.

In 1976 he waged an independent, antiparty campaign for president that initially showed some real grassroots support. But he was ten years ahead of John Anderson and twenty years ahead of Ross Perot. The press had trouble understanding the mechanics of an independent effort. Besides, in 1976 many voters were afraid of "wasting a vote" in what was projected to be, and was, a close race between

Jimmy Carter and Gerald Ford. Liberals, particularly, said that we could not afford to have Bob Dole "a heartbeat away" from the presidency.

So is McCarthy bitter? Sometimes. Mostly, he seems remarkably cheerful, resilient, and untouched by the crassness, duplicity, and mean spirit of Washington, where he still lives and works. He always kept a part of himself in reserve, his admirers and critics said. This reserve (call it poetic, the religious sense, or simple dignity) probably kept him sane.

His hatred of cant and pretension, his reliance upon reticence, his stoicism, and his distrust of cheap emotional postures and pat solutions have sometimes been mistaken for lack of passion. Actually, as the writer Wilfred Sheed once remarked of McCarthy, all of these traits are evidence of a deeply sensitive person who insists on behaving like a grown-up.

•

Two things are obviously true about McCarthy's political career. First, he has been consistently ahead of his time. He opposed red-baiting when many liberals ran for cover. He warned of potential abuses by the Central Intelligence Agency in the mid-1950s. He spotted the trend toward chronic unemployment in the early 1960s. He spoke out on the dangers of international arms merchants, often sponsored by the United States, in the mid-1960s. He saw the excessive costs of the automobile in the 1970s. He urged welfare reform in that same period. He spoke of the need for tax code simplification and restraining the IRS in the 1980s.

Second, this prescience has been *terrible* for his political fortunes. McCarthy not only has not been in office for twenty-five years, he has not been "in" for most of his political life.

Being prophetic and courageous is seldom a good career move in American politics. As McCarthy himself says, you can be forgiven for being wrong for too long in American politics, but not for being right too soon.

The exception was 1968, when his modesty and restraint were of enormous appeal to a wary nation. As Anatole France said of Zola, "He was a moment in the history of human conscience."

V

Gene McCarthy is a gregarious, warm, restless man; happy with people. He likes campaigns and campaigning and has stumped for scores of candidates since 1968—from Hugh Carey to Jerry Brown to Carol Moseley-Braun to Richard Lamm—as well as for himself. He works a room like an old-fashioned Irish pol. He shakes every hand at every airport baggage claim. He works over his speeches in the car and tests his lines on aides and friends—as if speeches or individual votes or friends and not handlers and political action committees were what mattered.

The McCarthy wit is an integral part of him—like his values, his skepticism, his sense of the possible. But McCarthy does not tell jokes. He muses and then amuses. The deadly serious notion is never far from the absolute put-on.

In a priceless moment in 1968, Johnny Carson asked McCarthy whether he would make a good president. McCarthy said he thought he would make an "adequate" one.

•

But it was not to be.

This unusual senator was not to become an unusual president. He finally returned, not entirely against his will, to the life of speaking and teaching and writing.

One of two things can happen to a man who has come so close to the brass ring on his own terms. He can be eaten alive with bitterness or he can become a sage. McCarthy has chosen wisdom and bemusement.

One by-product of McCarthy's "fate and fatalism" is a book like this one. His general topic is political folly. His specific target is political reform and what it has wrought. His eye surveys the goofiness of Congress, campaigns, and the media of today, and his wit is not short of targets. He never sticks too closely to the topic at hand, preferring to let his mind rove freely, which is McCarthy at his best.

McCarthy's tone is experienced, wry, detached, but not cynical or tired. His enemy is falseness and pretense. His faith is in reason and clear speech. His concern is his abiding one: the strength of our democratic institutions. His final grace note is laughter.

PART I
Against Reform

1

Triumph of the Innocent

"*T*here is no more frightening sound in the Universe," wrote the poet Robert Lowell, "than the harsh, high laughter of the innocent rejoicing over their victories." It's true, especially in politics.

Mark Twain singled out Benjamin Franklin as the first great American innocent. Twain said that Franklin had caused much needless distress, if not real harm, by afflicting several generations with virtuous-sounding nonsense statements, such as "A penny saved is a penny earned."

Donald Kaul, an Iowan turned Washington columnist and contemporary chronicler of innocents and cynics, agrees. He sees Henry Ford as a modern Franklin. Ford combined public relations and his own homespun philosophy in a crusade of and for Babbittry. Eventually, Ford came to believe that he had invented, or reinvented, the cause of world peace, the work ethic, and philanthropy.

Then came Dale Carnegie, an innocent who may have had more impact on human relations than anyone in our time. His recommendations on *How to Win Friends and Influence People* made the handshake dishonest.

Finally, we have Ross Perot—a contemporary Henry Ford, except that Perot never invented or made anything and his great cause is not world peace or jobs but campaign reform—clean politics. Politics is something Perot disdains, though he knows almost nothing about it and refuses to learn. His laughter is both harsh and high.

The innocent manages to turn good spirit into false piety, and sometimes bad faith.

During the past twenty-five years, the innocents have regularly despaired over the state of American politics. But they have reason to rejoice. They have won federal election reform, election reform in the states, congressional reform, and partial lobbying reform. Yet, they have failed to obtain federal financing for congressional races or term limits. This has caused much gloom among those who want "change," Left and Right. For the innocent are found in every wing and camp of every party.

In the last political generation:

- Reformers have limited campaign spending by the wealthy (except for themselves) but failed to limit political action committees, which in essence the federal election reforms created.
- Special prosecutors have become a way of life in American politics. The innocent have "cleaned up" politics to the point that the expectation of scandal is unceasing. (It is almost impossible to imagine a presidential administration without a major scandal.) One result is that half the eligible voters have virtually given up on the political process.
- Political gridlock and unrelenting partisanship are accepted facts of life, and competence in government is the exception rather than the rule.

But all this does not make the innocent doubt the rightness of his cause, the purity of his own intentions, or the importance of a "clean" and change-oriented political process. The innocent presses on—demanding more reform to correct the errors of the reforms that have failed.

In 1960 I published a book called *Frontiers in American Democracy*. In a section called "Innocence" I wrote:

> *Complexity or setback—even of a temporary nature—is difficult for the innocent to explain or bear, since he assumes that his intentions are good and his cause just, and that, consequently, immediate and continuous success is assured. . . . The innocent may postpone admission of failure by raising the hue and cry against "wicked men" who may be about to seek a scapegoat, a person to be blamed, a Jonah to be cast into the sea.*
>
> *When the innocent who has been reluctant to use government finally turns to it, he is likely to do so with great enthusiasm, to develop "so great a fever of goodness, that the dissolution of it must cure it," as the Duke observes in* Measure for Measure.
>
> *The innocent is disposed to favor massive effort and all-out war rather than containment or limited war, to demand action leading to final decision when postponement of trouble or limited or even temporary good may be the best that can be expected.*
>
> *[But,] vague protestations of innocence and simplicity will solve few problems in a world that is complex and beyond innocence. The need is for mature response—a response reflecting awareness of historical reality.*

The essence of political innocence—the chief attribute of many in politics today—is detachment from historical judgment, from tradition, from the tests of practical action.

There are many examples of innocence in politics in our day: the call for censorship of movies, television, and records; the one-man virtue industry of William Bennett; many in the press who now seek to police themselves as a profession rather than a craft; Ross Perot and his movement; many right-to-life activists; many pro-choice activists; most supply-siders; many in the Christian Coalition; many in the National Education Association.

But most harmful are the innocents who want to purify politics itself.

The continuing attempt to purify Congress, the political parties, political advertising (otherwise known as free speech), even the presidency and the courts is really worse for the republic than zealotry in behalf of abortion or choice or capitalism. Few clear victories are possible in these matters and a counterforce always reacts to a victory for one side or the other.

Political reform, on the other hand, is like motherhood. It appeals to Left and Right—campaign spending limits for the Left, term limits for the Right. Victories are quite possible in the quest to reform politics, for who wants to oppose reform, clean politics, or limits of the power of money? The fruits of such victories are hard to undo.

Some recent personifications of innocence, run amuck:

- Ross Perot, whose "vision thing" is that he would look under the hood of government and fix it.
- Hillary Clinton, in the cause of health insurance reform (a good cause), planned to accomplish her task on a massive scale in 100 days.
- The freshman House class of 1994, which came to office pledging to correct virtually every shortcoming of the federal government by defunding it.
- House Speaker Newt Gingrich, who says he is "a futurist" who believes technology can resolve most human problems.

- Ralph Nader, who reduces almost every complexity of government to a single motive or two: personal venality and class warfare.

The greatest myth of political innocence in our time is simply stated: The problems of contemporary politics and society are essentially a simple matter of process, and a purified process will yield good public policy. Hence a gimmick like public funding of campaigns or term limits becomes a deus ex machina—a magic key to resolve the conflicts of values and interests inherent in our democracy.

The myth is twofold: that process equals policy and that a good process is a clean or uncorrupted process. This is a mechanistic and simplistic view of public life and action—one that bets everything on procedural reform. But it is the vision of contemporary political innocence.

For the innocents of our time, politics can never be clean enough. So in the name of doing good, the innocents do much harm.

•

Consider these examples of "notable innocents" who meant to do good and actually did much harm:

1. **Common Cause, founded by John Gardner.** In representing what it claims to be "the public interest," Common Cause has effectively, with some help from other people and organizations, reorganized Congress and presidential politics—it has reorganized both into ineptitude.

- In the case of Congress, seniority was destroyed, and so the authority of committee chairmen. These were the power centers that kept Congress from degenerating into entropy.
- In the case of presidential politics, reform that sought to de-emphasize money actually increased the power of money by creating advantage for wealthy people (Steve Forbes, Perot) and

creatures of interest groups (or PACs), which is exactly what Bill Clinton and Bob Dole had become by 1996.

- Congress generally and the Senate in particular have been de-emphasized as an important breeding ground for presidential candidates, as several failed candidates in 1996 showed. A wealthy person like Forbes now runs himself rather than seeking out a more experienced representative of his views. Forbes might have backed Jack Kemp or Phil Gramm under 1960s rules. And either would have been a better candidate and a more competent president, had he prevailed.

I have said often that we could not have run the antiwar campaign of 1968 without wealthy donors, now banned under reform laws. Under today's rules, a lone antiwar senator could not have launched a challenge to a sitting president from the Senate. The nation would likely not have been given a referendum on the war in Vietnam in 1968 under the reform arrangements of today.

2. **The late Sen. Margaret Smith of Maine.** Smith was generally a sound legislator. But when in the Senate, she compiled a record of perfect attendance on 1,000 (she continued beyond that number) roll call votes. It is the most exceptional congressional attendance record in modern memory.

For her accomplishment, Smith was applauded by most of the press and by many politicians. It seemed like a virtuous and upright thing to do—come to work. Except that voting—especially on a great many routine and meaningless votes—is in many ways the least important thing that senators do.

Shortly after I left the Senate, a roll call vote was taken on what to do with the remains of Smokey Bear.

The Senate did and does vote too often on too many irrelevant things. It ought to deliberate more. This was the intent of the Founders.

Smith, a dignified and courageous woman, set a standard by which members of the Senate have come to be judged: their attendance record. But this is a measure of how many times they voted rather than by *how* they voted. It is an essentially useless standard. Yet it has been adopted as an important one by political scientists, by the League of Women Voters, and by publications like *Congressional Quarterly*.

Arguing about attendance has become a great game in re-election campaigns, a great preoccupation of political journalists, and overall a great irrelevance.

It is almost impossible for someone outside the Senate, or not following its activities day by day, to assess the context or importance of any particular vote. Yet, particular votes or absences from votes are often singled out by the press or challenging politicians. This is misleading and distracting. And we have the good Maggie Smith to thank for it.

Actually, any attendance, or roll response, by a senator in excess of 70 to 80 percent, indicates a waste of time and a lack of appreciation of what the role of a senator is.

3. **The Reverend Billy Graham.** Graham pioneered electronic religion, with a little advance work by Bishop Fulton Sheen.

Graham was a solid preacher of the Bible message. He taught the Gospel and performed his healing, not in TV studios but in mass meetings. However, he spawned a host of successors and contemporaries—Jimmy Swaggart, Oral Roberts, Jim Bakker, the Reverend Robert Schuller, to name a few—and these TV preachers have demeaned religious feeling, distorted the Bible, and taken advantage of a great many innocent people.

And now we have graduated to Ralph Reed—the Christian as Washington operative.

The Christian fundamentalists have gone into politics in a serious way, but not as Christians called to witness so much as Christians called to lobby—as another pressure group making demands. This too demeans—it belittles the mystery and complexity of belief.

If a Christian is serious about his faith, he *should* be involved, he *should* take a stand. What is not positive is for particular churches or churchmen to endorse a particular line, party, or politician. Jesus may be legitimately claimed as a revolutionary but not, I think, as a Republican or a Democrat.

Billy Graham made religion safe for TV, and also safe for presidents and corporation chiefs and those who had power—all of whom he seemed to bless. Instead of bringing Christian values to politics, he brought political techniques to Christianity; instead of serving as a conscience among politicians, he served as cover.

The Christian Right today simplifies politics as only innocents can. The assumption is, apparently, that Christian belief—the right kind anyway—confers an inherent wisdom in things political, even tactical politics. The Christian fundamentalist, simply because he exists, supposedly knows how to untangle a complex question like abortion or affirmative action. He may even know best who a candidate should pick as a running mate.

This is dangerous nonsense not only for belief but also for politics. Wisdom in politics comes hard and mostly through experience. To be born again does not make one politically astute or philosophically wise.

Graham is a sincere Christian and a mighty preacher. But he allowed himself to be used and he allowed religion to be used—mostly more for man's glorification than God's.

4. **George F. Kennan.** For many years Kennan was the nation's leading historian and foreign policy expert on Russia and what was once the Eastern bloc. Back in the early 1950s Kennan described and recommended the policy of "containment" of communist expansion

in Europe. Following World War II, and as applied to that time and to Europe as Kennan meant for it to be, the idea made some sense. But Kennan soon found his specific policy recommendations declared a "doctrine."

The doctrine of containment, applied by men who knew little of history or of ideas, was a disaster for the United States. Though Kennan protested for thirty years, his doctrine was used as justification for anticommunist and Cold War policy that included U.S. involvement in Vietnam, the invasion of Cuba under President Kennedy, and a number of "destabilizations" and rogue operations by the CIA.

Kennan is a brilliant man, a patriot, and a great scholar, but he sold U.S. policymakers an abstraction that became a substitute for the very thing Kennan knew best: diplomacy. Without containment, the Vietnam War and the Cold War might have ended sooner.

5. **The late Walter Heller.** Heller, as economic adviser to President Kennedy, broke with established Keynesian thought and in 1964 recommended a tax cut, despite a federal deficit, small though it was then; a high level of production; and relatively high employment levels. The Heller idea was to move a productive economy to higher levels.

Under the conditions of the times, the Heller recommendations worked. But subsequently, under different circumstances, the tax cuts and debt approach was applied with near-disastrous results. The Reagan and Bush "read my lips" era left the country with a downsizing economy and a national debt in excess of $4 trillion.

The idea of tax cuts paired with massive debt as good economics has taken hold of the Republican imagination, however. At least once a month someone celebrates the idea in *The Wall Street Journal,* and President Kennedy's name is usually invoked.

Of course tax cuts paired with a massive debt is *not* good economics, nor would the John Kennedy I knew and served with in Congress have approved of Reaganomics. But Heller helped to legitimize such folly.

6. **Paul Fisher.** Fisher invented the ballpoint pen. It made a cheap writing instrument available to nearly everyone in the workplace, those who could write and those who could not. People could now afford to carry a pen clearly displayed, even if they could not write well. The birth and distribution of the ballpoint pen came at the same time as two other indicators of upper mobility among Third World countries: the English bicycle, freeing its possessor from the ordinary limitations of space and human locomotion, and the Swiss watch, ownership of which indicated that human beings had some control over time.

The ubiquitous ballpoint pen was a sign that its possessor could leave a mark. At most, it suggested that his words would not die in air. The Japanese camera was to follow, an instrument challenging not only time but eternity.

And now we have fax machines and a world wired and talking to itself on "the Net."

But the negative effects of the introduction of the ballpoint pen were multiple. First, in the deterioration of handwriting. Second, in the increase of ink-stained shirts and coats. Third, in the progressive loss of the sense of ownership of private property. Few people now know whether the ballpoint in purse or pocket is their own. Fisher may have done more to destroy the sense of private property than Karl Marx.

The really terrible thing about the ballpoint pen, of course, was that it has contributed in some small measure to what might be called democratization by the innocents—not a democracy of rights or of access but implicitly of voice. Every person's opinion was now of a weight equal to every other person's, whether he knew a lot or almost nothing. Every person deserved access to his congressman, the pages of the local newspaper, the airwaves, whether he had something to say or not. This was the sort of delusional equality Alexis de Tocqueville said would destroy America.

7. **Walter Cronkite.** For a time Cronkite was credited with being "the most trusted man in America" (running ahead of presidents, popes, and evangelists in poll after poll in the 1970s). He developed the dubious function of the anchorman (now anchorperson or persons). Cronkite's lofty tone and impression of seriousness elevated TV news, which seemed a good thing once upon a time. But the emphasis on anchorpersons also personalized TV news, emphasizing star and glitz over substantive news coverage. The cult of personality eventually trivialized the news.

Network executives now consider the news divisions as no different in mission than the entertainment divisions. And at this point that is essentially so. Anchors are now performers—akin to the song-and-dance man, which is what Cronkite says he once wanted to become.

Television news alone virtually ruined politics in America by making it remote, abstract, dramatic, and impersonal. Politics became a thing the average citizen could not reach directly; he or she had to go through the media to get to it. TV news about politics was not old-fashioned reporting but filmmaking. TV news is not edited, after all—it is "produced."

8. **The late Robert Hutchins.** Hutchins left the presidency of the University of Chicago and founded the Center for the Study of Democratic Institutions. He was a worthy person. He managed many important studies dedicated to educating the people, to purifying our great democratic institutions, and to marketing the great books, which are basic to Western civilization.

But the Hutchins passion for self-analysis and criticism of democracy backfired. We now have a democracy that cannot stop talking to and about itself. We have instant and continual news analysis and polling, *The Reader's Digest,* speed reading, television courses on Plato and poetry, weekend seminars on leadership, and master's and Ph.D. degrees in management or employee relations. Plato and Jefferson for all is a good idea, but not if you must dumb them down to do it and not if you must deny that some must lead.

Americans are so busy evaluating and analyzing our democracy that we cannot live it. We are paralyzed by our critical awareness. Self-help democracy has actually contributed to the destruction of America's republican self-confidence.

The results of such programs—every man a social critic, no man a citizen—were evident in their effect on Robert McNamara, the defense secretary during the Lyndon Johnson years and later head of the World Bank. In a commencement address he gave near the end of his career as secretary of defense, he quoted theologians, philosophers, historians, poets, and others—one for every variety of cultural experience. At the end of his speech he added, rather casually, "And then there are Kafka, Kierkegaard, and Yeats." Thus, human wisdom becomes the Kmart of ideas, something to be consumed as concept du jour.

All of these people were either innocents themselves or badly misused by innocents, or both.

All of these people should make us skeptical about schemes to reinvent government or clean up politics.

Much of history really is, in Barbara Tuchman's phrase, the "march of folly." The ordinary myopia of human action and decision is only deepened, and usually compounded, by innocence.

The innocent believes there are solutions for problems available to the expertly trained. He believes there are no hollow victories. The innocent reads *The 7 Habits of Very Successful People* and takes it to heart, memorizing entire sections. The innocent does not count on unexpected costs. He does not believe in unintended consequences. He sees human history as linear if he thinks of history at all. He believes in social science, flowcharts, and the bottom line. Human affairs are not, for him, essentially complex. Human beings are not stubbornly mysterious. Politics is a thing to be fixed—a mess in Washington, as Ross Perot likes to say, that needs to be cleaned up by practical businessmen.

Innocents fail to see that out of even the purest and best motives chaos and confusion may follow.

But even the good notions of great minds cause confusion in the hands of innocents. For example:

1. Malthus, from whose works come contemporary statements such as "It's a population problem," when in fact the problem usually is one of human will.
2. Darwin, from whose theories come weighty expressions such as "I believe in evolution, not in revolution." (Evolutionary concepts turn up in strange and unusual texts, as when President Carter announced that he would "evolve a foreign policy.")
3. Einstein's theory of relativity was useful in physics, but is distracting when applied as a general judgment, as in the expression "Everything is relative."

Thus we should approach all reform with skepticism—as possible mischief by innocents. We should remember that political reform is dangerous and unpredictable because human beings are dangerous and unpredictable.

The best of reformers are hesitant and slow to change. They are driven to reform reluctantly as Yeats was "hurt into poetry." The wise reformer clings to old traditions and doubts any guarantees of a new human nature.

The worst reformers—the ones to watch out for—are missionaries—those who see the light and therefore should lead the way. They do not want a marginally better world but a *new* world. Missionaries have done much harm throughout history.

This was noted by Sam Houston in conversation with Alexis de Tocqueville during the latter's visit to the United States in 1831. Houston, a friend of the Indians, especially of the Creeks and Cherokees, warned Tocqueville that there were two things that should not be given to the Indians: "brandy and Christianity." Houston said the tribes should be left alone and respected for their own ways.

A similar thought was conveyed by the unsentimental prayer of a friend of mine. "God save us," he said, "from leading laymen."

2

Slaying St. George

"The Puritans," wrote Gilbert Chesterton, "wind up killing St. George and keeping the dragon." So it is with many political reformers today—they are really innocents or puritans, not practical liberals. So it is with the federal election amendments of 1975–76 and their complement of reform laws and codes designed to purify politics and politicians.

Bill Clinton is the latest and most conspicuous victim of puritanism. There is a special prosecutor devoted especially to him and to his wife, to all he did, or might have done, in Arkansas or Washington; to all he did, or might have done, with reference to the Whitewater real estate development and all like business deals; to all that Mrs. Clinton did or might have done; and to all the Clintons' staff or friends in Washington or Little Rock may have done or thought about doing. Or didn't do.

This is not really exaggeration. It is almost literally the official charge of the special prosecutor (more on the subject in chapter 3).

Perhaps Bill Clinton is as corrupt as Warren G. Harding. Perhaps he is not. But special prosecutors have been proliferating since the 1970s, and they don't go away. Nor do they ever seem to conclude that there is no ethical or legal violation of substance to be found and close down shop. No, they keep going until they have found a smoking gun, or something that looks like one.

The duties of these tribunes of virtue are almost infinite. They cover not only legal ground but also theological ground—not only corruption but also association with corruption, the appearance of corruption, or the possibility of an appearance of corruption. Plato's guardians could not pass such a test. And certainly the disciples of Christ could not.

How many in American business, medicine, or the law could stand the moral scrutiny of a special prosecutor working over a three-, four-, or five-year period to find and explore their ethical lapses?

The standard seems not to be personal honesty or legal property; these are not enough. One must be above suspicion, even above a hint of suspicion, and so must one's friends and associates.

The appearance standard was introduced by Common Cause in the 1970s. Common Cause said that candidates for office must avoid not only the fact of impropriety but also the appearance of impropriety.

The appearance standard required that politicians must not have tainted associates, and sometimes it seemed that they must not be tainted by any kind of association at all. Moreover, the appearance standard was expanded to include the undue influence and outside influence standards. We were told that too many officeholders were beholden to special or outside interests and that some of these interests exert undue influence on some politicians. And this, of course, was bad, even though most of the troublemakers of history, from Hitler to the so-called militias of contemporary America, have been notable for the lack of influences upon them, especially outside influences.

This culture of suspicion—the assumption of corruption—

achieved full force in the era of the special prosecutor. But for most politicians, politics without interests or influences is rather difficult to manage.

Since Richard Nixon, a huge number of American politicians have been either felled or badly damaged by questions concerning their personal morality: Edward Kennedy, Bert Lance, Geraldine Ferraro, Gary Hart, and the Clintons. Ironically, most were or are major advocates of campaign reform, public financing of campaigns, lobbying reforms, and so forth.

The principal arguments made for the election reform and financing laws have been that money is the root of all political evil and that the U.S. political system has been, or is being, corrupted by money, principally in the form of large contributions to campaign expenditures. Why is this bad? Because "fat cats" will have undue influence on politicians, that's why. An example is often said to be Clement Stone, the late Texas financier who gave so much money to Nixon. But what corrupted Nixon was arrogance, neurosis, and isolation. The people who helped this along were his palace guard, not fat cats. Stone was one of the better influences on Nixon. It is too bad there weren't ten of him.

Most modern reform arguments ignored the fact that the higher levels of political corruption come from the desire for power and pride in office, often demonstrated as excessive concern about what "history may say" about a politician. If Nixon and Lyndon Johnson were corrupted, it was not by money or the influence large contributors might have had upon them. Soft political money may have helped their drive for power and historical recognition, but it was not inherently corrupting. Nor is there evidence at levels of politics below the presidency that money has been the major corrupting influence it is supposed to have been.

One bit of evidence of corruption generally cited in presidential politics is what is usually called the "purchase of ambassadorships." Big contributors—or, in more recent politics, big fund-raisers—are given minor ambassadorships. Actually, political cronies, aides, and sidekicks have long been given diplomatic jobs that could be better handled by career diplomats. (President Clinton revived the practice somewhat by appointing Pamela Harriman, a major fund-raiser for the Democratic Party, ambassador to France, and Sen. Edward Kennedy's sister, ambassador to Ireland.)

It may be a questionable practice to award ambassadorships to large contributors or political royalty, but the record does not show that politics has been corrupted or foreign policy altered much over the years because of this practice. Far greater harm to American diplomacy has been done by historical ignorance—by presidents who listened to military advisers or would-be military advisers rather than reading diplomatic dispatches, or who knew little more about foreign policy than Cold War ideology.

Pride, not money, is usually at the center of any story of the fall of a nation, a government, or a leader.

Moreover, there is clear historical evidence that large contributors have been highly important in supporting controversial and maverick political movements and in challenging established ideas, practices, and institutions. The American Revolution, for example, was not financed by small contributions or with matching funds from George III. It was financed at critical times by large contributions from people such as Haym Salomon, John Hancock, and others, and even by contributions from foreigners we have long honored, such as the Marquis de Lafayette, whose help would be illegal under today's laws.

Even if more serious corruption because of money could be demonstrated to exist, that fact would not justify the broad attack on political traditions and on constitutional guarantees contained in the

1975–76 Federal Election Campaign Act, a law that violates—in some cases directly, in others indirectly—almost every personal and political right guaranteed by the Constitution.

- That law limits freedom of speech. It limits what a wealthy person can give to a nonwealthy candidate, for example, while allowing a wealthy candidate such as Ross Perot to give an unlimited amount to himself.

- It gives special privileges and advantages to the two major parties, in effect legalizing the Republican and Democratic parties. This is similar to the violation of the Constitution that would be inherent in the legalization of two religions. I am sure that if the Founding Fathers had anticipated a time when one, two, or more political parties would be given formal support by the government, an additional amendment would have been included in the Bill of Rights, forbidding the establishment or support of political parties by federal government.

- The 1975–76 campaign law does not provide for equal protection under the law or for due process, but consigns to a bureaucracy—the Federal Election Commission—legislative, executive, and judicial powers. A magisterial proceeding is set up—one of the very things that stirred Jefferson and Madison to support the concept of political privacy, which most Americans think of as a right. For 200 years, Americans have sought to extend and protect the secret ballot and limitations on public registration along party lines. Yet, through the FEC and the Federal Election Campaign Act, contributions become public record. At the same time, political action committees, which this law made legal, make it possible for employers to gently coerce employees to contribute to the company PAC, whose candidates may not be the individual's candidate.

Further, through legitimizing corporate and labor union political action committees, the law sets in motion a process whereby control over politics must certainly gravitate to these two sources of campaign financing, to the detriment of political parties, other political organizations, and individuals. Candidates of the future are more and more likely to be those supported by corporate funds, as is already being demonstrated in congressional elections, or by union funds. The only candidates who may be able to stand against this trend will be individuals of great personal or family wealth, who under the Supreme Court's residual defense of the constitutional guarantee of freedom of speech cannot be limited in their expenditure.

In effect the 1975–76 legislation consigns to the government significant control over the process by which the government itself is chosen.

THE IMPULSE TO REFORM

The most important reform impulse is the desire to tame the clerks: to make those responsible for "the administration of things" behave.

The cry of "Reform the bureaucracy" or "Reform the civil service" is as old as bureaucracy and civil service. It may be as old as the desire to clean up politics. It is a standard item in the catalog of demagoguery.

President Jimmy Carter used it in the 1976 campaign with some success, until his own righteousness and Ronald Reagan sank him.

Reagan ran against Washington for twenty years and as head of the federal government continued to campaign against it for another eight years. He shook his head in constant hurt and disappointment at the Washington apparatus, but there is no record that he made a single attempt to actually reshape the bureaucracy.

President Clinton, according to Bob Woodward of *The Washington Post,* dislikes Washington and hates "the Washington crowd." He put Vice President Gore in charge of overhauling the federal bureaucracy—a task Gore actually took seriously. One admires Gore for his sincerity, if not his gullibility.

The press generally applauds plans for reform of the bureaucracy. *The Washington Post* and *The New York Times* are particularly big on such plans. The *Post* does things like pronouncing a plan, say the Gore plan, an excellent one "on the whole." Whether the whole was greater than the sum of its parts, the *Post* never tells.

Business groups always favor reform of bureaucracy. During the Carter years, the Committee for Economic Development (CED) endorsed the Carter program to save the clerks. The CED spoke of ideas "evolved over the past thirty-five years." Apparently, ideas that have "evolved" are better than ideas that have come from mere reflection and observation.

There are two basic questions to be raised about the bureaucratic and civil service reforms.

- First: Is the civil service as ineffective as it is said to be?
- If the answer to the question is affirmative, a second question is: Do we want the civil service to be more effective than it is? The Internal Revenue Service, for example?

It may be that the nature of the bureaucracy is that it cannot be reformed. Perhaps President Reagan had the right idea: Either abolish a bureaucracy or simply oppose it. Don't even try to fix it. Of course Reagan picked some of the wrong bureaucracies to pick on and ignored some that should have been picked on (like the Pentagon). But here, as elsewhere (nuclear weapons), Reagan had the basic insight right, if not the application.

Perhaps Gore and his associates and supporters should have read the American humorist Mr. Dooley and reflected on his observations about reforms and reformers. "In the first place," said Dooley, "'tis a gr-great mistake to think that annywan ra-aly wants to rayform. . . . An' that's thruer in politics thin annywhere else. But a rayformer don't see it. A rayformer thinks he was ilicited because he was a rayformer, win th' thrush iv th' matther is he was ilicited because no wan knew him. He's ilicited because th' people don't know him an' do know th' other la-ad . . ."

THE "RE" FACTOR

An old congressman, elected in the time of Roosevelt's New Deal and surviving into the post–World War II years (as I recall it was either Brent Spence of Kentucky, chairman of the Banking and Currency Committee, or Robert "Muley" Doughton of North Carolina, chairman of the Ways and Means Committee during the Truman administration), advised new members of the House of Representatives to vote against any proposal carrying the letters *re* as a part of its title, prefix, or opening syllable. "You may be wrong once in a while," he said, "but over the years you will find that you have done well if you vote against all reorganizations, all recodifications, all reforms, all resolutions, and," he concluded, "all Republicans."

His judgment was sustained by Speaker Sam Rayburn, who at the same time noted that the only good thing in the Congressional Reorganization Act of 1945 was the salary increase, together with the pension program for members of Congress.

In the forty years since, most attempts at political reform in America have backfired.

- Reorganization of the military demonstrated the rightness of the old congressman's advice. Reform began with the name of the military agency of the United States. It was changed from the War Department to the Department of Defense, thus opening the way to unlimited expansion of that department and unlimited expenditures in its support.

The needs of war or of preparation for war are determinable; those of defense, infinite. Despite these two slips, the general thrust of the Truman administration was positive and forward looking. The emphasis was on advancing the New Deal and achieving the "Square Deal."

The Eisenhower administration, a kind of rest and rehabilitation period, was nevertheless marked by reforms and reorganizations of minor significance, but also by the development of the resolution as a major instrument of executive power over Congress.

- The Kennedy administration emphasized the *new* as in "New Frontier." Most frontiers are new, at least for a time, until they become old or former or lost.

- President Johnson returned to the *re* world in a significant way. In the tradition of Eisenhower, and John Foster Dulles, Johnson convinced the Senate to pass the Tonkin Gulf Resolution.

- President Nixon was a ready and frequent user of *re* as opening syllable. He promised to restore integrity in the government. He said that he would tell the truth, even if it hurt. He supported the congressional resolution for reform of the budget process—a process that contributed to the growth of fiscal irresponsibility, deficits, and mounting national debt—and the reorganization of Congress, even unto confusion and ineptitude.

Nixon also supported the election reforms that ultimately were signed into law by his successor and pardoner, Gerald Ford, and that all but destroyed open politics in the United States and opened or eased the way for major influence on politics and government by the corporations.

This same period was marked by the rediscovery and reintroduction of the rebate by the automobile industry, endorsed by at least one church near Lansing, Michigan, which offered a "rebate on eternal life."

• President Carter took up the idea of the rebate as a part of "reform" of the Internal Revenue Code. Perhaps the most notable *re* achievement of the Carter administration was, according to Vice President Mondale, the revitalization of the vice presidency. The office had again, according to the vice president, deteriorated in the body politic, as the vermiform appendix had in the human body, to the point of being completely atrophied. The vice president never explained why it would be good to revitalize either organ in either body.

• The *re* factor was strong in the Reagan administration, even manifest in the first syllable of the president's name. The emphasis in that administration was strong on return to the good old days—to the old values and, beyond that, to attempting the impossible task of "recapturing our destiny," which, although unrealized, seemed in the Reagan time frame to have escaped. President Bush was committed to continuing or completing the Reagan Revolution.

• Then came the Clinton campaign and administration. The emphasis in the campaign was on change, although *re* words were not altogether missing. They hovered on the edges, in talk of reinvesting and reindustrialization. There were suggestions of reform and of reorganizations, but nothing like what was to come.

3

Criminalizing Politics

SPECIAL PROSECUTORS:
A CURE THAT SPREADS THE DISEASE

*W*hat has the reform of the past two to three decades wrought? One result is a political culture of cynicism and scandal. And one reason for that, as I have said, is the constant resort to special prosecutors and special counsels.

During the years of controversy over civil rights legislation in the 1960s, there were proposals for a superior Supreme Court, a Supreme Supreme Court, to which cases decided in the Supreme Court would be appealed. It was a court that would have been, according to explanations given by its sponsors, above prejudice, above partisanship, above regionalism, above and beyond the corruption of intellect and will that besets even Supreme Court justices. Its wisdom would have been preternatural, just short of angelic.

In the same spirit, the Congress has undertaken to purify the judicial process with another office—that of the special prosecutor. President Clinton has had one after him and House Speaker Newt Gingrich, too. In the Gingrich case, we were really talking about an outside counsel, and this particular one's powers were somewhat limited. But Kenneth Starr's probe into the Clintons has been ever expansive and is now all inclusive and all intrusive. It began with

Whitewater and includes later but up-to-the-minute scandals—the Paula Jones and Monica Lewinsky cases.

There is, practically speaking, no limit to what the special prosecutor may investigate. It is also unlikely that any special prosecutor will end his tenure by announcing that no violation of law or morality has been found. Since Richard Nixon we have had two special prosecutors investigate two presidents. Just as their pursuit of scandal and their powers to pursue scandal are virtually unlimited, their desire for a catch—a big catch—is virtually undeterrable. They become obsessed.

The office of special prosecutor is an essentially undemocratic office with an essentially fascistic writ of power. It is also a guarantee of increased public disaffection, of legal distraction and expense on a grand scale, and of potential government paralysis.

What is the worst that Mr. Starr will prove about the Clintons? That they are guilty of conflicts of interest while in Arkansas, which most of us already believe, and of cover-ups while in Washington. Is this worth the ruination of another presidency? Especially if the culture of scandal is perpetuated and the grand inquisitorial powers of the special prosecutor are strengthened?

How to limit the monster we have created?

Once appointed, the special prosecutor could be removed by the attorney general for "extraordinary impropriety," or by the constitutional process of impeachment. But the political cost of a president removing a special prosecutor could be impeachment.

The justification given for the office of special prosecutor is Watergate, which was also the justification for passage of the Federal Election Campaign Act. In its first examination of that act, the Supreme Court held that it violated freedom of speech in two major aspects and that it violated the constitutional provisions for separation of powers.

Advocates of the act evidently thought that such violations were a small price to pay for purification.

The special-prosecutor law is an attempt to avoid the constitutional and political responsibility of the Congress to sit in judgment of the president and the executive branch. The attorney general of the United States, as an agent of the president, is responsible for enforcing the law against everyone in the country except the president. The president is subject to impeachment by the House and conviction by the Senate for "high crimes and misdemeanors" and also for felonies, which fall somewhere in between. This is a rational process, one that has satisfactorily met the test of history, even in the case of Watergate.

Congress has avoided its ultimate responsibility by defining conditions in which the appointment of a special prosecutor has become all but automatic. Moreover, it has encouraged the courts to become deeply involved in prosecution at a high level of politics. The function of the courts is to judge, not to prosecute or appoint prosecutors.

Again, the attempt has been made to purify politics and the result has been to confuse and corrupt it. But no matter how hard Congress may try to eliminate them, the elements of politics—corruption, large and small, human vanity, and the need for judgment—will remain.

Consider the process by which special prosecutors are selected. Two political questions should be asked. The first is: Who appoints the attorney general? And the second: Who appoints the three judges who in turn appoint a special prosecutor? The attorney general, by tradition, is a partisan. The federal judges are where they are because of partisan support. No judge in American history has been nominated by an independent, nonpartisan Congress.

Hence, Archibald Cox (the precursor) and Lawrence Walsh and Kenneth Starr (both appointed under the current statutes) were all white knights with political pasts. All of them came to be seen by those who either opposed them or were their victims as deeply partisan.

Under a partisan system, no matter how many layers of partisan appointees are placed between the action and the actor, a whisper of doubt, or a stage whisper of suspicion, will remain.

As a rule of government, it is better to place the area of doubt within the range of popular judgment rather than to pretend that partisanship does not exist. Cynicism about the inquisitors themselves cannot be significantly reduced by a process that camouflages or obscures the fact that partisanship is built into the American political system.

We should abolish the special-prosecutor laws and practices and let Congress, the press, and the people make the judgments. Better to overdo the impeachment process than to continue to abuse the silly and destructive special-prosecutor process we now have in place.

A CASE HISTORY IN CRIMINALIZING POLITICS

More than 200 years ago, John Adams, along with his cousin Samuel and others, inspired and led the American Revolution. John Adams believed in self-government. He believed that politics should not be controlled by the British government or any other government. Adams warned against the dangers of partisan politics, and he especially warned against the dangers of two-party politics. In 1770, commenting on the new Massachusetts Constitution, he wrote: "There is nothing which I dread so much as a division of the republic into two great parties, each arranged under its leader, and converting measures in opposition to each other. This, in my humble apprehension, is to be dreaded as the greatest political evil under our constitution."

In the Revolutionary era, Adams was no favorite of the British government. Had he been captured, he might well have been hanged for his political activities. He escaped such a fate and eventually became the second president of the United States.

Some 200 years later, another man named John Adams, a New Englander who evidently believed in open politics but was unaware that politics in the United States is not what it was before passage of the Federal Election Campaign Act, encountered the power of the state.

In 1976 Adams was moved to run for the Republican nomination for the U.S. House in New Hampshire. He was a war hero, but he was unemployed. He had no campaign chairman, no campaign fund or apparatus, no media ads, no handlers, in fact, no income to speak of. He was living on a navy disability pension of $173 a month. Nevertheless, Adams, the modern, filed for the Republican primary and (one assumes because of his good name) won.

Next, the Federal Election Commission, the administrative agency of the Federal Election Campaign Act, entered the picture. Adams came under official watch because he had not filed financial reports required by the law. When he entered the campaign, he apparently did not know that such reports were required.

The FEC sent notices and forms and, eventually, threatening letters; but it received no information about John Adams. Adams did, however, respond in one way to the call of the state. After receiving one of the FEC threats, he made a collect call to the FEC office in Washington, saying that he had asked for no money for his campaign, had received none, had spent none, and had called collect because he did not have thirteen cents (the cost then) for a stamp.

This information might have satisfied the commission, since it had no evidence that Adams had collected or spent any money. But the FEC staff had no written reports with which to paper their files.

The case against Adams was, as the bureaucrats say, "activated."

The power of the law and of the courts was turned on Adams, as it might have been turned on his illustrious predecessor of the same name had the Revolution failed. Adams, the latter, became a hunted man and a wanted person—not by the agents of the Crown but by the agents of the FEC.

The FEC proceeded against Adams in federal court, asking that he be required to file the information demanded and that he be fined up to $5,000. Adams neither responded to the suit nor appeared in court. The commission continued its case against this great menace to clean elections even after he was trounced by the Democratic incumbent in the November election.

Since Adams did not respond to its suit, the FEC filed a default motion in federal court. A hearing was held in Concord on January 12, 1977. The commission sent one of its top lawyers to appear before the federal judge. (It is rumored that the judge asked the lawyer if the FEC didn't have better things to do with its time.) Adams did not appear. The judge ordered that he be made to file the required information and that he be fined $100.

The majesty of the federal government, in the person of U.S. marshals, proceeded to search for John Adams. They found him in an old soldiers' home in Massachusetts. He filled out an FEC report, listing a total of $150 in spending—$50 for his primary filing fee and $100 for telephone calls. But he did not pay the fine, possibly because he did not have the money.

The FEC evidently did not think either of attaching the culprit's disability pension or of making him sell his war medals in order to settle the fine.

POLITICS, LIKE LIVING, CAN BE CRIMINAL

America is fast becoming a felonious society.

The old saying "There ought to be a law" scarcely applies today since almost everything that can be made the object of a law has been covered.

Individual action has always been risky in America. Social critics from Alexis de Tocqueville to David Reisman have noted the drive toward conformity, which modern society and postmodern politics have merely accentuated. Under the federal election laws, individual action can land you in court. It has become increasingly risky to run for office for fear of violating the criminal code.

But voluntary association has become risky, too. Citizens who would petition the government, especially in an organized way, are threatened by lobbying reform bills with possible criminal penalties. Citizens who contribute to candidates their bosses may dislike must hope their secret is not discovered lest they lose their jobs. Some businessmen who want to back a cause or candidate they believe in find that they have been operating within close range of criminal prosecution. Citizens who attempt to fill out their own tax returns have long been in danger.

Citizenship, along with the professional practice of politics, has been criminalized in the United States. So has humanity in many instances.

Some years ago a report of enlistments in the armed services stated that thousands of 22,000 enlistees concealed criminal records, which made them subject to a $10,000 fine and to imprisonment. (The military, in this case exercising commendable restraint, kept two of three of those who concealed criminal records, and prosecuted no one.)

Even legal betting involves relatively high risk. Nonbettors know that the only winner in the long run, and often in the short run, is the track or the house. But federal tax law was changed to require race-tracks to withhold 20 percent of any win over $1,000. Andrew Beyer, the track and betting expert, once said that those who bet on the horses and participate in other forms of legal gambling are treated worse than any other persons subject to the Internal Revenue Code. They usually find, he writes, that it is impossible to prove their losses to the satisfaction of the IRS. They cannot carry losses forward. They are allowed no deductible expenses. Certainly, it is true that the cost of collecting taxes on gambling earnings bears no relationship to what is collected.

I prefer the attitudes toward gambling held in Australia, a nation I visited a decade or so ago. In the course of a ten-day visit to that country, there were at least two news stories reflecting this difference.

The first story involved the secretary-manager of the Fitzroy Foot-ball Club, who was convicted of stealing more than $11,000 from the club's treasury. The defense lawyer pointed out that his client had lost most of his savings in 1974, when he loaned to a close friend a large sum of money that was not repaid. It was also acknowledged that gam-bling was involved. In view of all the circumstances (including the fact that restitution had been made), the club committee had passed a unanimous resolution recommending that no charges be pressed against the former secretary-manager. He was fined $1,000 and re-leased on a three-year good-behavior bond. It was difficult, the judge said, to sentence a man who devoted his whole life to the community and to football, with little or no reward.

The second story involved the Reverend Frank Mulcahy of St. Mary Roman Catholic Church, Grafton, New South Wales. There is a track at Grafton, which sponsors an annual race known as the Grafton Cup. Father Mulcahy included a tip on the race in his weekly parish bulletin. He did not give the name of the horse but drew a cartoon of a horse leaning across a fence and smelling flowers, with a caption reading, "How sweet it is. Good punting."

The faithful got the message, which was to bet on a horse named Sweet Aroma. The mare won at 36-to-1 odds. The St. Mary parishioners were such big winners that the track did not have enough money on hand to pay them off, and a bank was opened to provide the funds.

If the same had happened in the United States, Father Mulcahy probably would have been arraigned before a diocesan council for discipline. He might have been found in violation of state or federal law for encouraging gambling or giving suggested odds without a license. And the IRS probably would have been waiting at his church the next Sunday, demanding 20 percent of the collection.

4

The Fever to Do Good

"There is so great a fever on goodness," says the Duke in Shakespeare's *Measure for Measure*, "that the dissolution of it must cure it."

The fever on doing good, or of trying to make offers do good, virtually consumes the United States today. The fever has now run through the executive branch of the U.S. government, and several recent presidents have been found wanting. There is little—personal or political—we do not know about any of them. Even vice presidents these days must adhere to full—and indecent—disclosure. Who knew anything about John Nance Garner or Alben W. Barkley? Who cared? The vice presidency was a charming constitutional anachronism. Now the vice presidency is relevant, even important, and so we must know all about vice presidents, too.

Naturally, cabinet members also must disclose their financial affairs. Under the law, most federal officials above a certain rank are required to list their financial holdings so as to disclose any possibility of conflict of interest.

The interest of the purifiers has also turned to the judiciary. Under the Constitution, federal judges are nominated by the president and confirmed by the Senate. This procedure was settled on, after long debate in the Constitutional Convention, as the best way to ensure judicial independence. Proposals to have federal judges appointed by the president without any confirmation by the Congress also were considered and rejected, as were other variations. To further ensure the independence of the judiciary, the Constitution provided that judges were to hold their offices "during good behavior" (that is, for life, as a rule); that their salaries could not be diminished during their terms of office; and that they could be removed only by impeachment.

The importance of this independence was underscored by others besides those who wrote the Constitution.

The wisdom of the drafters of the Constitution has been demonstrated by nearly 200 years of history. The resistance to Franklin Roosevelt's effort to "pack the Court" is perhaps the best example.

With only a few examples of judicial misconduct and incompetence, the purifiers moved on the judicial system. Their attack was two-pronged. One focus was, and still is, on the process of appointment. It is proposed that this process be removed from politics, or at least from politicians. While it has been around for a long time, this idea was given new vitality by President Carter. He proposed having citizens' commissions instead of senators recommend judicial appointees. Just how the citizens' commissions were to be set up without politicians being involved, Carter did not specify. Nor did he explain how the constitutional power of the Senate to confirm judges was to be isolated from any possible advance influence on the choice of nominees.

The Carter proposal might work in a Platonic society, with guardians trained (as Plato suggested) to be protectors of the state. In our society guardians would undoubtedly be a part of the civil service.

Even the intervention of bar associations in nominations to the fed-

eral judiciary, a practice encouraged by some senators, is questionable. Few senators, in the course of a six-year term, are called upon to
recommend more than one or two nominees for federal courts. If a
senator does not know his constituency and the lawyers and judges in
it well enough to pick one or two persons every six years, he should
resign.

The second prong of the purist attack on the judiciary consists of
proposals to make it easier to remove judges once they have been appointed. Over the years the Senate has passed several bills establishing special disciplinary procedures that could investigate, censure,
and help remove judges for misconduct, intemperance, or anything
deemed prejudicial to the administration of justice.

The third attack on the judiciary is the so-called litmus test on fundamental issues such as abortion and affirmative action. In this instance a president or presidential nominee sounds out a prospective
judge or justice to make sure he leans "the right way." Ronald Reagan
had a litmus test on abortion. So did Bill Clinton, though his test was
in the other direction. George Bush claimed there was no such test on
any issue in his administration. And Clarence Thomas told the Senate
he had never thought about abortion and was still thinking about
quotas and affirmative action. (Bush also said Thomas was the best-
qualified candidate he could find to sit on the court.)

What is at work here is the puritans' or innocents' attempt to rein in
or humble an independent judiciary. The result, were they to succeed,
would be jurists who are apolitical (or transpolitical) or jurists who are
totally political. History shows that while there are potential abuses in
an independent judiciary, judges who are neither wholly political nor
political eunuchs are most likely to at least observe the higher law and
seek to do justice.

Fine justices—like Earl Warren, William Brennan, and Harry

Blackmun—and fine judges—like Learned Hand, Miles Lord of Minnesota, James Buckley, and Ralph K. Winter—are political animals. They are nominated and approved by the Senate on the basis that they can be trusted to do their duty—to seek the common good. Some trust must remain.

To demand that judges be totally political would make it impossible for them to do their duty. To demand that they be totally above politics would make it impossible to see their duty clearly.

The puritan desire for efficiency, order, and virtue does not always translate into positive—or even intended—political results. Look at Jimmy Carter: a good man and a limited leader. Then look at Bill Clinton: perhaps a less good man and a master politician. Consider Herbert Hoover: a very good man and a poor president. Then think of Franklin Roosevelt: a complex mix of personal morality and motive and a great president.

Nor does puritan virtue always translate into compassionate justice. Oliver Cromwell is the extreme example, but perhaps the most telling one.

One need not be a follower of Machiavelli to see the wisdom of his view that too much virtue (of a certain kind, anyway) can be an impediment in politics. Covering oneself in self-proclaiming virtue can make one rigid, strident, uncompromising, shrill, and vengeful: generally ineffective.

The Christian theologian (and part-time liberal politician) Reinhold Niebuhr said politics requires the wisdom of the serpent and the gentleness of the dove. He was right.

And the American Founders were themselves mixes of worldliness and intellect, self-interest and nobility. If they had been only brilliant and noble, they might not have won the Revolution. If they had been only worldly and self-interested, there would have been little to win.

Certainly Madison and Adams would have scoffed at the idea of politicians as eunuchs or monks.

To the Founders and the other great thinkers of the Enlightenment, virtue had to do not with purity of lifestyle or motive but with public duty: service to the commonwealth. It is a sad irony that as we have raised the standards of personal purity to an impossible level, we have also allowed public morality—which I would define as the ability of public men to keep their words and stand by their convictions—to wither. Moreover, citizenship itself, when not attached to power, position, or interest, has become essentially meaningless in the minds of most Americans.

We are becoming a society ever in search of purity but devoid of moral strength, sacrifice, or high purpose.

THE SCATTERSHOT PURSUIT OF A BETTER SOCIETY

The fever to do good can be both intoxicating and corroding. Consider the Americans for Democratic Action.

Americans for Democratic Action has long been a good organization to belong to. After all, it had the words "American" and "Democratic" in its name. Moreover, its three letters, *ADA,* did not lend themselves to use as an acronym.

Unexplained, the letters might indicate a safe organization like the American Dental Association, which never got into as much trouble as the American Medical Association, which drew the wrath of many liberals in the U.S. House and took on Hillary Clinton when she proposed to reform the entire health insurance system (after 100 days of study).

President Carter said of the AMA that while most individual doctors were fine persons and professionals, as organized in a medical society they were something else. He never said anything like that about either individual dentists or organized dentists. The most critical thing ever written about dentists was the poet Robert Thy's observation that "Dentists water their lawns even when it is raining."

ADA might also stand for the American Dairymen's Association, a reputable organization.

The real, original Americans for Democratic Action got its start in the late 1940s and ran on strongly into the 1950s as a liberal organization set up to protect the country from communist influence and the liberals from being confused with communists or fellow travelers. Its members were people like Hubert Humphrey and Reinhold Niebuhr. It accomplished its mission so thoroughly and successfully that by the 1960s it moved to higher ground and, as an adjunct to the Democratic Party, helped repel the conservatives and the Republicans for the better part of a decade, including noble service in opposing the war in Vietnam.

In the 1970s, however, the ADA fell into the reform trap, along with Common Cause, the League of Women Voters, and other organizations. ADA was in this situation a little like the March of Dimes, which after the polio vaccine was discovered found itself at a loss and went searching for other diseases and disorders. It was never the same again. And so it was with ADA when it got into reform, always a dangerous venture for liberals.

Liberals should be more naturally wary of reform. It was the liberals of their day who supported the introduction of the guillotine as a substitute for the executioner and his ax. This, on the grounds that the guillotine was more humane. It was, but it was also more efficient.

In any case, in the 1970s, caught up in reform, ADA supported such things as the Federal Election Campaign Act, the reorganization of Congress, codes of ethics for the House of Representatives and the

Senate, legislation to control lobbying, etc., until finally, in the 1980s, acting through its Consumer Affairs Committee, ADA began making a study of toys.

The study was not a simple one. It covered price, quality, safety, and psychological effects of some toys. Its price reports were about what one might find in any consumer study: prices of toys vary from store to store, and FAO Schwartz charges more than any other store, something known for a long time.

The quality and safety research turned up more interesting results. Unhinged toy boxes were found to be the most dangerous. The toy that broke the quickest was an oil derrick–refinery play set. The worst doll, the ADA said, was a Bye-Bye Diapers doll. The complaint of the ADA researchers was that the doll leaked not only at the proper place but also at the neck. (Well, I have changed babies who were wet from the neck down.)

Somewhere in the 1980s—about when it went after toys—I concluded that the ADA had given up on politics and education as a way to reform society. Of course, we soon elected a president whose concerns seemed to be midnight basketball, school uniforms, and more wholesome TV.

This sort of thing, I suppose, is in keeping with presidents who say they want to be moral leaders, somewhat in the manner of Andrew Fletcher who in 1703 said, "Let me make a nation's song, I care not who makes its laws."

The new ADA slogan may well be, Let me make a nation's toys, I care not who makes its laws or songs.

The president's new slogan may be, Let me write the nation's dress code, I care not who makes its laws or picks its judges.

The administration developed, under the direction of a revitalized vice president, a master plan for "reinventing government." Just how one reinvents an invention was left unexplained. In any case "reinvention teams" were organized in various government departments. Treasury, for example, had a reinvention team, which proposed to reduce the agency's staff of bond salespersons. Then Secretary of Agriculture Mike Espy set up "review boards" for conducting "re-evaluations," and he noted that rewards were to be given to employees who made particularly "outstanding" contributions to "reinventing" the Department of Agriculture.

After or near the end of a midsummer meeting on reinventing the National Aeronautics and Space Administration (NASA), the directors of that agency reaffirmed their loyalty and restated their commitment to reshaping and reutilizing the resources of that agency's centers. (There was no report of any original affirmation preceding the reaffirmation.)

Not to be left out, according to report, 99.9 percent of the civilian managers of the Defense Department signed on for reinventing the department, possibly by bringing back the cavalry.

Where is Brent Spence, or was it Robert "Muley" Doughton, now that we need another rewarning?

CELIBACY AS THE ULTIMATE REFORM

But beyond a pure bureaucracy, reform demands even more—power husbands, power wives.

It was certain to come: the "substantive" comparison of the wives of presidential candidates as potential first ladies (or, assuming that a woman may be elected to the presidency, of potential first gentlemen). First lady is no longer an honor, a title, or even a job. It is now an office. It was even suggested that there be a first ladies' debate between Hillary Clinton and Elizabeth Dole in 1996.

The daily commercial press, after publicizing the idea, did not endorse the office of first lady. So the Hillary/Liddy contest was left to those who write letters to the editor. The results were not unlike those reported to have occurred in those primitive societies in which captured women were turned over to the female members of the tribe.

In the 1960 presidential debates, only the presidential candidates were included in the debates. In 1976 the vice presidential candidates were added to the show. We can anticipate that something new will have to be added to enliven the interest in the 2000 campaign. And that following the conventions and the selection of the vice presidential candidates, the only business remaining to be accomplished in either convention—the question of the qualifications of the spouses of both the presidential and even vice presidential candidates—will again be raised.

The Commission on Presidential Debates, which has assumed, or been given by some unknown authority, the power to determine who is to participate in the presidential campaign debates and to establish the conditions for such debates, may be moved to add this third debate between wives of the candidates.

It would not be wholly unreasonable to do so, as candidates almost without exception declare in their campaigns that their wives are their special confidantes and advisers. Jimmy Carter, for example, said that Rosalynn was "closest to his consciousness." And Nancy Reagan regularly gave her husband cues or answered for him. It might be helpful to the electorate to get a better idea as to what kind of advice they might give their husbands.

There is precedent for concern over the character and qualifications of spouses; it comes from fields other than politics. Major corporations, for example, make careful evaluations of wives before promoting husbands to high corporate offices. Now that women are rising in the corporate world, the corporations may be expected to exercise greater foresight in advance of marriages. This might be done by promising corporate employees counseling as to what kind of person will best serve the long-term interests of the corporation.

Years ago a congressional inquiry discovered the fact that the navy (this was before Tailhook) required in advance of promotions of junior officers not only an evaluation of the officer but also of his wife. It was never made clear who evaluated the younger wives—senior naval officers or their wives.

The State Department, not to be caught short, required ratings of wives of foreign service officers. Under congressional questioning, the personnel chief of the State Department, when asked about the evaluations and the extent to which he relied on them in making appointments, reported that he had not found them very useful and that after studying many reports, he had concluded that every foreign service officer was married to the same woman. This woman was intelligent, virtuous, socially acceptable, patient, loyal, dedicated, attractive, etc.

An alternative to this increasingly complex approach to picking a president would be to look to religious history, with the rule of celibacy for clergy. Today, this long-standing practice is being challenged within the Catholic Church. Compromising positions are being offered, such as allowing priests to marry but to insist on celibacy for bishops and for the pope. One can assume that if the ordination of women is approved, similar variations may be applied. In the application of a limited celibacy rule to politics, House members might be allowed to marry, but celibacy would be required of senators and certainly of the president.

Presidents are beginning to claim powers previously reserved to religious leaders: a kind of infallibility, reflected in statements such as: "If you knew what the president knows and had to carry the burdens of the office as he does, you would agree with him."

And presidents now assert moral authority, as evidenced in President Nixon's statement that the president is the moral leader of the country, and a comparable statement by President Carter that only the president can speak the moral judgment of the country to the rest of the world.

Celibacy would seem to be a small price to pay for the possession of such powers. Certainly, if it were required of presidents, it would simplify the electoral process.

5

The Postmodern Presidency

THE FIRST 100 DAYS AND THE FEBRUARY FACTOR

*T*he modern presidency is as removed, possibly more removed, from the people as the imperial presidencies of Lyndon Johnson and Richard Nixon. From Jimmy Carter on,
our presidents have been more and more distanced from their party
organizations, from the traditional ideology of their parties, from the
cabinet, from Congress, and from any sense of continuity with the history of the presidency.

A merely modern president might break with the past, as Roosevelt
did. Roosevelt had a reason for his break—the Great Depression. His
new order, however, was based upon refinement of the old. FDR reformed capitalism to save it. Hence, the antithesis was drawn from the
thesis in good, rational Hegelian fashion.

What we are into today is not rational or historical. The nature of
change and reform today is free floating, an end in itself, unattached to
anything in particular. It is self-contained reform.

A different kind of president is called for today. The president must
be all change, all motion, all strategy, existential, as one wag said. President Clinton reinvents himself by the month, week, day, and sometimes hour.

But this is not all a matter of personalities. Our society and politics have changed. Our laws, rules, and folkways have changed—all in ways that have undermined tradition and made public life rootless and textless, what one might call *postmodern.*

To begin, the president is not even sworn in on the day the Founders intended, a day that worked out very well.

On January 21, the day after President Clinton was first inaugurated, *The Washington Post* declared that the "clock" was ticking on President Clinton's 100-day plan.

After stating that the first 100 days was a "self-conscious, sometimes silly standard for measuring presidents," the *Post* proceeded to apply that standard. Even though as a candidate, Bill Clinton had invited a judgment on his first 100 days, that invitation should never have been taken seriously by the press when it was offered, or when the 100-day deadline was reached. Nor should it be accepted as a standard for historical judgment in contrast with Roosevelt or Kennedy or any other president.

Presidential candidates should not be encouraged to make irresponsible promises or projections in campaigns and then, subsequently, be judged for having fulfilled them or having failed to do so. And judgments should not be accepted by those who encouraged the initial act of irresponsibility. Applying the first-100-days standard as a measure of the success or failure of an administration is both irrelevant and unfair.

Franklin Roosevelt's countdown did not begin until March 4, 1933, the date of his first inauguration.

Today the presidential term begins on January 20. Roosevelt's evaluation did not begin until 116 days after his election. Bill Clinton's began, in 1992, 72 days after his election. Roosevelt's 100th day did not arrive until mid-June. Clinton's time ran out about the first of May, giving Roosevelt approximately 44 more days, following his election, before the judgment of experts, pundits, and the press was passed.

Roosevelt undoubtedly made some tentative decisions before he was sworn in as president, but he made no official or binding ones until after March 4. In consequence of the "lame duck" amendment passed in 1933, Clinton was called upon to make offical decisions in February.

Why the amendment was passed is unclear. There was no record of constitutional or governmental crisis in any way related to the March inauguration date. There was no prospect of such crisis in 1933. And February is not a good month for decision making, especially in the Northern Hemisphere; it is not a month distinguished by any significant natural phenomenon.

February has no equinox, as do March and September, and no solstice, as do December and June. It is not named after a god or an emperor. For the ancients it was a month reserved for purification, preparation for renewal. The date of February 2 marks the Christian feast of Purification. The Romans dedicated February to the netherworld. During February they worshiped Pluto and their dead ancestors.

In medieval times February was looked upon as a dangerous month; even a good February was suspect. "All the months of the year curse a fair February" runs a Welsh proverb. "February bears the bier," wrote the poet Shelley.

Even the animals shun decision making in February. It is a month of deep hibernation. Bodily and mental functions are at the lowest level of the year. Only the groundhog, by reputation, breaks the pattern and then only for a quick look for his shadow. His response is not reflective but automatic. If he sees his shadow, he returns to his burrow to hibernate for another six weeks. If he doesn't see his shadow, he, according to groundhog experts, also returns to the burrow for six weeks. A few years ago a groundhog found in Wisconsin in February had a body temperature of thirty-eight degrees and a pulse count of ten beats to the minute. Higher mammals—human beings—are comparably depressed, physically and mentally, in February.

The drafters of the Constitution, when they set the March 4 date for the inauguration, may well have known that February was no time for an outside inauguration program and no time in which to begin making important decisions.

Since we cannot repeal February, we should repeal the Twenty-second Amendment. Until that is done, no newly elected president should be encouraged to make any decisions in that month and should hold off until after the Ides of March. President Clinton failed twice in attempting to appoint an attorney general and succeeded only after March had come.

A POSTMODERN RITUAL:
SEARCHING FOR THE MANDATE

The argument, possibly the dominant one among political commentators, columnists, editors, politicians, and others, in the early weeks of the Clinton administration (1993) was over whether or not the president had a mandate. Clinton supporters insisted that he did have a mandate, at least for "change," vague and ill defined as change might be. Robert Dole, leader of the Republicans in the Senate at the time, said flatly that the president did not have a mandate of any kind.

An administration, a president, without a mandate is in deep trouble. This deep truth has been recognized since the Carter administration. Walter Mondale, commenting on the Carter administration's defeat in 1980, said that the failure of the administration occurred, first, "because it had no mandate," and second, because it did not have "an agenda to lean on."

The first Clinton administration, of course, was not without an agenda. It had many. One of its problems was choosing among agendas. But even if an administration has one agenda or several, it is in trouble, the experts say, if it does not have a mandate.

Mandate hunting and identification are much like bird-watching. In 1978, for a book he wrote with James J. Kilpatrick and myself, the cartoonist Jeff MacNelly was called on to represent the mandate in graphic form. MacNelly chose a bird, something between an eagle and a vulture, and then distinguished among mandates, two major types, Greater Mandates and Lesser Mandates. He reported no such thing as a simple Great Mandate. Greater Mandates included Impressive Mandates, Overwhelming Mandates, and Irresistible Mandates. None of these rare species has been seen since the Roosevelt administration, until they were seen or said to have been seen in the Reagan administration.

Elizabeth Drew, an experienced and credible mandate watcher and observer, reported in the first year of the Clinton administration that she had sighted, or discovered, and identified a previously unknown species of mandate, possibly a subspecies or a hybrid or a genetic sport, the "Pale" Mandate.

The Drew mandate is purely "pale," not pale blue or pale yellow but absolutely pale, possibly the color of the pale horse of the Apocalypse, neither white nor gray.

Such discoveries must be a great relief to the news administration. Any kind of mandate is better than no mandate. As Gertrude Stein might have said, "A mandate is a mandate is a mandate."

THE GOVERNOR OF THE UNITED STATES

Among the Founding Fathers and the authors of the Federalist Papers, Alexander Hamilton demonstrated perhaps the least disposition to be overly trustful of human nature. Thomas Jefferson was optimistic. James Madison was chary. John Adams saw blackness in the human soul, but hoped for republican democracy anyway.

Writing in Federalist Paper No. 17, Hamilton undertook to answer the charge that under the proposed Constitution the federal government might become so strong that it would absorb "those residuary authorities, which might be judged proper to leave with states for local purposes." "Allowing," he wrote, "the utmost latitude to the love of power which any reasonable man can require, I confess, I am at a loss to discover what temptation the persons entrusted with the general government could ever feel to divest the states of authorities of that description." He then listed some of the things he thought would never be "desirable cares of a general jurisdiction." Among them he included domestic police, supervision of agriculture, and general local needs, and, he concluded, "It is therefore improbable that there should exist a disposition in the federal councils to usurp the powers with which they are connected, because the attempt to exercise those powers would be as troublesome as it would be nugatory; and the possession of them, for that reason, would contribute nothing to the dignity, to the importance, or to the splendor of the national government."

Hamilton did not anticipate the move to shared funding of local activities by the federal government and state and local governments, or the confusion, actually competition, for responsibility and possible political credit in many parts of the Great Society program, which in its farthest reaches had the federal government taking some responsibility for even garbage collection and disposal.

The state of confusion, of the mingling of responsibilities that has been developing, was clearly manifest in the campaign of Bill Clinton in 1992. The thrust of his campaign was more that of a campaign to be governor of the United States than to be president. The principal responsibilities of governors and of local authorities traditionally have been law enforcement, education, maintenance of roads, problems of poverty, and health. Clinton said that if elected, he would be known as the "education president," as some claimed he was the "education governor" of Arkansas. He declared that he would handle the welfare and poverty problems through a program of "workfare, not welfare," which he sort of tried as governor and which almost all governors now say they believe in.

In 1992 Bill Clinton said he was going to develop a program to help governors and mayors build "empowerment zones," as governors have with some success done, by attracting foreign industries with offers of special tax concessions, use of new facilities financed with tax-exempt bonds, right-to-work laws, etc. Clinton promised to be involved in law enforcement, through providing financing for 100,000 more police officers. And he said he would help them build roads and bridges.

In 1996 the president announced he had done all that. And he added that he had turned welfare back to the states and the governors (a Republican program), come out for school uniforms and midnight basketball, disposed of innumerable tons of toxic waste, and extended phone service to Cuba (in the hopes of whetting Cubans' appetites for capitalism).

The confusion of responsibility implicit in the Clinton presidency ran far beyond anything in the Great Society program or concept and beyond the imagination of Hamilton.

Though his interest in foreign policy and his sense of how to deal with Congress have grown considerably, the president's early performance in office reflected his gubernatorial experience and indicated that he did not comprehend the differences between a governorship and the presidency, thus sustaining a commonly held axiom in the U.S. Senate—that it takes roughly six years for a governor elected to the Senate to get over being a governor.

The transition from governor to president may not be as shocking or traumatic as the transition from governor to senator.

And it may be that at this point in our history the country needs a governor rather than a president.

But some of the procedures and practices in place that preceded the election of President Clinton in 1992 remind one of state government:

- Some states operate under constitutional requirements that their budgets be balanced every year. Budget resolutions comparable to those now popular in the federal Congress are common in state legislatures.

- Budget conflicts are regularly settled in state government, by trade-offs in the closing hours of legislative sessions. Some governors have therefore been given line-item veto powers. One popular reform of recent years—now law—is the line-item veto for the president at the federal level.

- Earmarking of revenue is a common practice in state governments: a special tax for education, for example; gasoline taxes for roads and bridges; special fees for special purposes, and so on. In the federal government, the use of earmarking has traditionally been very restricted; the one major exception was the earmarking of the gasoline tax imposed in the Eisenhower Administration to finance the federal highway-building program. Earmarking is more and more often advocated as a way to retire the deficit. And the Clinton administration proposes much wider and more varied use of the practice: So-called sin taxes are proposed on tobacco, to be used for cancer research.

Earmarked funds are often borrowed against (in the states they are sometimes called rainy-day funds) until they are needed. The federal government now does this with Social Security funds, to help finance debt and deficits (much to the dismay of Sen. Daniel Patrick Moynihan).

- Caps are proposed to be placed on expenditures; trade-offs, such as $2 in reduced expenditures for every increase in taxes, and comparable Rube Goldberg procedures are common in state government. In Washington the think tanks are now thinking about them.

The acceptance of transferred state procedures to the national level reflects the growing influence of governors and former governors, the most prominent being Bill Clinton.

But a trend of generally unrecognized significance is the number of former members of state legislatures now present in the House of Representatives. According to congressional research studies, their numbers increased from 165 in 1970 to 225 in 1992. Just as Bill Clinton's first instinct was to attempt to model his presidency after his experience as a governor, the new members of Congress elected in the classes of 1992 and 1994 were often inclined to act like state legislators. Whereas Clinton spent his early months in office thinking about how to manage a bureaucracy (the basic job of a governor), the new breed in Congress was overly driven by partisanship and theatrical tactics, such as holding bills and fellow members hostage in various ways. This finally culminated in the shutdown of the federal government, the sort of midnight tactic that has often been employed at the state level but that backfired at the federal level.

President Clinton learned to think of himself as something more than a governor of the United States—though when in trouble he still acts a bit like the old-fashioned first lady, urging school uniforms and literacy volunteers.

The younger members of Congress have some things to learn as well. The federal government is far more complex than state government; the national media are more skeptical; it is not like Columbus, Athens, Hartford, or St. Paul. And historically Congress has worked best when most of the real work was done in a bipartisan way and ideology was kept at bay.

POSTMODERN POLICIES, POLITICS, LOGIC, AND VALUES

I now understand that in the higher levels of culture—art, music, poetry, etc.—we have been moving out of the age of modernism into a new age or era labeled "postmodernism."

At first the term gave me some trouble. Modernism, to me, had always indicated the now and could never be post, unless the word was to be fixed, as having no future use. There could never be a postmodernism. But now the line has been broken. We may look forward to new-modernism, or neomodernism, possibly neo-neomodernism, to indicate new eras and ages, as we do Stallone movies. Thus, what may be ahead is Postmodernism II, III, etc.

Then I learned from President Clinton that we in the United States are in a postmodern *political* era. This took me somewhat by surprise. The politics of most of the modern era had been a mixed bag of democracy, communism, fascism, and colonialism with a polarization into two camps, communism and capitalistic democracy, following the end of World War II. With the breakup of the Soviet Union and the general abandonment of communism, some political observers said we were back to the end of World War II, while others said we were back to the beginning of World War II. None of these early analysts identified the beginning of a postmodern age of politics that now apparently is upon us.

Since I can find no orderly or systematic exposition of postmodern politics, even from those who say they are practicing it, I have been trying to define it by noting differences between current and past politics, hoping that, as in the method of music-minus-one, a melody may emerge.

Apparently, the logic of postmodernism is not traditional or Aristotelian. It is what computer experts call "fuzzy logic," the logic of the computer, which under some circumstances is said to be more reliable, at least in the short run, than classical, rational logic.

The strength of the new logic lies in the fact that it uses, or manipulates, imprecise facts (nonfacts?), or what may not be a fact, or even a nonfact, but an imprecision (a word once used by a Reagan aide to explain a presidential misstatement). Everything in the new logic is approached as a matter of degree. Key words are not absolutes, like black and white, or hot or cold, but gray, or cool.

Consistent with this use of logic and language, President Jimmy Carter described what some called a failure in the attempted rescue of the American hostages held in Iran (they were not rescued) as an "incomplete success." It might as well have been described as a partial failure.

Early indications of unrecognized postmodernism in both the Reagan and Carter administrations, obscured by the deconstructionism (linguistic and political) of the Bush administration, should have forewarned us of a new politics, which is becoming more clearly manifest in the Clinton administration and what might be called "the Clinton generation" in politics.

The postmodern generation in politics has several distinguishing marks. First, it is indifferent to tradition. People in the new politics are unlikely to have had the experience of participating in satisfying and sustaining history. They missed the days of high patriotism and sacrifice of World War II and came to political awareness during the years of the Vietnam War, many experiencing the distressing and difficult test of patriotism, as in the case of President Clinton.

Second, postmodern politics discounts loyalty and personal relationships. Appointment to office or election to office, which used to reflect cultural and personal ties such as religion and nationality, is more likely to depend on physical or physiological or biological differences, such as race, sex, or accident of time of birth.

When Zoë Baird, President Clinton's first choice to be attorney general, looked for help, having experienced difficulty after being nominated by the president, she found no personal support even from Mr. Clinton. But she did receive the depersonalized support of her generation and fellow members of the female sex. Her situation moved one political writer with historical memory to report a prepostmodern rule of Chicago Democratic politics (a rule probably still in effect in Chicago): "Don't send us nobody that nobody sent."

Third, postmodern politicians and persons are lonely. Many of them have not known community—not the community of family, not family loyalty, or loyalty to place, to city or town, or to employers or corporations, or even loyalty to baseball teams. They are isolated. Many are like a child alone in an airport, smiling too readily, too soon, or too long, bearing a name tag with both a return and a forwarding address.

Fourth, postmoderns are not greedy as often described. They are insecure, seeking security in making more, and in using more, rather than having more.

The music of the postmodernist age, if not all postmoderns, is rap—instant in composition and in performance. It is wholly impromptu—produced and consumed in one disposable presentation.

Postmodern persons are more likely to say, "I represent," or "I am a client," than "I am."

They spend a lot of time redefining themselves and looking for new meaning.

They have many friends who seem to be not just friends but best friends. There seem to be no casual friends or former friends, and all friends are mutual, shared with others like investments in a mutual fund.

Postmoderns are advocates and practitioners of zero-based thinking. I tried it once and passed right through the zero mark into the range of subzero thinking. The climb back was too difficult.

I now try to start thinking not only above zero but also well above the freezing point.

Postmoderns believe that both life and politics can be reduced to problems and solutions. They say things like, "If you do not know what the problem is, you are part of it." They are not only problem solvers but problem finders. Postmodern political campaigns and offices have issues persons. Meetings are advanced by the use of facilitators. And proposals are challenged not by the traditional devil's advocate but by contrarians.

Postmoderns are quite free with language. They make nouns into verbs, like "expense," and then, for general use, into gerunds. A man used to father a child and then become a father. A woman would have a child and then become a mother. Husbands and wives now "parent" their children. Books on parenting are popular in postmodern America.

Postmoderns quantify and extrapolate and, without history but with fuzzy logic, are the power in postmodern politics. David Gergen said, on his joining the Clinton administration, that he became more "centered." Dick Morris said that writing a book after he had disgraced himself and the president he worked for was "healing." Gergen said he "intersected" with members of the administration, "bonded" with them, and experienced a "psychic return." Perhaps it was the same for Morris.

The postmodern politician is, in a sense, the reformer without clear ends or convictions and without historical context, which is the sort of reform we have today. Reform that is free floating, existential, and believes above all in "change" is the essence of postmodern policies.

As Leon Wieseltier wrote in *The New Republic* (July 1993), the postmodern politician, as exemplified by President Clinton, is marked not by nonbelief but by belief in everything, a belief that eliminates the rule of contradiction and leaves one with only one working principle—belief in "process."

6

Postmodern Bureaucracy:
The Military-Industrial Complex

*O*ne factor that has helped to remove the presidency from democratic politics, from the representative process, and at times from reality itself, hence rendering it postmodern, is the military industrial complex.

In some measure, the military-industrial complex has come to control the parameters of presidential decision making and of the presidential image and style of leadership.

Presidents Johnson, Nixon, Bush, and Clinton have all been preoccupied by military policy, to the exclusion of foreign policy, properly considered. All of these presidents were preoccupied with their roles as leaders of the military, as commander in chief, to the exclusion of diplomatic leadership on the world stage.

The "military-industrial complex" was named by President Dwight Eisenhower, who in his farewell address in 1961 sounded a warning. He said, "We must guard against the acquisition of unwarranted influence, whether sought or unsought, by the military-industrial complex. The potential for the disastrous rise of misplaced power exists and will persist."

In that address President Eisenhower restated a warning first given to the United States by Alexis de Tocqueville in 1840, when the translation of his book *Democracy in America* was published in the United States. In that book the French political philosopher anticipated the threat to a democratic government and society from a military establishment that was larger and stronger and more powerful than was needed for any immediate or reasonably predictable military threat to the nation. Such an establishment, Tocqueville predicted, could become a political force in itself, exercising independent power not only over military and foreign policy but also over the domestic civilian society it was designed to serve.

At the time Tocqueville made his observations, the U.S. military establishment was a limited power. In 1831, the year of his visit, the number of active duty enlisted personnel was 9,913, of whom roughly 5,000 were in the army and 4,000 in the navy.

The number of military personnel increased to approximately 50,000 at the time of the Mexican War. There was no accurate count of forces in the army during the Civil War, but the number in the navy and in the marines totaled about 55,000. From the end of the Civil War until the Spanish-American War, the total numbers in the armed forces varied from approximately 35,000 to 40,000. During World War I, peak enrollment occurred in 1918, when the number of persons in the army was recorded as over 2,250,000 and in the combined navy and Marine Corps as over 465,000. The numbers quickly declined after the war and hovered in the range of 300,000 from 1920 to 1940.

In 1945 enlisted personnel on active duty for World War II came to about 10,795,000. By 1947 the number was down to 1,385,000 and remained at about that number until the Korean War, when it increased to as high as 3,254,000 in 1952. Vietnam counted numbers at about 3,000,000. Following that war the numbers leveled off at about 2,000,000.

Within the complex of people with ties to the military at the beginning of the nineties were some 1,155,000 civilian employees; 1,700,000 reservists; dependent persons numbering over 1,000,000; and over 1,300,000 retired military annuitants.

It was not until after the end of World War II and the Korean War that anything comparable to the kind of establishment that Tocqueville warned against developed in the United States. That establishment did not spring full blown from the wars. In the interim, between the end of World War II and the beginning of the Korean War, defense budgets were reduced to as little as $15 billion to $16 billion a year. Defense costs for the Korean War rose to $40 billion and more annually and did not come down after the end of the war, rising to approximately $100 billion a year by 1978, to $200 billion by 1988, and to over $300 billion by 1990—in advance of the special increases accompanying the war in the Persian Gulf area.

There were other factors that fed into the development of the military-industrial complex: Before World War II, ships were built in the U.S. Navy shipyards. Tanks were built in factories operated by the army. There were naval gun factories and torpedo factories, army arsenals and munition plants, and no air force.

Major involvement of civilian production facilities in military supply came with World War II, which was a war of production, of supply, and of logistics, requiring much more material and service than could be provided by existing military operations. The entire U.S. industrial base and service establishment was mobilized in support of the war. Privately owned shipyards built ships for the navy. Automobile companies became manufacturers of tanks or trucks or jeeps. Private companies expanded production of guns and ammunition.

The military-industrial establishment as a powerful influence on domestic and on foreign policy, on politics, did not come into being by accident or as an afterthought or incidental development.

Long before the complex was in place, in fact, scarcely before World War II had ended, there was evidence that the military and those interested in it were making plans for the future. An executive committee was organized that made recommendations to Congress.

Congress took up the recommendations and in 1947 and in 1949 passed military reorganization legislation. There were two provisions in these reorganization acts that had significant bearing on the future. The first provision, bearing upon the force and function of the military, was the abandonment, or rejection, of the word "war." The War Department was no more. It was replaced by the less aggressive but more enduring and unassailable Department of Defense. The need for a large war department might be challenged if there was no war. The department, so named, might be called upon to report on future war plans.

Moreover, a defense department could not fairly be subjected to demands for plans for war. The demands for defense are potentially without limit. No matter how thorough its defense efforts were, the animal in Kafka's "The Burrow" remained fearful and insecure. A scratching sound was disturbing, as was silence. *Defense* is really unlimited. Defense on earth must be supplemented by defense in space or at least by a defense initiative in space.

The second significant provision of the reorganization was the establishment of the United States Air Force within the Department of Defense, with status equal to that of the Department of the Army and the Department of the Navy.

Airpower advocates, riding on the popularity achieved by airpower during World War II, prevailed despite opposition from both the Department of the Army and the Department of the Navy. Establishing the third department resolved the dispute between the army and the navy relative to unification. Each department evidently believed that with unification, one or the other of the departments that had been unified would dominate. The accepted plan introduced into defense the principle of the trinity, with the internal assurance that any two of the three departments could unite against the third if it threatened to become dominant.

The military-industrial complex was strengthened and consolidated through procurement policies that added a powerful political strength to its inherent economic power. This strengthening was achieved through careful distribution of defense contracts and subcontracts. The procurement program proposed for the building of the B-2 is exemplary.

As originally proposed, the procurement would have been distributed among forty-six states, with the possibility that ninety-two senators would then have some interest in the economic fallout from the program, which had the potential to supply work for tens of thousands of workers and contracts to hundreds of suppliers. An early Defense Department press release named more than 150 possible contractors and subcontractors.

The economic and political logic has endured. In defense of our involvement in the Persian Gulf area, then Secretary of State James Baker noted that *jobs were at stake.* Military suppliers ran advertisements telling of their contribution in helping fight the war and providing jobs at the same time. The president of the United States visited civilian production facilities. The military proposed that payments made by foreign countries in support of the war should not be passed through congressional appropriation procedures but be made directly to the Defense Department. This process, if allowed, might have opened the way for direct contracting between the Pentagon and foreign countries for mercenary services.

The way that the military-industrial complex entwines itself in the culture and economy of the United States is most clearly seen, of course, when the matters at issue are such as the closing of shipyards or military bases, or the competing of states, regions, and companies for major contracts.

Tocqueville, with all of his gift of foresight, could scarcely have been expected to anticipate how accurately the Pentagon, as a covering label for the whole military-industrial complex with its outside support, would fulfill his forecast: becoming a republic within the republic, with its own welfare program (including health care, an educational system, housing, recreational and retirement programs, and veterinary services. This, even though the cavalry is gone, and only the canine corps, some experimental animals, dolphins, and homing pigeons remain in the service). The Pentagon has its own retail service: the post exchange, or PX, which became the largest retail operation in the country, or of the country, behind Sears, Roebuck (and probably behind Wal-Mart today).

The full extent of this duplication or replication of civilian life and culture became evident in the debate on the first Reagan defense budget. It was found that the administration, while cutting other elements in the budget, both military and nonmilitary, not only planned no cuts in money for military bands and other musical units but also was proposing an increase in the appropriations for these operations. The bands included the traditional military bands, supplemented by a variety of unconventional, nontraditional, and irregular musical groups, such as the U.S. Army Chorus, the Navy's Sea Chanters, and the Air Force's Singing Sergeants. In the jazz theater of operations, the army deployed a unit known as the Army Blues; the navy's able-bodied jazzmen were called the Commodores; and the air force unit, Airmen of Notes.

The army arsenal had a chamber orchestra, a brass quartet, a string quartet, a unit called the Herald Trumpets, and a fife-and-drum corps. The navy countered with an elite instrumental combo, Cross Current. The navy also had a bluegrass group and Port Authority, which played rock 'n' roll as well. It had no string group. The air force, however, had the Strolling Strings and a rapid-deployment rock band called Mach I.

The Marine Corps makes a point of not breaking its musicians into specialized units. This is consistent with the corps's tradition of going anywhere and of doing anything it is called upon to do. A spokesperson for the marines at the time said that the marine band had members who could be called on to perform any kind of musical mission from Bach to rock, from band to orchestra, and from combo and ensemble to solo work on instruments like guitar and harp.

The final prop or support for the independence of the military-industrial complex was put in place when the draft law was allowed to expire in the Nixon administration, to be replaced with what was called the Volunteer Army program. In the post-Vietnam period, both the militarists and civil libertarians looked for an alternative to the flawed and discriminatory draft program that had been in effect during the closing years of the Vietnam War.

The militarists argued that under the volunteer (better called mercenary) program, only those who wanted to be in the military or were willing to enter it for money would have to serve. The antimilitarists and the libertarians were satisfied that under the new program those who wished to stay out of the military would be free to do so. Both sides seemed either unfamiliar with, or indifferent to, the debate between Hamilton and Jefferson when the nation was being established. Hamilton wanted a mercenary, professional army, and Jefferson held for a citizens' army drawn from the general public. Neither view prevailed until the 1970s. Until then our military forces had been a mixture of citizen and of professional personnel, made up of a corps of professionals supplemented by a citizen's draft for major wars.

The war in the Persian Gulf was not a clear test of the military, political, and social implications of a mercenary army, but it gave evidence that Tocqueville's warning was and is worthy of attention. It was asserted at the time of the war that the few in the Persian Gulf forces who questioned the operation had good grounds for challenge since these persons were being paid, and had contracted to perform military service. The military-industrial complex, with its supporting forces, was in place not only as a military institution but also as an economic, diplomatic, and social one.

7

The No-Fault Presidency: Who, Me?

*H*arry Truman was noted for saying of his presidency, "The buck stops here," a phrase that has nothing to do with dollars, but is one drawn from poker and referring to the marker designating the next player to deal the cards.

President Eisenhower accepted responsibility for the U-2 flight over Russia during his administration. John Kennedy did the same for the failed Cuban invasion. Both Eisenhower and Kennedy could have justifiably given excuses.

Subsequent presidents have been less ready to accept and acknowledge blame for either foreign or domestic policy failures.

As U.S. involvement in Vietnam deepened, President Johnson invoked the Tonkin Gulf Resolution as a protective defense and noted that he was carrying on a policy in Vietnam accepted and advanced by the three presidents who had preceded him in office. President Nixon, in turn, noted that he was carrying forward, even in Cambodia, what four of his predecessors had sustained. He labeled the Vietnam War a "Democrat war."

President Carter attributed domestic failures during his administration to the "malaise" that he said had settled on the nation. He occasionally gave examples of those stricken with malaise: Members of the medical profession, he said, were fine as individual doctors but were suspect as members of medical associations.

President Reagan took credit for military success in Grenada but passed over the deaths of marines in Lebanon as a kind of biblical event.

This progressive rejection of presidential responsibility came full term and possibly reached institutional status in the Bush administration. President Bush blamed the budget deficit on the Democratic Congress. He might have gone further, in Carter style, and blamed it on the American electorate, since that electorate chose a Democratic Congress in both 1990 and 1992, despite the president's appeal for the election of Republicans. But Bush settled on Congress. It was Congress, he said, that controlled the federal budget. The president, according to Bush, was a sort of regent, basically unable to do much about federal spending and fiscal priorities. Harry Truman would have been astounded at such an abdication.

Bush took no responsibility for the savings and loan debacle or for related difficulties in the deregulated banking industry or in the Department of Housing and Urban Development.

Bush did not even take responsibility for his choice of a running mate. Other presidents and presidential candidates had been held responsible for their vice presidents and running mates. And none had even attempted to dodge responsibility. Franklin Roosevelt had rejected two vice presidents, John Nance Garner and Henry Wallace, as running mates. Dwight Eisenhower answered for Richard Nixon in 1952. George McGovern was held responsible for his choice and subsequent rejection of Sen. Thomas Eagleton (a good man who, incredible as it might seem today, was driven from the ticket in 1972 because he had been treated for depression). Nixon, belatedly, had to take the blame for his choice of Spiro Agnew. And Walter Mondale suffered for his choice of Geraldine Ferraro. George Bush treated Dan Quayle as a kind of accident or an act of nature—something found on the doorstep one morning. Bush may have wanted to dump Quayle in 1992, but finding no one who would do it for him or make the decision for him, he failed to take responsibility for removing Quayle from the ticket.

Bush's distancing of himself from responsibility was not limited to domestic and official actions.

Whereas Lee Atwater, manager of the Bush campaign, apologized a few months before his death for some of the things he had done to help defeat Michael Dukakis in the 1988 campaign, especially the racial exploitation of the Willie Horton ad, there was no comparable expression of regret from George Bush, the beneficiary of Atwater's work.

The most glaring demonstration of denial of presidential responsibility by Bush occurred on April 7, 1992, following the successes of the Gulf War, when the president, in a church in Houston, publicly absolved himself—and, by extension, the United States—of any responsibility for the condition of various Iraqi rebel and refugee groups.

We had, he acknowledged, encouraged them to revolt against Saddam Hussein, but the United States had not, he asserted, promised those who responded to that encouragement any support in arms or otherwise.

Moreover, the president noted, bringing legal support to his abdication, any assistance would have been an intervention in the internal affairs of another nation, an action not allowed by the United Nations. This was an assertion almost breathtaking in its hypocrisy and intellectual dishonesty. Had the United Nations been in existence as

World War II was about to begin and had Adolf Hitler (Bush had called Saddam "Hitler") promised to give up conquered territory, to suspend production of weapons of mass destruction, and to make reparations or the promise of them, he might have been allowed to go on—as long as he executed only German Jews.

Bush's denial of responsibility for refugees created by the Gulf War was in line with similar denials of responsibility for other actions related to the Persian Gulf War. For example, the death and destruction that resulted from the liberation of Kuwait and the attacks on Saddam's fleeing or retreating troops were, the president said, attributable to Saddam and were on *his* conscience. Moreover, Bush held that the shelling and bombing of troops, tanks, trucks, etc. during the retreat of Iraqi forces were justified under the Geneva Conventions since the forces had not surrendered and were assumed to be moving to a new position from which they would resume hostilities. The president, during these early days of the war, attempted to insulate himself even more clearly from responsibility, saying that he was doing what the military recommended. In later stages of the war, claims of presidential intervention in policy making began to surface.

A further question of responsibility was raised regarding earlier tacit and under-the-table support for Saddam Hussein. The United States certainly tilted toward Iraq in its war with Iran. And the United States under Bush may well have initially given Saddam reason to believe that his disputes over oil and borders with Kuwait were of little concern to the United States. Moreover, our friendly relations with Saddam had continued long after it was suspected, if not known with certainty, that he had used chemical weapons against the Kurds.

Yet, Bush acknowledged no responsibility or fault. The explanation of U.S. policy toward Iraq was left to a career foreign service officer, April Glaspie, who served as ambassador to Iraq. The ambassador's explanation of the apparent contradictions between policy and action was as follows: She said that the United States had made the mistake of not realizing how "dumb" Saddam was in believing that we meant what we said. When we indicated our indifference to what he might do about Kuwait, he should have realized that we did not really mean it.

Glaspie did not report at what level in the State Department the mistake (of not realizing how dumb Saddam was) was made. Nor did she explain whether the mistake occurred because our officials were too "dumb" to realize how dumb Saddam was or because the general level of intelligence in the administration was so high that no one in the department could comprehend dumbness of the level at which it evidently exists in Saddam Hussein.

In any event this was the level of explanation or justification by the Bush presidency for a de facto alliance with a man against whom the United States was to soon wage war and whom the president called as evil as Hitler. Bush created an intellectual and moral void out of which emerged the "no-fault presidency": If things went wrong, no one was responsible and no one was to blame. If things went well, everyone was responsible and it was to the credit of the president.

It may be that President Bush's disposition to avoid responsibility was nurtured by his experience in the political offices that he had held prior to his election to the presidency, mostly unelected. Moreover, even his record in electoral politics, prior to seeking the presidency and vice presidency, was one of fundamental compromise. Bush first ran and was elected to the House of Representatives as a liberal Republican. He subsequently ran for the Senate twice, unsuccessfully, as a Goldwater and then as an Agnew conservative.

Bush then became ambassador to the United Nations. He was appointed to the post by Richard Nixon, who wanted to downgrade the job. For Bush, who had just narrowly lost his second Senate race and had nowhere to go in elective politics, it was a political lifesaver and a huge step up from former congressman. Bush was most grateful.

His next job was as chairman of the Republican Party, where he replaced Robert Dole. Again, Bush was appointed by Nixon. Bush's job was to defend the integrity and honor of Nixon during Watergate. Chairmanship of the Republican Party (one can say the same of the chairmanship of the Democratic Party) is not recommended for character building.

Bush was also liaison to China—not even ambassador but the president's personal liaison and Henry Kissinger's. In this post Bush reportedly played a great deal of tennis and perhaps arranged for Kissinger's visits.

The other office held by Bush before he sought the presidency and vice presidency in 1980 may have profoundly affected his attitude toward personal responsibility and his sensitivity to truth: He became head of the Central Intelligence Agency.

Bush's last post before he became president was the vice presidency, where he served eight years. Bush accepted the vice presidential nomination after having vigorously denounced Ronald Reagan's economic views as "voodoo economics." He then became a most enthusiastic and dedicated convert to Reaganism and Reaganomics.

It is hard to imagine any politician who had followed this career path emerging as a decisive and responsible national leader.

Peggy Noonan, in her book about the Reagan administration, *What I Saw at the Revolution,* makes several observations that may help explain the Bush detachment or flight from responsibility.

According to Noonan, a speechwriter for Bush, her early offerings were rejected, principally because the pronoun "I" was used too often. According to Noonan, candidate Bush hated to say *I.* If she wrote an *I* in a speech for him, he would drop the phrase or construction containing the pronoun or drop an entire sentence rather than say the *I* word. Eventually, she accommodated her texts to the candidate's desire. Instead of writing, "I moved to Texas," she would write, "moved to Texas." Instead of "We joined the Republican Party," she wrote, "joined the Republican Party."

Noonan speculated as to whether when he took the oath of office Bush would say "solemnly swear," not "I solemnly swear," and "preserve and protect," not "I will preserve and protect," in keeping with his favoring naked predicates, rather than complete sentences with both subject and predicates. Noonan suggests that Bush's disposition to avoid the use of the pronoun *I* had its beginnings in Bush's childhood. His supposedly stern mother admonished him, when he was a boy, not to use the *I* word.

Noonan later was accepted into the speechwriters' group and took, or was given, credit for adding the "thousand points of light" and "read my lips" lines to the standard Bush campaign speech. So even the phrases for which George Bush is remembered are the work of someone else. Bush said them, but Peggy Noonan was responsible.

GEORGE BUSH'S WAR

The labeling of the original U.S. military action in the Persian Gulf as "Desert Storm" followed a little-noted precedent by which the Pentagon named its wars in advance. The Grenada invasion was officially known in military circles, or pentagonals, as "Urgent Fury" and the Panama action as "Just Cause." Neither of these titles took hold as historical markers, possibly because the action in each case was relatively short-lived and both interventions were of limited objective.

Neither did Desert Storm or the sustaining action, "Rolling Thunder," make much impact. Neither will make it into the history books as major chapters in military history, great or not so great—like the Battle of Britain or the Battle of the Bulge or the Vietnam War.

The Gulf War has become a sort of nonwar—almost immediately forgotten except for the U.S. soldiers injured or disabled there. Indeed, the only "heroes" of the war were Gen. "Stormin' Norman" Schwarzkopf, Gen. Colin Powell, and President Bush. Two soon went into civilian life, and one was soundly beaten in a national election.

A whole (or a half) presidency later, nagging and basic questions remain: Why did the United States fight the Gulf War? What did we hope to accomplish? What do we think we did accomplish? And have we stabilized the region? Neither the press nor Congress has seemed very curious.

President Clinton's parenthetical bombing in northern Iraq in the summer of 1996—during the presidential season—seemed to be in keeping with what is now the established U.S. stance in the gulf: When things heat up, do something. Since George Bush, we have taken actions without aims or even clear military strategy. A president, by these lights, must "show strength" and "not go wobbly," but long-term diplomatic goals are optional.

The purpose of the Gulf War as first stated—namely, to protect access to Saudi Arabian oil supplies—was wholly defensible. The United States had a clear right and obligation to intervene in our own interest, but also in consequence of obligations accepted under NATO and under our treaties with Japan.

The justification for our intervention was comparable to that underscoring our intervention in Korea: principally, to assure nations dependent on us in the Far East of the seriousness of our commitment and of our integrity.

But as the magnitude of our military movement grew, so did the magnitude and number of reasons given for our being engaged, just as purposes magnified and multiplied and the commitment of arms and men had increased in Vietnam.

There are many questions that President Bush should have been asked and that he should have answered as conditions for advancing and extending the Gulf War. Most of them remain unanswered today:

- Was the liberation of Kuwait contemplated?
- Was the deposing of Saddam Hussein considered?
- Was the destruction of Iraq's potential to produce nuclear weapons and its real capability to produce chemical and germ warfare a primary objective? Or was the war to protect American pride?
- Why was the advice of military experts or those reputed to be experts, for example, retired Admiral William J. Crowe, Jr., ignored?
- Why were the military forces of the Arab nations aligned against Iraq, most of them armed with U.S.-made weapons, not asked or urged or required to assume major military responsibilities in the war? These aligned Arab nations had a combined population of approximately 100 million people versus an Iraqi population of about 12 million. Egypt, alone, had an army strong enough to have fought the Israeli forces to a draw in 1973. The Saudis and the smaller oil-producing countries had advanced U.S. equipment. And the Syrians, one of what were called "the coalition allies" had arms enough for continuing military action in Lebanon.
- President Bush spoke of "the new world order." What was, what is, the new world order to be established?
- How was this world order to be maintained?
- What were the plans for meeting the costs of the war, since it appeared early that Saudi, Japanese, and German contributions

would fall far short of what we might have expected them to contribute? Did our government know this would be the case from the start?

- Immediately after the war, why did President Bush not take the initiative in setting up a general conference on the problems of the Middle East, or indicate a willingness to follow the initiatives of others, especially since the changes in Russia and the accompanying possibility of constructive participation by the Russians greatly increased the chances of success in efforts to establish peace and order in the area?

- Why were efforts not being made to make the Middle East a nuclear-free area as part of a more comprehensive nuclear nonproliferation and nuclear disarmament effort?

- With chemical and germ warfare a possibility (even, it appears, a reality) in the Middle East, why was there no significant effort or disposition in evidence on the part of the United States to move toward banning such weapons, including our own neutron bombs?

- Can anyone explain U.S. support of Saddam Hussein during the Iran-Iraq war?

- After we "won" the war, why did the president not propose a world conference or U.N. action to re-examine the 1923 mapping, principally by the British, in the Middle East?

- Why were the Israelis not permitted to "take out" Iraqi nuclear installations, thus establishing a basis for respect and appreciation among the Arab nations threatened by Iraq's nuclear arms?

- Is it true, as some have said, that the strength of Iraq's army was never what the president represented it to be and that the sending of 500,000 military personnel with supplies, weapons, and other material to the Middle East was primarily an exercise in logistics and a test of acceptance by Congress and by the people of the United States of presidential power?

These questions still matter today, not only so that we may clearly see where we have been and how some of the peoples of the Middle East might see recent history but also because it might help U.S. policymakers to clarify our aims and objectives in the future. U.S. policy at the moment remains utterly vague, almost random, despite the best efforts of President Clinton to "bring people together" in that part of the world.

Before you fight other nations or attempt to bring them together, it helps to know what you are trying to accomplish.

The Gulf War and subsequent gulf policy are prime examples of the pattern of no-fault presidential leadership, which President Clinton has continued.

President Bush acted as if he had inherited a military and political posture whose purpose had never been made quite clear to him. Such posturing is exactly what did happen to President Clinton, but it did not move him to attempt to understand the war, its aims, or its consequences. He merely assumed the rhetorical pose—"I will do something"—and continued the posturing.

THE BUSH PRESIDENCY:
REPRESENTATION WITHOUT TAXATION

War or no war, the Bush presidency was marked by some of the silliest personal behavior of a president in this century, beginning with a post-election pre-swearing-in photo of the president-elect and his wife, Barbara, in a large bed, surrounded by dogs and grandchildren. This was followed by sports scenes: tennis, golf, baseball, and even horseshoes, plus almost daily excessive and intensive jogging. (One

reporter who jogged with or near the president said that near the end
of the first two miles, there came a period lasting about 200 yards
when the president spoke clearly and in complete sentences.)

There was a succession of baseball-type caps, and the president, in
a golf cart between holes, pausing to give short press conferences on
war, taxes, and unrelated matters. The president would then move on
with his standard phrase of dismissal: "Gotta run now."

Silliness extended beyond personal and incidental behavior. It was
demonstrated most clearly with the president's persistence in appropriating stock and macho political phrases, sometimes spoken by
President Reagan and sometimes borrowed from Clint Eastwood
movies: "Go ahead, make my day," "There you go again," etc. This
became the basis of taxation or fiscal policy. "Read my lips" became
the moral basis, such as it was, of the Bush presidency.

In the course of the history of our country, revolts against taxes
have been a standard bill of fare, although the general and continuous
thrust has been against particular taxes, not taxes in general. The pa-
triots of Boston, anticipating the Revolution, opened the antitax action by dumping tea into the harbor in protest against what they
declared to be a discriminatory tax on their favorite drink (next to
rum). James Otis took up the cause, not by denouncing taxes, even
particular ones, but by his bold declaration that "taxation without
representation is tyranny." The implication of the Otis thesis was that
taxation *with* representation was defensible.

This thesis was challenged soon after the adoption of the Constitution and the election of George Washington as president. Washington,
with whom George Bush claimed some connection in a campaign slogan, "From George to George," never indicated orally or in writing or
by lip movements or even by hand signs whether he was for taxes in
general or in particular.

But he put down a tax rebellion during his presidency, and so the matter rested, more or less, until the imposition of the income tax and the various tax rebellions of the twentieth century. (There were minor protests along the way.)

For most of the past fifty years of this century, the continuing position of the Republicans has been to assert that "Democrat" taxes discouraged business expansion and stifled the free enterprise system. The Democrats, in turn, have asserted that taxes favored the rich, were unfair, and fell as a heavy and inequitable burden on those least able to pay, who, if relieved of their tax burden, would purchase more goods and thus stimulate the entire economy. Neither party seriously challenged the actual right and necessity of government to impose and to collect taxes.

George McGovern in his 1972 campaign proposed using taxes or the tax system as a direct, if not automatic, means of moving income closer to equality among the American people. Under this proposal, the government would collect taxes and then distribute collected revenue to all eligible persons, in the amount of $1,000 per person—to those who had paid at least $1,000 and to those who had not paid that much, or to those who had not paid *any* income taxes. The $1,000 was to fall like the biblical rain on the just and on the unjust alike and on the taxpayers and the nontaxpayers.

The proposal was not well received by the electorate. This was not surprising since it violated one of Machiavelli's fundamental rules, which is that in taking something from the people, the prince should take from everyone in one act and then return it slowly and selectively. McGovern proposed the opposite.

Jimmy Carter, as a candidate, asserted that the U.S. Tax Code was a "disgrace to the human race," a declaration not wholly endorsed by Democratic members of Congress or former members, who through the years had labored hard on the code. (I myself spent twenty-two years on the tax-writing committees of the House and Senate.) As president, Carter proposed a variation on the McGovern proposition. It was also a variation on the rebate programs being offered by the automobile companies at that time. The rebates proposed by Carter were to be smaller than those proposed by McGovern and spread out in monthly distributions.

As a former peanut processor, President Carter was prepared to think small. But his rebate proposal was not accepted. Instead, as his fiscal policy, he opted for what in his campaign he had called the "cruelest tax": inflation. The inflation rate rose from approximately 7 percent a year at the beginning of the Carter presidency to 13 percent by the end of it.

Carter, because of his declaration not against taxes but against the tax code, was a precursor to President Reagan. The Gipper was the first American president to oppose taxes per se. Reagan's position on taxes was comparable to the Carter position on the war in Vietnam. Carter was for it, he said, but against the way it was conducted. Reagan was not against the way the tax code was written, as Carter was; he was against the code itself. An appropriate slogan for Reagan tax policy was a variation on the James Otis declaration—in effect that "taxation even with representation is tyranny."

Reagan proceeded, with a supporting Congress, to cut taxes, substituting federal deficits and borrowed money—what had previously been called fiscal irresponsibility—for taxation. Reagan thus made future tax collections by the federal government a most popular investment for Japanese, Germans, and other foreign investors.

The political secret of the Reagan policy was laying the burden of accumulating debt not on the next generation of taxpayers—who, anticipating it, might reject it—but on the succession of generations succeeding them. The *children* of the next generation are not in a position to do much about what will happen to them as a consequence of current policy.

President Bush in his no-new-tax policy carried tax policy to a neo-revolutionary postmodernist stage. Bush went beyond Otis and beyond the advanced variation on Otis—Ronald Reagan—to the ultimate formulation of tax policy in a postmodern democracy: simply, representation without taxation.

The House of Representatives, under Newt Gingrich, proposed and passed legislation along these lines—the line-item veto and the balanced-budget agreement. The danger is that in the interim, before this idyllic state of zero taxation is reached, simple-minded or logical or patriotically motivated taxpayers may accept that Bush and Gingrich are right—that all new taxes are bad and that most old ones should go.

More and more Americans may come to accept the declared wisdom of the antitax politicians: that the people's money is best used if kept from the government and used according to the determination of the people who earn it, or gain control of it, through investment or inheritance.

Logically, then, we should all on our own stop paying taxes, thus serving the common good and bringing on immediately the happy state of a democracy without obligation and representation without taxation.

SELLING POLLUTION RIGHTS

Not as irresponsible as the no-tax policy but bordering on its ridiculousness was the Bush approach to pollution control. Under the terms of clean air legislation, a cap was proposed on the total volume of sulfur emissions allowed for the entire United States. Each utility company would then be given a share of the nationally allowed rate of pollution. Any utility that did not pollute up to its allowed amount would be permitted to sell the unused part to another utility that was polluting above its quota or had in mind to do so. Under the terms of the bill, emission credits could be saved against future need and carried on company books as an asset. Thus, in effect, the policy accomplished what *The Washington Post* described as "monetizing dirt," or at least capitalizing it.

There were precedents, or near precedents, for this action in such things as allowing companies and people to sell losses, to sell unused investment credits and depletion allowances, or to receive payments for unused tax credits under the negative income tax concept. But this pollution proposal was the first clear instance of financially rewarding people or companies for not having done what was judged to be socially and environmentally undesirable.

The potential for extension of this practice raises interesting possibilities. One can conceive of a society in which every person or business is allowed a level of irresponsible personal or social activity with the concomitant possibility of being rewarded, either directly or indirectly, by society for good behavior by being allowed to sell or transfer the unused portion of the quota of antisocial action allowed. Thus, if one were permitted, say, twenty points of traffic violations, and had used none or only a portion of the quota, he or she might sell the unused points or transfer them to someone who had exceeded the twenty-point limit. There might be special treatment under the law for first offenders: unused points might be sold or transferred to second offenders. Thus, a general level of corruption, lawlessness, pollution, and generally antisocial behavior for the entire society could be established and regulated, and selling and transfer below the socially tolerable level encouraged.

This is a kind of modern, secular application of the religious institution of indulgences. The underlying concept, the working principle, of indulgences was that some people were better than they needed to be in order to escape temporal or purgatorial punishments, whereas many others—the sinners—fell short.

Under the terms for granting indulgences, credits built up by the good could be transferred to those who had fallen short and even to those who anticipated falling short. The transfer in its early stages could be gratuitous, an answer to prayers and petitions. Money-based transfers were soon introduced.

The anticipation of fault and need to build up credits moved William of Aquitaine to establish the monastery of Cluny in the twelfth century, with the instruction that the monks pray continuously for his salvation while he went on with his work of war and pillage. When the church ran short of saintly credits and a balanced program, it established a kind of central bank of credits, which could be sold directly.

The New York Times of March 29, 1993, reported that the Environmental Protection Agency's first auction of pollution rights had attracted more participants than had been expected and had brought in $21 million. The report included the disappointing news that the utilities that were trying to piggyback on the auction, in order to sell the pollution rights previously granted them, had been less successful in their sales efforts. EPA said it had received 106 bids for the 50,000 spot allowances it was offering. Each spot allowed the utility that had bought it to emit a ton of sulfur dioxide.

Evidently, the bidders for pollution rights preferred to buy their rights directly from the government, which may have been offering so many spots that it had underminded the market for private sales pollution rights. In the same way, those seeking relief through indulgences, in the religious realm, preferred Rome as their source of indulgences over what might be offered by traveling pardoners.

The sale of indulgences did not serve the church well in the long run, nor did it, insofar as the record shows, discourage sinners. The sale of pollution rights will likely do for the commonweal what the sale of indulgences did for the soul.

But this is the sort of end we reach under the doctrine of taxation without representation and democracy without obligation.

FULL EMPLOYMENT FOR EX-PRESIDENTS

What to do with surviving ex-presidents, or what they should do or be allowed to do, has become a matter of some national concern.

Of the four surviving presidents and former President Nixon, who is only recently departed and still very much in the news, the popular judgment is that former President Carter had made the most useful contributions as well as the most healthy adjustment with his work in Habitat for Humanity. Indeed, this is an outstanding organization designed to encourage volunteer nongovernmental efforts to provide housing for the poor. In lending his reputation and his person to Habitat, in supervising elections in various countries of the world, and in acting as a diplomatic middleman, Carter *has* made a mark. His more recent efforts—some call them intrusions—into peacemaking in Bosnia, on the other hand, have had mixed results.

Before his death, Nixon, according to some, was rehabilitating himself and his reputation. He did this principally by making foreign policy recommendations, as events and time gave him openings. (Recent revelations from the finally public Nixon tapes, as to what might be called his Oval Office temperament, have set the rehabilitation campaign back a bit.)

President Ford plays golf, often with Hollywood types, and sits on several boards. He has made little claim to continuing a public role of any significance.

President Reagan, after one lucrative commercial trip to Japan, settled for making occasional ceremonial appearances at Republican Party affairs, riding horses, and cutting wood. He then became ill with Alzheimer's disease and withdrew from public life. Some pundits have said he has "done a lot" for the disease, just as he did for colon cancer, just by contracting it and then guarding his privacy and dignity.

Perhaps. But one still feels we may know too much about our leaders without much real benefit from the knowledge. Reagan's predecessors had not "done much" for their physical disorders or disabilities. President Eisenhower, although he had ileitis and also a heart attack during his administration, was not said to have done a lot for either. John Kennedy did not make public reports on the state of his health. He did publicly relate the use of a rocking chair to his bad back, an action that may have done something for rocking chairs.

Lyndon Johnson, although he publicly displayed the scar left over after his gallbladder operation, was not credited with having done a lot for gallbladders or their removal. Nixon played down his phlebitis, and Carter, who in his physical report noted that he had occasional problems with hemorrhoids, let it go at that. And as president, George Bush did not make a case for fellow sufferers of thyroid deficiencies.

But presidential retirement is apparently no day at the beach, even with good health.

It is, we are told, hard to adapt to driving again. And supermarkets are a bit of a mystery. And there is the weighty issue of one's "continuing role," if any.

Bush does seem inclined to accept the postpresidential role carved out by Ford: virtual retirement. Nor has Bush fit easily into the elder statesman mode of Carter or Nixon. After five years at it, he seems rather lost and forlorn.

What Bush might consider, possibly setting a precedent for future ex-presidents, is taking up some of the unfinished business of his presidency:

1. He could broker the sale of arms to Saudi Arabia.

2. He could lobby for the sale of more tanks to Kuwait.

3. He could take up the private sale of pollution rights.

4. He could take up the sale of radio licenses and commercial television channels, as proposed by ex-Sen. Bob Dole (they could be limited partners) and use the proceeds to pay for various cut-back or underfunded programs such as Head Start and welfare. The program might be extended to include the offering, under competitive bidding conditions, of all existing radio and television licenses when they come up for renewal. Those proceeds could balance the budget—an old Republican goal.

Most networks have carried programs or news stories about the bargains cattlemen are getting in leasing public lands for cattle grazing. The right to graze on the public mind and will, now given free to television and radio licensees, is much more valuable than the right to graze on western grass and sagebrush.

5. The former president might have another try at selling cars in Japan, roughly comparable to selling coal in Newcastle.

6. And he might also handle the sale of the five ex-presidents' autographed group photograph, which was sold to raise funds for their individual libraries.

8

How Not to Make a President (Or an Administration)

Suggestions for reforming the election process are mostly doomed to failure, since basically what is called for is responsible decision making on the part of the electorate, sustained and assisted by a creditable press.

Both are getting harder to hope for.

Meanwhile, we are inundated every four years with proposals to reform American politics. In 1997 the postelection guilt of 1996 caused politicians of all stripes to promise campaign reform and the press to promise to somehow make itself grow up in time for the campaign of 2000.

Some procedural changes may be necessary as a matter of self-defense against more ambitious reforms. Other minor changes might do some minimal good, clearing the way to responsible decision making. There are at least five such changes that would be useful and easily achieved. They could be effected without seriously interfering with freedom of speech or assembly—the two basic constitutional rights that bear on political choice in the United States.

• *The office of vice president should be abolished.* Provisions for replacing a president in an orderly, rational, and prompt way could be applied, similar to the procedures outlined in the constitutional amendment on presidential disability. They worked well enough when Gerald Ford was chosen to replace Spiro Agnew, following Agnew's resignation.

There are at least three good reasons for abolishing the office of vice president. First, having a vice president on the ticket clutters the election campaign, offering the voters an apparent choice when in fact only the presidential candidate will—while he lives—be in a position to direct and significantly affect policy. And in principle a ticket made up of two unbalanced persons might well appear to constitute a balanced ticket.

Second, the existence of the office of the vice president puts people in line for the presidency who would not necessarily be the best choice to run for that office. Recent examples include Richard Nixon, who probably could not have made it to a presidential candidacy had he not been vice president under Dwight Eisenhower. The vice presidency can appear to dignify a fool; it can make a nonpresidential person *seem* almost presidential. This certainly applies to Spiro Agnew, who had no national political reputation and no known qualifications for the presidency when chosen to be Nixon's running mate.

Third, the office can waste the abilities of a good politician for four or eight years—years during which he or she could serve more effectively in some other office. Examples include Lyndon Johnson and Hubert Humphrey, whose talents went unused when they served as vice president. Holding the office may also seriously impair the office-holder's chances of being elected president, even though it may help to get him nominated. It is commonly held that both Humphrey and Walter Mondale were hurt as presidential candidates by their vice presidential services.

If it is too much trouble to abolish the office, we at least ought not to fill it: Leave the post empty and use the offices in the Old Executive Office Building to house the many presidential commissions that are forever being formed to study problems Congress and the president could not or would not solve.

• *The Federal Election Campaign Act and its amendments of 1975–76 should be repealed.* This would open up the political process as it was open before that legislation was passed. A politics that brought to the country such presidents as Franklin Roosevelt, Harry Truman, Dwight Eisenhower, and John Kennedy—in contrast to Jimmy Carter, Ronald Reagan, George Bush, and Bill Clinton—cannot be judged to have been all bad.

• *Televised political advertisements should be abolished.* Or, if that is not possible, severely regulated so as to minimize the conditioning effects of current ads. (For example, candidates would have to speak for themselves, à la Ross Perot.)

The country has long accepted the idea of a de facto ban on televised advertising of liquor and cigarettes, presumably protecting U.S. citizens from physical corruption. Similar bans should be applied to the other end of the spectrum of human needs and wants—namely, politics and religion. Television could continue to carry ads for deodorants, detergents, pain relief, and automobiles.

• *The equal time and fairness doctrines should be rigorously applied to televised reporting of political campaigns, even though the presentation of such news might be severely limited as a result.* The spoken word (primarily radio) and the written word remain the best means of political reportage. For it was in the period approximately from 1930 to 1960—after the advent of radio and before the coming of television—that the best communication of political ideas took place.

• *Finally, televised debates should be eliminated unless used as a device to attract the attention of voters during primaries—a compromise justification.* But they are best wholly banned in the showdown campaign between major candidates. Presidents, unlike senators, do not have to be great debaters. Once elected, they will not be debating anyone.

Most candidates admit that the people who most influence them are their spouses (and second, their vice presidents). If a debate is to have significant bearing on the presidency, perhaps it should be held between the presidential candidate and his or her spouse, or between the presidential and vice presidential candidates of the same party. A Dole-versus-Kemp debate would have been more interesting than the Dole-Clinton debates were. And Al Gore, whom we now know to be an aggressive debater, might have forced President Clinton to actually talk about something real, rather than just emoting.

With the course cleared by these changes, there would be time to look to the positive and substantive basis upon which presidents should be chosen—job creation, debt reduction, foreign policy, and global economics—and to the actual means of selection and election of presidential candidates. Those means are now utterly chaotic and unrepresentative, and the way to fix them is not more primaries, a national primary, more caucuses, or campaign reform, all of which will lead to the further triumph of corporate money and special-interest domination of the process. The cure is a more *representative* process.

JUDGING THE CABINET

In a parliamentary system, like that in England, voters usually know before an election who the principal members of the next cabinet will be. In the United States voters can only speculate, with the help of columnists, who have not been very accurate in their predictions on who will be appointed by the newly elected presidents.

Occasionally, a candidate will hint at prospective appointments. In a recent campaign, only one likely candidate, Robert Dole, named a possible appointee. He said that he would give Colin Powell "almost any job he wanted."

Twenty years before, Gerald Ford proclaimed a similar confidence in Henry Kissinger. Ford said that, if elected, he would make Kissinger secretary of state—Henry and God willing.

Both the Dole and the Ford pledges were looked upon as signs of political weakness, and perhaps they were. But a pre-election announcement as to major cabinet appointees would also be good government.

Immediately after the election, the timidity, secrecy, and hesitation that marked the former candidate disappear. Presidents-elect begin to talk about the important choices they are prepared to make, and soon they begin to leak prospective cabinet officers through friendly (or willing) members of the press. It is as though election had given them the special grace of office, not unlike the gift of infallibility that follows from a papal election.

President Clinton, who is generally thought to have stumbled a bit in naming his cabinet the first time, did much pondering and much leaking before naming his second cabinet. It had to include at least one Republican, we were told, yet still remain diverse ("looking like America") and still reward the politically loyal.

In judging the choices future presidents make, it is useful to recall the qualifications, characters, and performances of cabinet members in past administrations.

• I would rate George Marshall as the best secretary of state in recent decades. Marshall was experienced in war and in peace; he was pragmatic. He saw foreign policy as an extension of national character and interests. He was a historian. The worst secretary of state was

Dean Rusk, although pushed hard by John Foster Dulles. Dulles laid down the ideological lines for the Cold War "confrontation": "massive retaliation," "the immorality of neutralism," and so on. He also arranged covenants, executive agreements, and treaties to sustain these moral judgments. Rusk, succeeding Dulles after a brief interlude, accepted the ideological dicta and took action to support them. He was to Dulles what Oliver Cromwell was to John Calvin.

The general conclusion is that the secretary of state should not be an ideologue. The appointee should not be from a family with strong traditions in the religious ministry, nor be a geopolitical thinker, nor be schooled in the balance-of-power theory of the Austro-Hungarian empire. And, preferably, he or she should not have been "with" a foundation or, as they say, "of" an institution, like Brookings. He also should not be a former campaign manager, fund-raiser, or corporate lawyer.

• The best secretary of the Treasury in the past fifty years probably was Henry Morgenthau of the Roosevelt administration. He was skilled in politics and in finance, informed of world affairs. Among recent secretaries, three deserve praise: Henry Fowler, his successor, Joseph Barr, of the Johnson administration, and George Shultz of the Nixon administration. All three understood that the U.S. dollar was a force for stability and economic growth at home and a force for order in world affairs. The worst recent Treasury secretary was John Connally, who in a short term achieved a significant failure by cutting the dollar free and letting it float—or, in a more appropriate Texas image, letting it loose on the world monetary range with no more than a hair brand to identify it.

• The best attorney general of modern times was Francis Biddle, who held that office under Roosevelt and under Truman, with William Rogers of the Eisenhower administration as a runner-up.

Both Biddle and Rogers kept the office above politics. Both understood that the attorney general was the top law officer in the land. Both probably would have resigned if it had been suggested to them that a special prosecutor be appointed to handle matters under their jurisdiction. The worst attorney general of our times was John Mitchell, for politicizing the Justice Department even to the point of involving it in campaign politics. The attorney general should not be the campaign manager of the president who appoints him. Preferably this person should not be from the president's own political party. Nor, for that matter, from the president's family.

Cabinet positions other than the three above are of lesser order, or should be if properly conceived and administered. They are primarily service and executive offices rather than policy-making ones.

• Louis Johnson, secretary of defense under Truman, was the last secretary to stand against the growth of the military-industrial complex. Melvin Laird, secretary of defense under Nixon, was a militarist, but he directed and controlled the expansion. Laird's political experience was a good preparation. His record supports the argument that the secretary of defense should be drawn from Congress.

The worst secretary of defense must be Robert McNamara. He brought to the office the arrogance of the automobile industry, which previously had been represented by Charlie Wilson of General Motors. One sure conclusion is that the secretary of defense should not be a former automobile executive. A football coach might do or possibly two—one for defense and one for offense.

The postmaster general is no longer a member of the cabinet. But without question, the best postmaster general was James Farley of the Roosevelt administration. He ran the post office, and also the Democratic Party. He kept politics in the post office, where it could do little harm. He recognized that politics is like pigeons: If it is concentrated in one building or in one department, you should not scatter it to others.

The worst postmaster general was Arthur E. Summerfield of the Eisenhower administration. He let politics get out of the post office and let the service deteriorate. Then he took up pornography and censorship (he was against the former and for the latter). *Lady Chatterley's Lover* was banned from the mails under Summerfield, as was Aristophanes' *Lysistrata*. The ban on the second item was lifted when Summerfield learned that the play had been written more than 2,000 years before he moved to ban it.

• The best secretary of labor was Frances Perkins. The poorest was Martin Durkin of the Eisenhower administration. Durkin had been a union member. Perkins was a graduate of Mount Holyoke. The lesson is obvious.

• The best secretary of agriculture was Charlie Brannan, who delighted in arguing with Agriculture Committee members. The worst was Ezra Taft Benson, an elder of the Mormon Church. A good rule for picking a secretary of agriculture is to get someone from the opposite party to take the job, someone who will not introduce religion into the department, and someone who knows that ethnic jokes, which may be accepted quite without prejudice by farm audiences, are not generally acceptable. If hard pressed, the president might look to Minnesota, which in recent years has become the mother of secretaries of agriculture.

• Harold Ickes of the Roosevelt cabinet was a model secretary of the interior. He not only was a conservationist but also was a capable defender of his policies, able to draw criticism away from the president, and unquestionably politically helpful. Ickes was credited with typing Thomas Dewey, Roosevelt's opponent in the 1944 presidential election, as "the little man on the wedding cake." He once defended the government policy of killing young pigs to reduce the supply of pork during the Depression by saying that he had "never known a pig that died of old age." The worst secretary of the interior was Douglas McKay of the Eisenhower administration, appointed for no discernible reason other than that he had been governor of Oregon, a state with many trees. Before becoming secretary, he had owned and operated a Chevrolet dealership.

• The best secretary of health, education, and welfare (HEW), now the Departments of Education and of Health and Human Services, was Wilbur Cohen, a nonpolitical career person. Cohen knew the programs and knew how to administer them. He never complained of the burdens of the office or suggested that they were beyond his powers. He left the proposing of new programs to the elected politicians. The worst HEW secretary possibly was John Gardner, who resigned from the office in protest over "priorities" and other things. Gardner was miscast; he misunderstood the office. Gardner would have been a good person to preach the Crusades or proclaim the westward movement in the United States, but he was not the person to be put in charge of the march to Jerusalem or of a wagon train passing through Indian territory. The guiding rule in picking a secretary of health and human services is that his or her motto should be "Sufficient unto the day are the problems already assigned to this department."

• Appointing a secretary of commerce is one official act in which no president should fail. The secretary of commerce should be a nice person, decent, contented, full of pleasantries, with no further political ambitions—ideally with no ambitions of any kind. He or she should be able to report encouraging or discouraging business reports with equal assurance and optimism. The best secretary of commerce in recent administrations was Luther Hodges of the Kennedy administration. Luther wore a fresh flower in his coat lapel each day.

The departments of energy and education have not been in existence long enough to permit objective standards for secretaries like the ones I have discussed. Moreover, a number of members of Congress, like Dole in the last campaign, have come out for eliminating both.

Presidents should pay some attention to fit: Former Senate majority leader George Mitchell of Maine, for example, had no reputation as an expert or advocate in foreign policy, but was touted for secretary of state. (Madeleine Albright ultimately got the job.) Mitchell *would* be a superb attorney general. (He is a former federal judge.) Sen. Richard Lugar, a Republican from Indiana, who spurned the president's advances, would have been much better equipped for the post. He has worked on foreign policy for twenty years.

William Cohen, also of Maine, named secretary of defense, had no particular reputation as an expert on the military. Cohen worked on intelligence and civil liberties. Sen. Sam Nunn was the man most people in the Senate turned to on defense matters, regardless of party. (This is in the tradition of the late Richard Russell.) Nunn was almost overqualified for this job, while not particularly qualified for state, which he sought and lost.

The U.N. ambassadorship should be an important post but is generally treated as a door prize. Clinton awarded it to a professor in 1992, and Madeleine Albright did a good job. But the person appointed to this position should have some national standing and some standing with Congress as a sign of respect for the United Nations. Dwight Eisenshower sent Henry Cabot Lodge to the U.N. John Kennedy sent Adlai Stevenson. Gerald Ford sent William Scranton. All had been contenders for national office. All did well at the U.N. Richard Nixon sent George Bush, at that time a defeated congressman, while Bush sent a former CIA man (and retired general), and

Ronald Reagan sent Jeane Kirkpatrick, another professor, whom he admired for her articles in *Commentary* magazine.

Clinton's top possibility for the U.N. in 1996 was Richard Holbrooke, author of the Dayton, Ohio, peace accord for Bosnia. At least he had experience and stature. Instead, Clinton picked a little-known congressman from New Mexico.

The post has also been taken in and out of the cabinet. It ought to be in the cabinet and occupied by a national figure of independent status.

It would be good for the nation if each candidate for the presidency were compelled to announce his three or four top cabinet choices during the presidential campaign. The country ought not to be surprised or generally unenlightened about who, along with the president, is running the government.

Strange and almost indefensible cabinet choices in recent years include Edwin Meese as attorney general, William Perry as secretary of defense, Warren Christopher as secretary of state, Donald Regan as treasury secretary, Hazel O'Leary as energy secretary, and James Baker as secretary of the Treasury and then state (he was not qualified for either job).

For the most part—with the exception of Ford, who made some good appointments—all of our presidents since Truman have downgraded the cabinet and turned the cabinet secretaries into personal assistants to the president. This practice has made for a mediocre as well as undistinguished executive branch, sometimes an incompetent one.

The president is not a plant manager; he is more akin to a CEO. He cannot run the federal government by himself or out of the White House.

When the country elects a president, it elects an executive branch.

It would be well to act as if this is what we are doing when we hold national elections. The person a president is likely to appoint as attorney general or secretary of state matters far more to the good of the republic than does the candidate's party platform on school prayer or abortion.

We are a government of people as well as laws. Yet our national campaigns give virtually no attention to the people who will make up a candidate's future presidency.

Often the candidate himself does not know. He is focused on election, not government (like Clinton in 1992). We ought to make him think about his government and then tell us what he thinks.

AN ANTIREFORM REFORM

The Constitutional Convention in 1787, after prolonged debate and after having considered procedures for choosing a president—election by the national legislature or by state representatives or directly by the people—finally, by a vote of nine states to two, approved the principle of electing the president by a body created specifically for that purpose, namely, the electoral college.

In the first presidential election some electors were appointed by state legislatures. A few other states, including Pennsylvania, Maryland, and Virginia, provided for popular election of the electors.

By 1796, the first election after George Washington's two terms, electors were chosen by the people in six states and by legislatures in ten states. By that time, within eight years of the adoption of the Constitution, partisanship had reached the point that, in every one of the sixteen states then a part of the union, electors were picked as men pledged to one candidate or the other: John Adams or Thomas Jefferson. The electoral college as conceived by the Founding Fathers—a body of responsible, trusted persons—was already effectively discarded. (And it had hardly been tested.)

As partisan politics has become more dominant in the republic, the independent role of the electoral college has been all but forgotten, and electors have come to vote automatically for the party candidate to whom they are committed. Because of the development of partisan politics, and for other reasons, the original conception of how the electoral college was intended to work has been confused and neglected. A popular opinion has developed that the electoral college is either a bad idea or one that is unworkable. It is neither. The trouble is that it has not been used as it was intended.

The original conception was that electors would be chosen for one task only—a very important one in the new republic: the selection of a president of the United States. As electors they were to be agents of the people of their states. It was anticipated that the electors would be wise and responsible, but more that they would be free of immediate involvement with politics and legislative matters because they were not themselves members of Congress or of state legislatures.

The electoral college, as it was called, was designed to deny both Congress and the voters total, direct power over an election. Whereas the Founding Fathers were familiar with political factions—division being the mark of every political society—they hoped and believed that these divisive and power-seeking organizations would have a limited influence in the choice of the president.

Ironically, the electoral college in its more or less original form would be more useful and more rational today than ever. It would involve popular sovereignty over the nomination process—quite absent now—but with the popular wisdom, and reactions, molded and refined by those elected by the people to choose a president.

A revised electoral college certainly beats what we have now.

Our political parties—as armies of political organization and as platforms of principle—are dead. Our presidential candidates are therefore now picked by those who have great wealth; the media, those whose profession is the packaging and mass marketing of politicians; and a very small number of primary voters in a few states. It is not a democratic method of selecting presidents but a manipulation and perversion of democracy, and it is not reflective democracy because the process is not representative in any way.

How to get back to the electoral college?

The states could, by individual and separate actions, restore the electoral process to what it was intended to be. But they are as unlikely to do so as they were to extend the vote to women or to people between the ages of eighteen and twenty-one before constitutional amendments accomplished those purposes. Maine is the only state that has moved, even modestly, to conform to the constitutional intent.

The Maine system—by which one electoral vote goes to the winner of the popular vote in each congressional district and two electoral votes go to the winner of the statewide popular vote—is clearly better than the winner-take-all rule applied in the other forty-nine states in the current operation of the electoral college.

But even better than the Maine district system would be one dividing the states into presidential electoral districts, each smaller than a congressional district, which now includes about 450,000 people.

If each presidential elector represented, say, a district of 100,000 people, a candidate for the electoral college could campaign effectively without spending great sums of money. One person with a few volunteers in the course of a presidential campaign could reach all voters in his 100,000-person constituency. If the country were divided into some 2,000 such districts, 2,000 presidential electors would be chosen. Obviously, if a majority of those chosen were Democrats, a Democratic president would be chosen; if a majority were Republicans, a Republican would be president. If neither party had a majority, the third- or fourth-party electors would hold the balance of power, and their votes would have to be solicited by other parties.

This procedure is no different from the one followed within U.S. political parties at their conventions (or on the way to conventions). In Great Britain it is used in choosing the prime minister, under the parliamentary system.

A president chosen through this process would clearly be a constitutional president, and he or she would be chosen by electors who represented a majority—if not of the voters, almost certainly of the citizens.

We should follow the advice of John Holcombe, who in the early years of this century argued that "in no reactionary spirit, therefore, but with views thoroughly progressive," we should "return for relief to the wisdom of the fathers by making effective their admirable device—the electoral college."

In so speaking, he sustained the judgment of James Madison, not only as expressed in the Constitution but also as late as 1823, when he wrote, "One advantage of electors is that, although generally the mere mouths of their constituents, they may be intentionally left sometimes to their own judgment, guided by further information that may be acquired for them; and finally, what is of material importance, they will be able, when ascertaining which may not be till a late hour, that the first choice of their constituents is utterly hopeless, to substitute in the electoral college the name known to be their second choice."

The need for purifying and perfecting the process of the selection of the president is most important today, because of the complexity and weight of the demands of the presidential office and because voter knowledge of the qualifications of the presidential candidates is obscured or distorted by spin doctors and media hype. It is better to improve the representative process, as conceived by Madison, than to propose that it should be done away with.

The electoral college has not worked because, mostly, it has not been tried—its function as a means to perfect the representative process was abandoned or forgotten.

The problem is not a defect in the conception of this unique constitutional institution but rather the intrusion of partisanship and faction between the people and the executive branch of government. It is the electoral college that should stand between the two.

9

Postmodern Foreign Policy

LOOK, NO PRINCIPLES

*I*nterventionism has been a mark of U.S. history almost from the beginning of our national existence, but up to and through World War II, interventions were generally justified as necessary to defending the nation, freeing oppressed people, or saving democracy. Most interventions were pragmatically determined and of limited purpose.

The foreign policy of the Truman administration in the post–World War II period was consistent with this tradition. Dean Acheson as secretary of state, speaking for President Harry Truman, defined U.S. postwar foreign policy as to both its purposes and its methods. Seldom did he make the case for either policy or program on an ideological basis, although he was not indifferent to ethical and moral considerations. He was, with presidential concurrence, a great treaty-maker, but his treaty proposals were based primarily on historical conditions, rather than on ideological assessments and projections. The NATO commitment, the Marshall Plan, the Truman Doctrine, the aid programs to Greece and Turkey were not against communist ideology, but against particular communist powers. Nor was the Korean War defended as an involvement based upon a general policy of the containment of communism, but as an action directed toward carrying out World War II in the Asian theater.

The Acheson-Truman conception of national defense was one of a defined perimeter, described simply by President Truman when he said that anytime a pig stuck its snout under your tent, the thing to do was to hit it on the snout. This foreign policy was classical, therefore restrained and limited.

Following the Truman administration and the departure of Acheson, foreign policy came to be dominated by the ideas and historical philosophy of John Foster Dulles, secretary of state under President Dwight Eisenhower. Dulles had committed himself to foreign service early in his life and seemed to look upon that service almost as though it were a religious vocation. His approach to foreign policy was essentially moralistic, which is one thing, but it was also highly ideological. Communists were to be treated primarily not as nationalists but as part of monolithic world communism. In contrast with the limited and defined objectives of Truman and Acheson, Dulles's objectives were open-ended and global. Even "neutralism" was, in his view, "immoral." The line between noncommunists of all kinds and communists of all kinds was clear to Dulles.

Dulles, like Acheson, was a treaty-maker. His treaties, for the most part, in contrast to those engineered by Acheson, were not limited to defined historical situations and geographical areas but encompassed things that had not yet occurred and might never occur. They transcended territorial limitations, reaching out for ideological conflicts that might arise in the future.

In this spirit, and in anticipation of trouble, he advanced the Southeast Asia Treaty Organization (SEATO). He advocated adherence to the proposals of the Military Committee of the Baghdad Pact, designed to put together an anticommunist bloc in the Middle East, and was reported to have sought a combination of African nations to contain Egypt and Gamal Abdel Nasser. He supported passage of mutual anticommunist defense treaties between the United States and South Korea, the United States and Nationalist China, and the United States and Japan. Dulles was the great covenantor of modern times, combining in documentary form both legal and moral obligations.

In addition to his bent for entering into treaties, Dulles was a great proponent of congressional resolutions—some to sustain current policies and governmental actions, others in anticipation. Whereas Truman went into Korea without special congressional support, Dulles, acting for President Eisenhower, was quick to come to Congress for endorsements of administration commitments. Thus, he presented and secured the passage of the Far East (Formosa) Resolution in 1955, which he said put the Peiping (later, Beijing) government on notice that if it attacked Formosa, the United States would instantly be in the war.

Again in 1957, following the Suez Canal crisis, Dulles came to Congress asking for a joint resolution on the Middle East that would state the determination of the United States to assist any country in the Middle East that asked for help from threatened, communist-inspired aggression. (President Lyndon Johnson, following this precedent, sought and obtained the later controversial Tonkin Gulf Resolution in 1964.)

During the Eisenhower administration, the United States continued its policy of indirect intervention through supporting the French in Southeast Asia and by sending military advisers there. It also came to the defense of Quemoy and Ma-tsu and landed troops in Lebanon. Eisenhower's administration threatened retaliatory action against our traditional allies, the British, the French, and the Israelis, at the time of the Suez conflict and planned an invasion of Cuba.

Meanwhile, secret, interventionist foreign policy was being carried on by the Central Intelligence Agency, directed by John Foster Dulles's brother Allen. Independent of Congress, not limited by treaty obligations or accepted standards for judging the methods by which international affairs might be conducted, the CIA enmeshed itself in foreign policy. It took credit for the overthrow of Jacobo Arbenz Guzmán in Guatemala and of Mohammad Mossadegh in Iran and acknowledged its involvement in anticommunist activities in Laos, Vietnam, and other parts of the world.

Interventionism in the Kennedy and Johnson administrations was conducted under the guidance and inspiration of Secretary of State Dean Rusk, a kind of Cromwell to Dulles's Calvin. Under Kennedy, the invasion of Cuba was attempted and some 17,000 special forces were sent into Vietnam. The CIA continued to be active in Southeast Asia and in Cuba.

President Johnson escalated the war in Vietnam into a major military engagement and sent troops into the Dominican Republic to "stabilize" the government. The doctrinal justification was based on a kind of amalgamation of the Monroe Doctrine and the Eisenhower Middle East Doctrine transferred to the West.

President Richard Nixon carried the Vietnam War several stages beyond the level that it had reached under Johnson. New tactical and strategic measures were introduced, including what was called an "incursion" into Cambodia—the first incursion in our history, or certainly the first use of that word to describe a U.S. military action. It was an interesting choice of a word, since there is no verb form for incursion (as the verb invade goes with the noun invasion). One cannot incurse. An incursion is therefore existential, a kind of happening.

The Carter administration demonstrated its anticommunist zeal and willingness to intervene by embargoing grain sales to the Soviet

Union and by keeping U.S. athletes out of the 1980 Olympic Games because of Russian intervention in Afghanistan.

Although the Reagan administration proceeded with a massive military buildup, and used the violent language of cold war, its actual military interventions were modest, although numerous. Libya was bombed. A few shells were fired into Lebanon by U.S. warships. Marines were sent into Lebanon, with no very clear mission, and subsequently withdrawn. Navy vessels, one of them the frigate *Stark,* were assigned to protect oil shipments in the Persian Gulf. Grenada was successfully invaded. The U.S. government, or part of it, supported the Contra troops in Nicaragua, the Iranians, and possibly also Iraq in the Iran-Iraq war.

And then we move to George Bush and the no-fault, buck-stops-nowhere presidency, followed by Bill Clinton and his postmodern presidency with its existential foreign policy—the buck begins anywhere and ends nowhere.

President Clinton, said Bob Dole, had a "photo-op foreign policy." This is actually putting it kindly. The president has a photo-op response policy regarding foreign affairs and foreign crises. He feels he must respond in some way, even if the response is meaningless, to world politics, at least when it boils over or reaches U.S. shores. This is what his efforts in the gulf in the summer of 1996 amounted to. And this is what his White House summit with the Middle East principals that same summer amounted to.

All in all this sort of policy—engagement without mission and without definition—is probably more dangerous than simple, old-fashioned isolationism, as the U.S. response in Somalia and Bosnia showed. Certainly, the United States under Clinton created false hope in both places.

Multilateralism might be a fallback for a president without a foreign policy, except that the United States lacks allies (more on this in a few pages) and has systematically waged war upon the United Nations as an institution. One may disagree with much that the United Nations does and dislike many who seem to run it, but U.S. policy since President Reagan and Ambassador Jeane J. Kirkpatrick has been to manipulate, undermine, displace, and denounce the United Nations *as an institution.* It should not surprise anyone when the United Nations is little help to us in trouble spots of the world.

IS THERE A DOCTRINE IN THE HOUSE?

For too much of our history, presidential decisions have been justified, and also insulated from historical reality and from congressional review, by the intrusion of presidential "doctrines," some sustained by congressional approval, others only by tradition or by the popularity or power of an incumbent president.

The two presidential doctrines that have had the clearest bearing on foreign and military policy are the Monroe Doctrine and the Eisenhower Doctrine, operating separately or in variable combinations.

The doctrinal approach to foreign policy began with President James Monroe's statement of December 1823 when he declared that the American continents were not to be considered subjects for future colonization by any European powers, that the political system of the European allied powers was essentially different from that of America, and that any attempt on their part to extend their system to any portion of this hemisphere would be considered dangerous to "our peace and safety." The statement also promised that existing colonies or dependencies of any European power would not be interfered with and that in matters relating to European wars and other matters involving the European powers, "we have never taken any part, nor does it comport with our policy so to do."

Commentators and critics point out that the Monroe Doctrine was a mere declaration of presidential position, which in itself could not prevent intervention or commit the country to war without congressional declaration and support. Although the critics were undoubtedly technically and constitutionally right, the declaration subsequently took on doctrinal force, encouraging any number of succeeding presidents to interfere or threaten to interfere in South American and Central American affairs. They did not seek congressional support, and they carried out their interventions with little fear of criticism or effective opposition.

The "doctrine" has been modified and has taken on new and more comprehensive meanings with the passage of time. President Eisenhower, with the passage of the Middle East Resolution in 1956, was credited with having established a doctrine that stated that the United States could intervene militarily in the Middle East if it were asked to do so by a government threatened by communist takeover. The doctrine was not long confined to applications in the Middle East. It was later combined with the Monroe Doctrine as a preliminary justification for the planning of the Cuban invasion and for the Bay of Pigs venture. The basic political plan was that once a beachhead had been established in a country, that government would invite the United States to come to its aid because it was being threatened by a communist or communist-inspired or -supported movement—in this case, the Castro government. An extension of the Monroe Doctrine accepted that a foreign ideology could be treated as an actionable threat, whereas a century or more earlier, the threat had to be a foreign government.

This defense was used to explain and justify the intervention in the Dominican Republic by the Johnson administration. Thomas Mann, the chief administration spokesman for Latin American policy at the time, said that the landing of U.S. troops in the Dominican Republic was not intervention but a "response" to the "intervention" of communist subversives.

The Russians announced their version of the Eisenhower Doctrine in the Brezhnev Doctrine, which justified their invasion of Afghanistan.

The Reagan administration's action in Grenada carried the combined Monroe-Eisenhower Doctrine a step further. There was no invasion by a foreign country, and there was no request by a noncommunist government in power for help against communists or communism. The action seemed to be based on the proposition that there should have been a request for a noncommunist faction and that there might have been one if such a faction had existed in Grenada, but since there was no such faction to make the request, the Reagan administration could take the initiative. And it did.

Another proposition that gives support to continuing U.S. intervention attempts to justify presidential or governmental military actions on the grounds that the president in office is continuing policies and programs initiated or carried on by a previous president or presidents. Although President Kennedy never offered continuity as an official or personal defense for the Bay of Pigs operation, some of his supporters occasionally pointed out that the plans for the invasion had been prepared by and for the Eisenhower administration.

President Johnson used continuity as a defense of his escalation of the war in Vietnam. He was, he said, only supporting and advancing a policy that had been supported by three presidents who preceded him: President Truman, who had helped the French indirectly by giving them aid under the NATO program and the Marshall Plan while the French Indochina war was in progress; President Eisenhower, who had sent in advisers; and President Kennedy, who had sent in special forces and had given other help to the South Vietnamese.

President Nixon endorsed the concept of continuity, saying that he was pursuing a policy that had been supported by four previous presidents.

Foreign policy purely by extension—or continuation—may be worse than foreign policy by resolution and doctrine.

President Clinton's brand of interventionism is in keeping with the man. It exists free of doctrine, unless one considers the defense of democracy and promotion of capitalism a doctrine. Like most of Clinton's policies, his foreign policy is free floating and without context.

And yet, the president did "act" militarily, if minimally, in the gulf in the summer of 1996, and he has attempted to act as a broker for peace in the Middle East. In both cases, one could, by inference, conclude that Clinton was continuing the policy of George Bush. His top Middle East adviser, Dennis Ross, was Bush's top Middle East adviser. And the Clinton policy in the Gulf was the vague and firmly-held-to policy of George Bush—to stand firm against Saddam or to appear to stand firm. But it is interesting to note that President Clinton never explained *how* he intended to stand firm or why it was important that he should.

The Clinton foreign policy in China and Cuba also has been a continuation of the Bush policy, but with no apparent attempt to evaluate or anlyze the old policy.

There was no Bush doctrine. And no one has accused Bill Clinton of having a doctrine. Both are postdoctrinal, and Clinton's foreign policy in particular is truly postmodern: It is reinvented daily, with no reference to time past. It derives from no specific principles (even faulty ones like those of Dulles). It is reactive and virtually spontaneous.

American foreign policy today has little connection to historical alliances. It has little basis in partisan or electoral politics. It used to be that the American foreign policy debate was based on competing principles—isolationism versus internationalism, free trade versus what is now called managed trade or protection of U.S. industry (Jefferson was a protectionist), human rights versus national interests, containment of communism versus spheres of influence. And wise statecraft usually involved some sort of pragmatic balance of these varying principles and worldviews. What is notable today is the absence of such principles or worldviews.

Ronald Reagan was the last president with a clear view of world affairs, myopic though it was in some respects. Reagan knew two great things: Communism was bad, and there were too many nuclear weapons. His policy therefore was half cliché and half prophetic, and, with considerable Russian help, he moved to end the arms race.

Bush and Clinton both engaged in world affairs but engaged free of clear purpose, precept, or long-range plan.

Contemporary foreign policy derives from photo opportunities, as Dole said, and from a vague continuity coated with pieties (boost democracy and capitalism). Contemporary foreign policy is not made by strong personalities with strong views—like Dean Acheson, George Marshall, and Arthur Vandenberg—but by faceless processors of official reaction—like Cyrus Vance and Warren Christopher. Both were corporate lawyers, not statesmen or diplomats.

Bush's lack of definition almost made sense, given his career as a member of the apparat and the way he came to the presidency—after Reagan. It is more disappointing coming from a Democrat like Clinton, who had a different tradition to build upon. But Clinton has done little to tame the military, little to reform the United Nations, little to reverse the U.S. reputation for bad neighborism in the Americas, little to combat Asian economic power, little to restore historical friendships and alliances, and little to promote or defend human rights.

Even in the crisis areas—Bosnia, Northern Ireland, the Middle East, the gulf—the Clinton response has been, at best, mere response, often too late to be meaningful or effective. Initiative and imagination have been almost nonexistent, even in these hot spots.

It is a long way from the foreign policy of Woodrow Wilson and Franklin Roosevelt and Adlai Stevenson to the foreign policy of Bill Clinton—the distance being that between a foreign policy rooted in ideas and American tradition and one rooted in polling and posturing.

LOOK, NO ALLIES

American government officials, from presidents on down—as well as most editors, political columnists, commentators, essayists, and historians—commonly assume that the allies of the United States include the members of NATO; Israel, Japan, Australia, New Zealand, and South Korea; plus some smaller countries scattered about the globe. But the fact is the United States has few, if any, true allies. What it has instead is a number of nations that it maintains in a dependency relationship. This is a relationship that Washington has approved and cultivated—a relationship, in fact, that it insists upon whenever any of these dependents shows any sign of independence. Some of these nations truly were American allies in World War II. Others, such as Japan and Germany, were added to the list later because they were no longer enemies, they needed the United States, and they were willing to accept the dependency relationship.

The German and Japanese surrenders after World War II were essentially unconditional surrenders, leaving those two countries militarily and (especially Japan) economically dependent on the United States. In reality, though, it was not only its enemies who surrendered to the United States after the war but also its former allies in Western Europe. The North Atlantic Treaty was for them not so much an agreement among allies and sovereign nations as it was an acknowledgment of the economic and military realities of postwar Europe, a treaty of dependence—almost an unconditional surrender of a different sort to the United States. That is also what was required of other nations later added to the list of "allies," including South Korea, Iran for many years, and, in a somewhat different context, Israel.

The vestiges of sovereignty and national self-respect that survived the formal NATO agreements were largely wiped out by Secretary of State John Foster Dulles's arrogant, moralistic domination of American relations with Europe, as well as with non-European friends such as India and Egypt. Dulles generally proceeded without consulting, or even caring about, the opinions of other nations. He insisted that they (especially members of NATO) accept and support American policy.

He attempted to force the European nations into what he called a "European defense community," the effect of which would have been to require them to give up their last, limited claims to military independence. To push his plan, Dulles threatened an "agonizing reappraisal" of the American role in Europe unless his plan was adopted. He denounced Indian neutrality, specifically, as "immoral." He forced the British, the French, and the Israelis to withdraw from Egypt at the time of the 1956 Suez War. Subsequently, unhappy with the Egyptians because they were not antagonistic enough toward the Soviet Union, Dulles unilaterally decided—without consulting the European countries or the United States Senate, possibly without even consulting President Eisenhower—to pull out of the Aswan Dam project, thus leaving Egypt to the Soviets.

Although subsequent secretaries of state may not have acted as independently as Dulles, the presidents who followed Eisenhower showed great insensitivity to the dignity of our allies. John F. Kennedy displayed indifference toward the British, especially Prime Minister Harold Macmillan, on the matter of missile deployment. Lyndon B. Johnson forced the Australians and South Koreans to send token forces to Vietnam. Richard M. Nixon ignored everyone, including the U.S. Senate, with his incursion into Cambodia; he and his agent, Henry Kissinger, negotiated a new relationship with China without even the slightest nod toward the obvious interests of Australia and Japan.

In 1964 Ronald Steel published a book entitled *The End of Alliance*. The book correctly perceived the changed realities in Western Europe: the altered relationships of Western European nations to each other, to the United States, and to other nations in the world. The one major defect was the book's title. What Steel had observed was not the end of an alliance at all but the end of a dependency relationship. He noted the appearance of conditions and realities that required a reordering of relationships in NATO to reflect the growing independence, the self-sufficiency, and the desire for sovereignty among member nations. Those forces created pressures and demands that the NATO concept and form could not accommodate.

The first serious and open challenge to the old NATO concept— and the assertion, in fact, of a relationship much more like that of genuine allies—was made by Charles de Gaulle. When de Gaulle re-emerged on the European scene in 1958, the way was open for the liquidation of France's Algerian commitment, for its escape from dependence on American aid to fight its foreign wars, and for the restoration of France in the military and economic complex of Europe. But de Gaulle's return and the recognition of the reality of France as a force in Europe—an independent force—caused concern in Washington.

De Gaulle's conception of a united Europe, stretching from the Atlantic to the Urals—united not under a supranational political authority but by free-choice arrangements among sovereign governments—challenged the prevailing U.S. idea of European unity. Later, of course, it became the ideal.

What Washington had in mind at that time, however, was political, economic, and military unity—a dependence on the United States and an alliance against the Soviet Union.

Fearful that the West Germans would move to support the French position, the United States tried to force them to make a choice between Paris and Washington. Various devices for sharing power were suggested in order to influence the West Germans to select Washington's policy. The most noteworthy was a proposal that would have at least made it appear as though there were a shared responsibility for nuclear defense in Europe and a European finger on the nuclear trigger. How the finger was to be selected was never made clear.

Europe rejected the idea of a multilateral or multinational nuclear force. The British and French particularly opposed it. Verging on the ridiculous was the American proposal for multinational forces and the mixed manning of vessels, ideas urged especially by Secretary of State Dean Rusk. One ship was sent out on a highly publicized voyage to demonstrate the feasibility of the concept. But this was undertaken even before there had been an agreement on whether the cuisine and the chef should be French, German, British, or American, or on who would select the evening movies, let alone on more weighty matters.

De Gaulle's announcement of his intention to withdraw the French forces from NATO's integrated military command was not an announcement that he was leaving an alliance, but rather a repudiation of dependency. As André Fontaine wrote at the time of de Gaulle's action:

"The arrogance of the president of the republic is disagreeable and even incomprehensible to his allies, but it is not the arrogance of an isolated man, otherwise it would be only ridiculous. It is the arrogance of a man who is not resigned to anything which writes finis to a nation about which history has spoken without a break for a thousand years."

Four years earlier, in 1962, Raymond Aron had explained:

"It is an illusion to believe that the problems raised by General de Gaulle will disappear when he no longer 'graces the scene.' The privileged position of Great Britain in the atomic field is something which will never be accepted in Paris, no matter who may be in power."

The immediate American response was to try to isolate France from the rest of Western Europe. With difficulty, the United States obtained agreement from the thirteen other NATO participants on a common response to France. Yet the language of that response showed not only the caution and reluctance of the Europeans about agreeing to the American proposals for isolating France, but also how much the United States was relying on concepts that had become irrelevant during the preceding fifteen years.

In effect, the United States took the position that its policy toward Europe could be continued without France. The threat was that Washington might actually abandon its efforts for a united Europe, rather than accept any change in the elaborate structure of "military integration." Or NATO would simply pack up and move to Belgium. Plans would be made around France. Undersecretary of State George Ball, a leader of the move to isolate de Gaulle's France or to force him to keep France within the NATO military structure, announced to the Senate Foreign Relations Committee at the time that "the NATO crisis is over." The other countries of NATO, he said, were determined to press forward vigorously to maintain the integrated military structure without France. In fact, it was much better from a military point of view to have French military power back on the continent of Europe, even though formally outside the NATO command and yet physically in Vietnam and Algeria. But not so for secular and theological legalists like Ball and Rusk.

Despite the early warning and other historical changes, the United States has persisted in honoring and adhering to the exclusive NATO concept—even up to this day, when Poland, for example, badly wants to join. Washington has presumed its dominance.

The United States remained generally indifferent to the opinions of so-called allies about events in other parts of the world. Most Western European nationals had grave doubts about the wisdom of American involvement in Vietnam. Some openly criticized it. But Washington paid little attention to their point of view, in much the same way that it ignored Japan's attitude and its interests in that war.

Presidential candidates regularly reflect this arrogance of indifference. "If elected, I will reduce troops in Western Europe," one will say. "If elected, I will withdraw troops from South Korea," another will declare.

- Australia is a good example of a nation that is called an ally but is treated as a dependent. For almost two decades following World War II, Australian foreign policy was symbolized by Sir Robert Menzies. He accepted the Cold War as central to policy, and he gradually shifted Australian association and dependence from Great Britain to the United States, as British power waned and as Washington began to emphasize the threat posed by Asian communism to American interests—and also, therefore, to Australian interests. Australia was also somewhat fearful of the instability of the former colonial lands of the South Pacific that were becoming independent. The supposed alliance with the United States was formalized in the ANZUS Pact (Australia, New Zealand, United

States) and on a more comprehensive scale by Australia's joining SEATO. Australia followed American policy direction almost to the letter. Australian troops fought in South Korea and Vietnam. Australia allowed the United States to establish bases and tracking stations on its soil. And Australia declined to recognize China.

Following Menzies's retirement in 1966, and in view of the growing disenchantment with the Vietnam War, Australia also began to develop a spirit of independence and to demonstrate that a new relationship existed. Prime Minister Gough Whitlam's Labour government, elected in 1972 after twenty-three years of Liberal Party rule, withdrew Australian troops from Vietnam, protested the American bombing of Hanoi and Haiphong, and undertook to establish a changed relationship with China, quite independent of what the United States was doing or wanted done. Yet Washington proceeded as if the old relationship of dependency still existed. It continued to send ambassadors who reflected the attitude that Australia was a kind of semi-independent Texas populated by cattlemen, sheep farmers, cane-cutters, and beer-drinkers who would be ready when called upon to serve American interests.

• Israel is another ally that is not an ally, and it is mostly our fault.

During the forty years since the state of Israel was established—with the support of the United Nations and of the major nations of the world, including the Soviet Union—the United States has gradually moved to make Israel almost wholly dependent on the American government. French and English interests were repudiated at the time of the Suez war, and the United Nations was allowed to shed its responsibilities almost without protest when it withdrew in the face of Egyptian threats before the 1967 war. The Soviets, too, had more or less removed them-selves, leaving the United States as the chief supporter of Israel.

Progressively, the United States began to look upon Israel as a dependent and to treat it as such. Israeli ambassadors to Washington came to be selected on the basis of their good connections in the United States. Candidates for leadership in Israel had generally argued that they should be elected because of their support in the United States—until Menachem Begin suddenly took the position that Israel was a sovereign nation, an ally of the United States rather than a dependency. Distinct from his predecessors, Begin was not elected on the basis of widespread recognition or support among Americans. Rather, he believed that the United States had a political, moral, and even military interest in the independent existence of Israel. The establishment of the state of Israel was more than a humanitarian act, he felt. It was a political act, establishing a sovereign state of special character and purpose.

Begin, not unlike de Gaulle, declared that he would take the initiative in foreign policy, that he would seek to have not defensible boundaries but a defensible country, that he would not wait for a U.N. initiative relative to the problems of his country, or indeed wait for American initiatives or directions.

- Great Britain, with which the United States has the so-called special relationship, also has been treated more like a junior partner than a partner. This was true up until Margaret Thatcher, who, like Begin and de Gaulle, would not allow herself or her nation to be the object of condescension. John Major, however, returned to the lapdog mode with Bill Clinton. And Tony Blair, of course, has bonded with Clinton. But both England and Ireland have been treated like small children by the president and the administration on the Northern Irish question when there is no evidence that anyone visible in the Clinton White House or State Department has any real historical understanding or special insight into the problem.

In contrast to its attitude toward its allies, the United States treated its postwar enemies—principally, the former Soviet Union when it existed and the Chinese since Nixon, but also North Korea, Iran, and Iraq—with respect and deference. It attended to them. It often conferred with them. It deferred to them.

Since the USSR came apart, American treatment of Russia, and of Boris Yeltsin in particular, has been better than anything afforded a U.S. ally. And Yeltsin, though not a communist, is not exactly an ally or a champion of human rights. The other nation that has gotten the most attention, and the most favored attention, of our presidents and foreign-policy makers over the years has been China, whose interests and values could not be more opposite to our own.

Washington accepted the fact that these nations had nuclear bombs, and it has worried little about former Soviet nuclear armaments being more or less up for grabs. Yet Americans protest vigorously when nations that are defined as allies seek to build bombs or test them, or when they build nuclear reactors for themselves or other nations for nonmilitary purposes.

Proliferation, as now defined, means the possession of nuclear weapons by more nations than now have them. This definition, of course, excludes the failure to destroy unneeded nuclear weapons possessed by the the two great possessors, proliferators, and salesmen of arms: the United States and the former Soviet Union. (A number of former U.S. generals are now calling for unilateral disarmament. They are right. They are also forty years late.)

A nation that is asked not to develop its own nuclear weapons might well inquire as to what the Americans and the Soviets intend to do with the bombs they now do not need for deterrence or retaliation.

Obviously, the United States must adopt a new attitude toward, and develop new working relationships with, at least four countries: Japan, Germany, Australia, and Israel.

- The lopsided American relationship with Japan should be modified to give Japan fuller responsibility and even more military autonomy. Japan is no military threat to the United States or China or any other country. Japanese military problems are largely defensive and psychological. U.S. relations with Japan should not be based on pre–World War II conceptions or realities.

- The same is true of Germany, although in the German case the attitudes of other nations in Western and Central Europe, and of the Soviet Union, make any move toward giving Germany military autonomy and significant strength more difficult to justify. American troops and American-controlled military power must remain the principal armed force in Western Europe.

- Australia, too, deserves genuine allied status. It is one of the few countries in the world that has control of its own resources, both material and human. It is rich in critical raw materials, and it is underpopulated. Like Japan and the United States, Australia is a country that can do more than deal with its own economic problems. It should be viewed as a potential contributor to and participant in policies and programs that bear upon political and economic conditions in the South Pacific, Southeast Asia, and China.

    It should be remembered that Australians fought valiantly in both world wars and several smaller ones. More can be done to develop and integrate Australian naval power and airpower into whatever stable military structure is needed in the South Pacific. The country's real potential, however, is in its economic resources and especially in its role in the orderly, constructive, and morally controlled use of its uranium resources.

- The United States' relationship with Israel must become more mature. It has combined the worst aspects of a patron-client relationship and dysfunctional sibling rivalry. The United States reserves the right to be disappointed with Israel, to critique its leaders, and to threaten to cut off aid, even to take sides in its domestic elections. But it is not willing to be honest and independent in its dealings with Israeli politicians or prominent American Jews, or to separate historical and moral bonds from matters of U.S. national interest. The United States needs to be an ally of Israel without being an overbearing big brother.

Essential to any alliance is a shared purpose, perceived to promote the common good of members or participating nations—a common good that cannot be achieved as effectively by one nation acting alone or by two or three nations operating to the exclusion of others that have a vital interest in the goals of the combined effort. Nations participating in an allied effort need not have that perfect conformity of customs, habits, ideas, and manners suggested by Edmund Burke to be the real forces that hold nations together. But the greater this conformity, the greater the strength and durability of the alliance are likely to be. Movement toward such conformity among participants in an alliance is clearly desirable.

Agreement on methods is also desirable, but even with differences and disagreements, alliances can and have worked. Certainly there were major differences, both as to strategy and as to tactics, among the allied commanders, including Dwight D. Eisenhower and Viscount Montgomery, in World War II—not to mention the major ideological differences between the United States and the Soviet Union. Yet the war was waged effectively, at least to the point of military victory.

Alliance allows for differences in function and in physical, military, economic, and philosophical contributions. To be effective, alliance requires compromises and concessions, but only among nations whose sovereignty and integrity are clearly recognized. Without such recognition and respect, there can be no true alliance, only the appearance or the form.

Dependencies are dependencies, despite documentary declarations to the contrary. Allies are something else. There must be among them, with or without formal affirmation, a bond of intellectual and moral commitment. As Machiavelli admonished, the relationship of ally to ally is a better, more reliable, and more lasting one than that of patron to dependent or of conqueror to subject peoples. The United States needs allies, not dependencies.

NAME YOUR OWN WAR

Involvement in the Persian Gulf War was of another order from the other conflicts the United States had been involved in, in the last half century. Ideological distinctions that had marked, and in part determined, our policies in Europe, in South and Central America, in Africa, and in the Far East were not applicable. The communists were not coming. We were not invited in because of external or internal threats of impending communist takeovers. There were no covering treaties in place, no doctrines to invoke.

For months, even years, before the hostilities broke out, the United States was maintaining, certainly, not an unfriendly relationship with Iraq but rather a friendly one, involving diplomatic, economic, and military cooperation, sufficient to lead Saddam Hussein to think that he could move against Kuwait without fear of U.S. intervention.

It was not the invasion of Kuwait that moved the United States into action, but the belief that Saudi Arabia was in danger of invasion; also the consequent possibility that Saudi Arabian oil would be controlled by Saddam. Such control would certainly have threatened supplies of oil to the United States, to Japan, and to other nations of the world. In keeping with our national obligations to protect lifelines to vital resources, an intervention of limited measure was defensible. But almost immediately after our initial statement of purpose was stated, additional and more comprehensive reasons and objectives for intervention were introduced, progressively involving the interests and objectives of other nations.

The liberation of Kuwait was declared as a purpose scarcely separable from our defense of Saudi Arabia and its oil. Moreover, the liberation of Kuwait would signal to Saddam that the territorial lines and national distinctions in the Middle East were to be preserved. Such stability was of concern to oil interests and countries, especially to the British, who clearly cared about preserving the integrity of their 1922 maps. The objective, or incidental, benefit of weakening Saddam's military forces was added as something of interest to some other Arab nations and to Israel, as was the objective of destroying his chemical and germ warfare stocks and facilities and his potential to produce nuclear weapons. Added benefits, if not original purposes, were noted by President Bush and by the secretary of state, namely, to protect our way of life, to ensure jobs, and to take a major step toward establishing a new world order.

This multiplication, an escalation to a higher purpose or purposes, followed the Vietnam War pattern, according to which, as military force was increased in the area, more and higher purposes for the additions were given—from helping the French put down a colonial revolt, to helping anticommunist forces in a civil war in South Vietnam, to repelling an invasion from the North, to heading off the expansion of Chinese communism, to protecting the security of the Free World.

The changing explanations and justifications also were indicative of a groundless and aimless foreign "policy," literally being rationalized as it unfolded what I call a postmodern foreign policy.

The essence of postmodern foreign policy is this: The engagement becomes its own justification.

- The Persian Gulf operation demonstrated, on Pentagon-controlled television, how to deploy troops and materials. It was an amazing logistical achievement, even though unobstructed by enemy forces, with an assured place for landing troops and supplies and with a fuel supply in place. (One of the biggest military threats, as it turned out, was from friendly fire.)

- The invasion was accompanied by masterful diplomatic achievements, in getting the support of the U.N. Security Council, of the United Nations itself, and of most of the Arab nations. The operation was supported not only by the opinion of decent mankind but also by some whose opinions on the record had not been quite "decent."

- Even though loose ends and unfinished business remained in the area, and Saddam Hussein remained in power and undiminished, the war was declared "over," its mission accomplished. (A few years later, President Clinton would, in effect, fire his CIA chief for telling Congress that Saddam was stronger in 1996 than when the United States went to war against him.)

In any case the troops were brought home, and victory parades and celebrations were held. In addition to other precedents set by the Persian Gulf War, the Washington victory celebration may have set an example for comparable celebrations, following greater or lesser military victories, in the future. If it does (although new to the United States), it would not be a tradition new to history. In most major respects the D.C. victory celebration followed closely the example of Rome in the imperial period. In the early years of this epoch, the triumphant citizens noted the return of a general and his army from a victorious military campaign. The ceremony included an offering of sacrificial thanksgiving to the gods and included rites of purification of the top general and his troops. The purgative element was dropped in later triumphal celebrations.

Whereas during the years of the republic it was customary to hail the returning general as "imperator," in the imperial period this high honor was reserved for the emperor and his family.

President Bush did not wholly displace Gen. Norman Schwarzkopf in the Washington program, but he did share billing with him. The general was not hailed as imperator, but he was hailed by some as a possible presidential or vice presidential candidate.

General Colin Powell, chairman of the Joint Chiefs of Staff at the time, apparently had a somewhat mixed view of the Great Engagement. He later replaced Schwarzkopf as a potential candidate.

In the Washington triumph, as in the Roman, the victorious generals praised their soldiers collectively, and in special cases individually, and bestowed honors and decorations on the deserving. The dead were commemorated. But in strict keeping with the Roman practice, the booty should have been distributed among the soldiers and officers who served.

There was not much booty captured in the Persian Gulf War. The booty was saved, not captured. And oil is difficult to bestow.

But the two leading generals in the Persian Gulf War *were* rewarded handsomely, not by the U.S. government but by the lecture circuit and the networks and the publishing houses.

And the corporate business community, most notably those who were a part of the military-industrial complex, did quite well. As then Secretary of State James Baker said, in the ultimate justification/rationalization, "There are jobs at stake." Jobs, money, oil.

Meanwhile, many of the men who fought the war and have now come down with various strange ailments and fatal diseases have been told by the Pentagon that, though they risked their lives, their medical problems were not contracted in the Gulf War. The Pentagon is not responsible. Would even Rome have treated its soldiers so coldly?

PART II

Congress, Parties, and the Press

10

Congress: From Responsible and Representative to Reprehensible

*M*embers of Congress are responsible in some degree for the tendency to judge the work of Congress by quantity rather than quality. To justify their stewardship, some of them fill many pages of the *Congressional Record* with irrelevant statistics about laws enacted, nominations confirmed, roll call votes counted, and the days and hours spent in session. Since Congress has been in almost continuous session for the past two decades, the numbers alone are impressive. But they are not necessarily enlightening.

Neither Gingrichian rhetoric nor reports about quantity of legislation provide the standard by which to judge the effectiveness of Congress. Overstatement of existing weaknesses and extravagant claims of what may be accomplished through procedural reform will contribute little to a proper understanding of its role.

But the Senate and the House *are* out of order. They are out of sync with their own purposes, as set out by the Founders, and out of balance with each other and with the executive branch.

The Senate has gotten away from its proper role and become a kind of super House, while the House has become less representative, less of a people's House. The Senate also has given up much of its legitimate constitutional authority in the area of foreign policy, while the House has ceased to exercise its proper constitutional dominance over power of the purse.

In 1957 William S. White published *The Citadel*—a book that accomplished the mystification of the U.S. Senate. The Senate described in *The Citadel* was a place, according to White, "upon whose vitality and honor will at length rest the whole issue of the kind of society that we are to maintain." White, after examining the Senate of those days, found it to be good. He evaluated the members of the Senate and found many of them to be giants among men. He examined the rules of procedure and found them wholly satisfactory and appropriate, if not inspired, and sanctioned beyond time and history.

The popular judgment of the U.S. Senate today is something quite different from that of William S. White. The Senate is charged with failing to meet its responsibilities, with being unresponsive to national needs, and with being confused and incompetent. Some say the Senate today mainly serves as a platform from which to launch presidential campaigns. This is not completely untrue.

At times the Senate seems to be the last primitive society. Almost alone among American institutions, it still has respect for seniority. It has great respect for occupancy and for the territorial imperative; you can scarcely move a senator out of an office, even after he has died. And the Senate has its own trial by ordeal, the filibuster.

The Senate of today is not the Senate of 1957; neither is it the Senate as described in popular criticism. Despite certain similarities to a primitive society, it is more than that. Working under difficult circumstances, it has in recent times made a record of positive achievement.

When I entered the Senate in 1959, the reputedly strong men of the past—Democrats like Tom Connally of Texas and Walter George of Georgia—were gone. And on the Republican side, such stalwarts as the senior Robert Taft of Ohio, Arthur Vandenberg of Michigan, Eugene Milliken of Colorado, and others listed by White were gone. The Senate had new leaders, new members, and new problems.

In the years immediately following World War II, the Senate was involved in settling the postwar world. It ratified the peace treaties and helped establish the United Nations, the North Atlantic Treaty Organization, and the Marshall Plan. These were important tasks that the Senate performed well.

In this same period, especially after 1948, the Senate was largely immobilized in dealing with domestic problems because nearly every issue—whether it was housing, education, or labor law—became a civil rights issue. And on civil rights the Senate was deadlocked. Consequently, from 1948 until 1959, the House of Representatives generally pushed ahead of the Senate in dealing with domestic problems.

A significant change occurred in the elections of 1958. In that year twelve new senators, liberal on most domestic issues, were elected: E. L. Bartlett of Alaska, Thomas Dodd of Connecticut, Clair Engle of California, Ernest Gruening of Alaska, Philip Hart of Michigan, Vance Hartke of Indiana, Gale McGee of Wyoming, Frank Moss of Utah, Edmund Muskie of Maine, Harrison Williams of New Jersey, Stephen Young of Ohio, and myself. The immediate effect was that the initiative on most domestic issues shifted from the House to the Senate. Now the Senate began to move ahead of the House in advocating new legislative programs, increasing appropriations to support established programs, and facing the civil rights issue. But it was not until the 1964 presidential election, when Barry Goldwater's candidacy gave the House a clear liberal majority, that Congress as a whole could deal with the great mass of domestic legislation that had needed action for many years.

The Senate's concern with domestic problems had both good and bad effects. The good effect was that much necessary legislation was passed. The bad effects were two:

First, preoccupation with domestic problems caused the Senate to cease giving proper attention to international relations. As a result, there was the gradual usurpation of power in this field by the executive branch of the government through the use of executive agreements and executive actions without formal treaties. In some cases, these merely continued wartime relationships. But new commitments—legal or extralegal—were made during the time that John Foster Dulles was secretary of state and his brother Allen was head of the Central Intelligence Agency.

The second bad effect of the Senate's concern with matters domestic was the change in the structure and operation of the Senate. This occurred especially while Lyndon Johnson was majority leader. The Senate became a kind of upper House of Representatives, with emphasis on committee work, roll calls, and quantitative measurements of success. Senator Johnson often announced the number of bills passed and made comparisons with other Congresses, both in terms of timing and in terms of the volume of legislative action.

(Johnson's attitude toward both houses of Congress caused him problems in the later years of his presidency. He had experience in driving cattle, where the technique is to start the cattle slowly and then stampede them at the end. But when you deal with Congress, you should know about the psychology of pigs, which is opposite that of cattle. In driving hogs, you start them as fast as you can, you make all kinds of noise, and you try to panic them. You shout at them in Latin. But once they are started, you slow them as you go along. When you get them right up to the pen you want them in, you come to a stop. The pigs will then look right and left and think that they have discovered it. And in they go.)

The Senate's influence on foreign policy was further weakened by the development of the Cold War into an ideological conflict and the formalization of that conflict in comprehensive treaties like SEATO and in resolutions like that of the Gulf of Tonkin in 1964. Congressional criticism was thus stifled, and congressional power yielded to the executive branch—sometimes even in advance of any defined problem, as in the case of the Middle East Resolution, passed under President Eisenhower in 1957.

The Senate itself in these years was a victim of the Cold War. The immediate manifestation of this was its intimidation by Sen. Joseph McCarthy and his two or three active supporters in the Senate. Both the Senate and the State Department retreated in the face of their challenge.

Another factor that in this period also weakened the Senate's role in foreign policy—a factor the Senate should have recognized and challenged early—was the inclusion, or intrusion, of the House into the field of foreign-policy making. This occurred in two ways. It happened directly because the Marshall Plan and other aid programs required authorization and appropriation of money by the House as well as the Senate. And it arose indirectly from the continued support by the House of a military establishment larger and stronger than was favored by the Senate.

Both President Johnson and President Nixon encouraged this shift of power to the House. Johnson turned to the House for support in Vietnam. Nixon encouraged the adoption there of the Hays Resolution in 1969, which affirmed House support of the president in his efforts to achieve "a just peace in Vietnam"—it passed by a vote of 333 to 55. Thereafter, Nixon often depended on the House to blunt the effect of Senate opposition to the war.

Only with the later escalation of the war in Southeast Asia did the Senate begin to give serious attention to what had happened to it and to reassert its rights and responsibilities. The road back has been difficult. Much of the high ground had been lost to the executive branch and the military, and low ground to the House of Representatives.

But the Senate did fight back. The effort was not so much one of individual leaders or even of the "club" (the inner circle that supposedly controls the Senate). Essentially, it was a response of the entire Senate.

In the 1960s the Foreign Relations Committee challenged the independence of the Central Intelligence Agency. The committee won a small concession within the Senate when it was agreed that a few members of Foreign Relations would join members of Armed Services and Appropriations on what was called an intelligence "oversight committee." There was more truth than was intended in that committee title. Sen. William Fulbright noted that the CIA would tell you only what it wanted to tell you anyway. (And some senators did not want to know everything. One of them said, "Just don't tell me; I don't want to know of it." Others on the supervisory committee said to other senators, "If you knew what we know . . ."— some of them had been at the front too long.) In any event, this led to a permanent oversight committee, which nonetheless encountered the same problems when attempting to exercise proper oversight. Sen. Daniel Patrick Moynihan was moved to resign as vice chair of the Senate Intelligence Committee and later to call for abolition of the CIA.

Another development in the late 1960s and early 1970s was a

stronger assertion of responsibility by the Senate. For the first time since the expansion of the military after World War II, Congress, but especially the Senate—and more particularly Sen. William Proxmire—raised serious and effective challenges to military spending. Opposition to the antiballistic missile (ABM) system reflected not just military, scientific, and economic considerations but also a reassertion in foreign policy by the Senate.

The device of the congressional resolution as a means of supporting administration policy was repudiated. In 1966 only five senators voted to take up the Gulf of Tonkin Resolution for reconsideration and possible repeal. (I was one.) In 1970 only five senators voted against repeal on the final vote. (But one can rightly say that repeal came after the resolution had been fully exploited.)

The Senate under the leadership of Mike Mansfield, and later Howard Baker on the Republican side, began to restore some of its collegiality and constitutional authority. And under Sen. Robert Byrd—a serious student of the Constitution and of history and a true guardian of the traditions and nobility of the Senate—the institution began to seem, once more, worthy of itself. Byrd is a statesman much underestimated and much underappreciated, especially by the Washington press.

The Senate leadership of Robert Dole and George Mitchell was, in my view, less successful. Dole was tethered to Republican presidents; Mitchell was bound to oppose them. Both men longed for the presidency, which may be a disadvantage in a Senate leader. Both were highly partisan. And neither was able to resist the influence of political action committees, pollsters and campaign consultants, the decline of senority, or the tendency of national political fads to overwhelm the Senate.

But the real purpose of the Senate is to stand *apart* from presidential politics and to resist the House, the executive, the bureaucracy, and the media in all things "popular," that is, trendy. When, for example, President Clinton sent the first lady across town to explain the flaws in the nation's health care system, there should have been grumbling, if not outright resistance, in the Senate. Instead, Hillary Clinton was received like a visiting head of state.

The years since the settlement of the Vietnam War have seen the renewed passivity and confusion of the Senate—less resistance to executive power and less consideration by members of what the Senate ought to be.

That is a shame. It makes national government more dysfunctional—or, if you will, postmodern.

As an ideal, the Senate should be one part House of Lords, one part Greek chorus, and one part Platonic guardians. Instead, the one institution of national government that could (and was intended to) provide wisdom, detachment, and balance when these qualities are most needed is reduced to acting as a second House and/or presidential breeding ground.

Two historical footnotes:

1. In the Senate's effort to reclaim its constitutional role in foreign policy, much credit must go to modern members of the Foreign Relations Committee: Democrats like J. William Fulbright of Arkansas and Frank Church of Idaho, and Republicans like Clifford Case of New Jersey and John Sherman Cooper of Kentucky. Special recognition also is due some Republican members of the Senate—such men as Jacob Javits of New York, Mark Hatfield of Oregon, Lowell P. Weicker of Connecticut, and Charles Mathias of Maryland—who, during their terms, showed greater concern for the constitutional role of the Senate than for uncritical party loyalty. The Senate is not meant to be a deeply partisan

place, and, and, at a minimum, it should be far less partisan than the House.

2. The Senate has made an important record—up until the Robert Bork and Clarence Thomas hearings—in improving the federal judiciary.

Although the initiative came principally from the executive, the Senate sustained and encouraged presidential efforts to improve the courts. During the terms of Presidents Truman, Eisenhower, Kennedy, and Johnson, the nation gradually began to move away from what until that time was a regional judicial system. There was one system for the North, another for the South, one for the Northeast, another for the Southwest. The practice was to clear all judges for a district court with the senators in that jurisdiction. It was almost as though senators were permitted to say to other senators, "You can have whatever kind of justice you want in your state if you leave us alone in ours."

The civil rights movement and the great civil rights legislation of the Great Society were the principal causes of the change of emphasis.

President Johnson's 1965 nomination of a former Mississippi governor for appointment to the Fifth Circuit was thoroughly challenged on the civil rights issue. Other nominees to the circuit courts were checked carefully. Also in 1965 a Johnson nominee for the District Court of Massachusetts was so strongly opposed on the ground of competence that the nominee's name was withdrawn.

Johnson's 1968 nomination of Abe Fortas as chief justice of the United States was challenged by senators who alleged conflict of interest. There was a filibuster against the nomination, and Johnson eventually withdrew it.

The Senate in 1969 and 1970 rejected two of President Nixon's nominees for the Supreme Court. In turning down the Clement

Haynsworth and Harrold Carswell nominations, the Senate clearly showed that it was not prepared to accept the Nixon theory of a Supreme Court on which regional differences were to be represented. The Senate preferred a national court whose members would be selected as qualified to deal with national problems on a national scale. Sen. Birch Bayh of Indiana led the fight against the appointment of Haynsworth and then, almost alone in the early days, against the appointment of Carswell.

At the same time the Judiciary Committee, and especially Sen. Sam Ervin of North Carolina, patiently and persistently defended the right of privacy and the right of every citizen to due process. Ervin was a good senator.

The Bork hearings, which totally politicized the process, and the Thomas hearings, which utterly demeaned it, set the federal judiciary, and the Senate's role in molding it, back roughly a political generation. These were all-time lows for the Senate and for the nation. The interest groups that politicized the hearings were at fault, but even more unforgivable was for a president to send up a nominee bound to exacerbate ideological partisanship. It happened with Bork, and it was worse with Thomas.

Also at fault were Senate floor and committee leaders who lost control of their chamber.

THE SENATE AND THE HIGH COURT

When Stephen Breyer became a Supreme Court justice, replacing Justice Harry Blackmun, someone remarked that the number of former circuit judges on the high court would remain at six. I found little to object to in the Breyer appointment and little to rejoice over.

Arguments made in support of Breyer included the standard one made whenever a circuit judge is proposed for the Supreme Court: namely, that he or she has been a good or outstanding member of the circuit court. Breyer may well have been a fine circuit court judge, as his supporters said, and as the supporters of recent appointees who were also former circuit judges, like Justices Clarence Thomas, Ruth Bader Ginsberg, and Anthony Kennedy, also argued.

But being a good or superior circuit court judge is not a reason to put that judge on the Supreme Court; in fact, it may well be reason to oppose such a nomination.

The Supreme Court is not a super or superior kind of circuit court. It is, in its essential functions, a court of a different order from any of the lower courts. Alexis de Tocqueville defined its role when he wrote in *Democracy in America* in 1831 that "a mightier judicial authority has never been constituted in any land." After listing some of the powers of the court, Tocqueville made this profound point concerning it: "One might say," he wrote, "that its prerogatives are entirely political, although its constitution is purely judicial."

The role of the circuit court, in contrast with federal district courts and the Supreme Court, is essentially conservative. Circuit judges should be credited with attention to precedents, thus curbing lower courts and protecting the Supreme Court from a flood of cases. When a circuit court justice on being nominated for the Supreme Court stresses regard for and sensitivity to precedent, he or she should receive credit as a circuit judge, but not as a prospective Supreme Court justice.

Gradually, and without much reflection, we have come to accept in the United States that all judges should be selected from the legal profession. A case can be made for appointing or electing lawyers to preside over the lower courts, especially the circuit court (more leniency might be allowed at the district level, where cases should be reviewed and settled within the limits of the law as written or interpreted by the Supreme Court). It might even be argued that creative imagination or a disposition to make legal judgments, beyond precedents and in the broader context of history and philosophy, is not desirable at the circuit court level. But the Supreme Court of the United States is another matter.

Students of constitutional history and of the Supreme Court's influence on the interpretation of the Constitution identify three periods of constitutional development preceding the current period:

- The first was from 1789 to the end of the Civil War, in which the court's right and responsibility in interpreting the Constitution and its application in changing circumstances were established.

    The judges and lawyers in the early decades of our national existence were not educated in a system of narrow professional definition or a professional curriculum. In those years, the study of law was incidental, or additional, to a broader education.

- The second era in the development of the Supreme Court runs from the end of the Civil War to the "court of revolution" of 1937. During that time the court was preoccupied with property rights.

- The third era after the court of revolution, allowing for the interruption of World War II, ran from 1937 through the civil rights struggle of the 1940s, 1950s, and 1960s.

The drift of the court in the past two decades has been due to preoccupation with "precedent" and the internal logic of "the law" itself, as the court has come increasingly to be made up of former circuit court judges. The court, in the time since the early 1970s, appears to be proving the accuracy of Mr. Dooley's observation made in the early years of this century that the Supreme Court "follows th' illiction returns."

The press has helped build up a general acceptance that this is the way the high court should operate, with reports of how the balance in the courts is likely to be affected by presidential elections and by new appointments. We have even been given projections as to the possible outcomes of cases—5 to 4, or 6 to 3, etc., as though the Supreme Court were a kind of super legislature.

In truth, cases easily settled by the appeal to precedent, or involving simple points of law, ordinarily are not taken to the Supreme Court. Important Supreme Court decisions do not deal with technical legal definitions and distinctions. In performing their most important functions, Supreme Court justices do not or should not "think as lawyers" or "speak as lawyers." The judgments they are called upon to make are much broader and deeper; they are beyond or above the "limits" of the law.

Today, nearly every right included in the Bill of Rights is in need of clarification and redefinition. Freedom of speech and of the press involves more than the right to say something in a public square or to publish a newspaper or pamphlet; the right must now be applied to monopoly press and to intrusive, controlling, and concentrated television and broadcast media.

Freedom of assembly is not satisfied by allowing people to hold simple meetings. Now it must include demonstrations, disruptive protests, and the right to belong to dissident groups. This right must also be considered in government definitions of "conspiracy."

The implied or derived right of privacy, traditionally a matter of requiring search warrants and not allowing the government to quarter troops in private homes, today is challenged by complicated technological developments, telephone records, phone taps, long-distance and hidden cameras, break-in potential in databases, and unlawful trespass on the "information highway."

In many areas the Constitution is pitted against, or has been interpreted so as to stand against, common practices (prayer in schools, for example). In the past, such confrontations were essentially at the pragmatic level rather than at the level of theory or principle. Today, many of the conflicts are between two concepts of law. One flows from the common law. It involves precedent and traditional relationships, such as those between husband and wife, parent and child, master and servant, and the possession or lack of property rights. The other flows from the rationalistic and individualistic concept of rights written into the Constitution and sustaining the proposition of the Declaration of Independence that all persons are created equal, have the same rights under the law, and are to be given the same protections.

Narrow training in law, or experience with case studies and precedents, can be of little help in dealing with challenges of the next century.

That a judge is a follower of precedents or a "consensus builder" or bicyclist or one who loves his wife and children is not reassuring when the subject matter of his deliberation is human rights in the age of nuclear biology.

It is easier for a historian or a philosopher to seek legal counsel when needed (from the Yellow Pages or from a computer) than it is for a lawyer/judge to find historical and philosophical counsel and to evaluate that counsel.

The Constitution sets no barriers to the appointment of nonlawyers to the Supreme Court. One might conclude that the record of the Supreme Court over the past half century would have been different—and better—if that court had had as members, even if for a short time, people like Henry Steele Commager, Barbara Tuchman, David Reisman, John Kenneth Galbraith, or Hannah Arendt. None of them could be, or has been, called a consensus builder, but all of them could think.

The Senate, in its constitutional role of protector of the integrity, independence, and dignity of the Supreme Court, should defend its trans-legal status and higher function. Members of the Senate should press for at least one social philosopher, one thinker, among the lawyers and circuit judges.

11

Premodern Senators:
Fulbright, Hatfield, Morse

*A*ccording to press reports, only about 900 people attended the memorial service held in the National Cathedral in Washington for former Sen. William Fulbright after his death. The cathedral seating could have accommodated 3,000. Attendance *was* disappointing, not so much as to numbers but as to composition—namely, the absence of senators, both current and former.

The most important contribution Fulbright made to the Senate was not in support or advancement of particular issues but in his persistent work in preserving and improving the Senate itself as an institution of rational, constitutional government.

Fulbright was one of three senators who served in recent times who have been distinguished by this kind of service—three whose conception of the Senate rose above considerations of partisanship, or personal political advancement, both within the Senate and beyond it. The other two were Wayne Morse and Mark Hatfield. These three rose above parochial or partisan issues when the national interest called for such action. They fit the description of great leadership defined by Edmund Burke.

These three senators, each in a distinctive way, demonstrated their understanding that the Senate has a special role in American government; that it is not, as noted, a super House of Representatives; that it has special obligations to protect the integrity of the federal courts; that it has a special obligation in the field of foreign policy; and finally, that it must watchdog government administration.

Responsibility for the judiciary was of special concern to Sen. Wayne Morse of Oregon. He shared Alexis de Tocqueville's view that the ultimate test of democracy in the United States would be made in the courts. Morse was a Senate activist. But he was also a Senate traditionalist. He engaged in debate on a variety of issues. He gave long and frequent speeches. He filibustered. He introduced resolutions seeking to direct or curb executive powers. In midcareer he left the Republican Party. After resting for a short while as an independent, he became a Democrat.

Fulbright demonstrated his dissent more quietly. His challenges were expressed primarily in words and very often the written word. He spoke quietly, sometimes on the floor of the Senate, sometimes out of the Senate. He developed ideas and challenged conventional wisdom by holding hearings. His strongest words came in the books he wrote. But occasionally, Fulbright did cast protest votes—sometimes alone, as in his vote to deny funds for Sen. Joseph McCarthy's investigative committee; sometimes with a few other senators, as in his support of proposals to bring up a resolution challenging the Vietnam War; and once, notably, against reorganization of the Senate.

Senators, editors, even columnists were uneasy when Fulbright disagreed with them. Presidents were disturbed even by his silence or nonsupport. His silence did not "bellow," as was said of the silence of Thomas More in his refusal to approve Henry VIII's marriage plans, but his silence was *heard.*

Fulbright spoke in judgment not only on foreign policy but also on domestic issues as well, sparing neither Republican nor Democratic administrations. In commenting on the results of an investigation of the Reconstruction Finance Corporation he conducted in 1951, he asked, "How do we deal with those who under guise of friendship accept favors which offend the spirit of the law, but do not violate the letter? What of the men outside government who suborn those within it?"

"One of the more disturbing aspects of this problem of moral conduct," he noted then, "is the revelation that among so many influential people, morality has become identical with legality."

It was statements like these, and like his suggestion that the United States should consider a change to a parliamentary government while it was experiencing the extreme obstructionism of the Eightieth Congress in the Truman administration, that moved President Truman to charge that Fulbright was "overeducated." Sen. Joseph McCarthy soon thereafter labeled him "Senator Half-bright." Fulbright just smiled.

•

Sen. Mark Hatfield, also of Oregon, showed his independence and his concern for the integrity of the Senate in his own way. He operated, for the most part, as a member of the minority party. Nonetheless, he spoke out and voted on issues with clear and rare impartiality. He was the only Republican to openly support the campaign against the Vietnam War in 1968. He was the one Republican senator who has spoken out against the passions and the bigotry of some of the religious right.

Hatfield stood against his party as the sole Senate Republican vote in opposition to the balanced-budget amendment to the Constitution. This he did in the face of threats of retaliation by some Republican senators. They seemed to underestimate Hatfield's integrity. Or perhaps they were unaware of his record on other critical issues.

Possibly, some of Hatfield's critics lacked his understanding of the special charge to U.S. senators—to defend the Constitution from partisan attacks.

These three senators—Morse, Fulbright, and Hatfield—were never members of the club in the Senate. Nor was nonmembership in the club a matter of personality or lack of opportunity. It was a matter of principle. These three did not conceive of the Senate as a club or as a partisan-dominated body, like the House of Representatives. Their conception of the Senate conformed closely to the ideal defined by Plato, who, in speaking of the guardians, said that they must never become "boon companions" of other guardians.

Nor did Fulbright, Morse, or Hatfield succumb to what C. S. Lewis called the "temptation of the 'Inner Ring,' " which, he said, can lead good men to do bad things. Lewis, had he written of the Senate, would undoubtedly have added that this temptation can lead to unsenatorial conduct.

THE FIGHT FOR THE SENATE SEAT AS SEEN FROM THE BLUE RIDGE

Almost twenty years ago now, seeking distance from Washington after an unsuccessful attempt to launch an independent presidential campaign, I bought a home in the Blue Ridge Mountains of Virginia. I have watched Virginia politics with interest.

I admired John Warner for his refusal to support Oliver North for the U.S. Senate in 1994. But this act of statesmanship brought the charge of party disloyalty. He fought a hard primary campaign and then faced an articulate, well-financed young opponent in the general election campaign, run mostly on television. This was Mark Warner, who became known as the other Warner.

Mark Warner let it be known that he was for family values, for fiscal responsibility, and for campaign reform. I was with him on the first two but questioned the capacity of one who has never campaigned for office, or been a member of the Senate, to make very good recommendations either for campaign reform or for reforming Congress.

I tried to make my evaluation of the Virginia Senate campaign by looking at some of the Virginia senators I had observed in action over nearly fifty years.

When I came to Congress, Virginia was represented in the Senate by Willis Robertson, father of evangelist and occasional presidential candidate Pat Robertson, and by Harry Byrd Sr. My first experience of Willis was at a prayer breakfast of members of Congress. It was the third and last such meeting I have attended. Willis gave the meditation, in which he stated that he would like to be for civil rights but that the Bible would not let him.

Willis was best known in the Senate as ranking member of the Gymnasium Committee, a post that carried with it the right to determine the temperature of the swimming pool. Willis liked cold water and set the temperature to satisfy his preference. When he left the Senate, there was rejoicing by those who wished to use the pool. Their rejoicing turned to near despair, however, when he was succeeded in the chairmanship by Sen. Henry Jackson of Washington, who set the water temperature at the level of Puget Sound.

I knew Harry Byrd Sr. only through the press until 1959, when I became a member of the Senate Finance Committee, of which he was chairman. Byrd had a traditional view of the role of the Senate and of its committees. This view was shared by most Senate committee chairmen, especially those from southern states in the 1950s and 1960s. Possibly because the issue of civil rights precluded them from having presidential ambitions, they concerned themselves not only with substantive issues but also with the constitutional and traditional structure and function of the Senate.

It was the Democratic senators from the South who provided the real strength in the move against Sen. Joseph McCarthy, not primarily because of the substance of the issues he was raising but because of his disrespect for the Senate and its procedures.

It was southern senators—Richard Russell and Sam Ervin, for example—who resisted presidential encroachments on Senate powers and actions, especially under President Johnson. As I've said, Johnson tried to make the Senate into a kind of higher House of Representatives, with emphasis on number of votes and measures passed rather than debate and deliberation on great matters. Senators like Russell and Ervin protected the dignity and the power of the Senate. This is a role now played by Sen. Robert Byrd of West Virginia.

The quality of senators elected from Virginia in recent decades is mixed, as in the case of those elected from most states. William Spong was a good choice, but he was replaced by William Scott, whom the press soon dubbed "Capitol Hill's dumbest senator."

Virginia Senate candidates have been mixed, too. Virginia did deny a Senate seat to Oliver North, which was good. But he was nominated for the Senate and came close. And Douglas Wilder, the able former governor of Virginia, was blocked from the Senate. He would have been a fine choice.

It is my hope that Senate candidates throughout the country will begin to take the purpose and traditions of the Senate more seriously and raise issues beyond the kind that Alexander Hamilton, in the *Federalist Papers*, said should be left to state and local governments, like busing and school prayer. (In the 1972 Florida presidential primary, I suggested that students pray on the bus.)

There are at least five issues of significant importance that should be raised and debated not only in the next presidential contest but also in all Senate campaigns of 1998:

- One is political economy: the matter of chronic unemployment and of the rise and acceptance of a poverty class of some 20 million persons. To accept that there is a permanent poverty class—or underclass—is really to accept the concept of surplus human beings.
- The second is that of the opportunity and wealth in America, not just the limited and much discussed balanced-budget issue, but the larger one of maldistribution of wealth and debt throughout our economy and our society.
- The third is that of election laws and practices, especially the law adopted in 1975, which effectively legalized the two parties, despite John Adams's observation that the worst thing he could anticipate was politics controlled by two strong factions. The law also set the stage for control of both parties by corporate PACs.
- The fourth is a complex of international economic problems, including the balance or imbalance of trade and immigration.
- The fifth is foreign policy, especially as it is operative or inoperative in Europe, in the Americas and in Cuba, in North Korea, and in the Israeli-Palestinian conflicts.

A further consideration, beyond issues, is the candidate's conception of the Senate. Virginia has a history of independent senatorial dignity and independence. Harry Byrd Sr. did not support the Democratic candidate in 1960. Harry Byrd Jr., in trouble with the Democratic Party, ran and won re-election to the Senate as a third-party candidate. In 1994 John Warner refused, as shown, to support the Republican nominees for lieutenant governor and senator (O. North).

These actions were consistent with those of three senators, who, I think, lived out a proper conception of what a senator should be:

Fulbright, Morse, and Hatfield. John Warner now approaches the level of these three.

What should matter in a Senate race is not the hot issue of the moment but the great issues of the age, the candidate's character, and his sense of the Senate as a unique American political institution.

HOW TO JUDGE A SENATE CANDIDATE

There are positive standards for judging senatorial attitudes and performance. There also are negative standards that, if they are the mark of candidates or incumbents, should serve as a warning.

Do not vote for a candidate who:

• Often quotes, as the sole authority in support of his or her position, dead politicians and asserts that he or she knows with certainty what the dead person would do if alive. Gen. George C. Marshall of World War II fame was announced as a supporter of the Vietnam War by one of its defenders long after the general had died.

• Lives off a trust set up for him or her by grandparents or great-grandparents. One living on a fund set up by his or her father is within tolerable range of acceptance. But if both grandparents and great-grandparents anticipated that their progeny were not to be trusted with the family inheritance even unto the fourth generation, there is small reason to accept that the same progeny should be given any part in handling a federal budget in excess of $1 trillion.

• Uses a spouse, or spouse and children, as an explanation or an excuse for a vote, especially if the vote is to increase congressional salaries.

• States that he or she was moved to run for office by sudden inspiration, or below the age of fourteen, on visiting Washington as part of a Boy Scout or Girl Scout group.

• Is touted by someone—friend, newspaper editor, or columnist—as having the potential to be a vice president.

• Regularly quotes from three of the following four documents: the Bible (all right if the candidate gives only book and author, but not chapter and verse); the Internal Revenue Code, by title and subtitle, and finer distinctions; the *Summa Theologica* of St. Thomas Aquinas, identifying question and answer; the rules of the U.S. Senate by title, chapter, and paragraph. (This strict rule applies only to incumbents, but can be applied to any challenger who says that if elected he or she will master the Senate rules.)

• Uses the family dog as a defense against any charges leveled against him or her, or is observed to change breeds from one election to another so as to have in the family picture a dog of the currently most popular breed. Defending one's dog from public attack is not only acceptable but commendable, as in the case of Franklin Roosevelt's dog, Fala, but only in and of itself. A candidate should defend his dog but not expect his dog to justify him.

• Publishes his or her income tax returns and challenges opponents to do the same; in most cases this is an act of indecent overexposure.

• Promises that he or she will have a perfect attendance record.

• Subscribes to a quotation service.

• Says that he or she will spend a lot of time listening to constituents.

12

Congress—It Used to Work

*I*n the roughly two and a half decades preceding the reforms of the 1970s (and also preceding the founding of Common Cause), Congress operated largely under the provisions of the Legislation Reorganization Act, passed in 1946. The major provisions of the act dealt with two matters: committee numbers and structure, and the budget process. Standing committees were reduced from 33 to 15 in the Senate and from 48 to 19 in the House of Representatives. Provisions were included to improve professional and clerical staffs, and salaries were increased from $10,000 a year to $12,500 a year. Members of Congress were brought into the Civil Service Retirement Program.

The second major matter addressed by the act was the budget. The act provided that the House of Representatives Ways and Means Committee, the Senate Finance Committee, and the Appropriations Committees of both houses should act as a joint budget committee and each year prepare a governmentwide budget. The report was to be accompanied by estimates of total expenditures and receipts. The law prohibited Congress from appropriating more than the estimated receipts without authorizing an increase in the public debt. A proposal to require that the president reduce all appropriations by a uniform percentage if expenditures exceeded receipts (a kind of early Gramm-Rudman Act) was rejected.

In its first test, in 1947, the budget procedure died in a House-Senate conference. The provisions were deemed unworkable and were suspended. In 1950 Chairman Clarence Cannon of the Appropriations Committee tried to control the budget by putting all appropriations ($37 billion was the amount that year) into a single bill. In 1951 the Appropriations Committee returned to the traditional method of Senate appropriations bills for each government department and agency. Cannon held that the $37 billion budget was too big and too complicated to be handled in one package. No such modesty has been expressed by current members of Congress, who now take on in one appropriation expenditures in excess of $1 trillion.

In any case, without complying with a controlling budget procedure, without reforming Congress, without codes of ethics, without the purifying effect of the Federal Election Act, without Common Cause, Congress—sometimes in support of presidents, sometimes in opposition—between 1947 and 1970 paid off the World War II debts, met the costs of the Korean War, initiated and financed the Marshall Plan, extended Social Security to include nearly all U.S. citizens, established and financed Medicare and Medicaid, built and paid for the interstate highway system, financed the hospital-building program and the development of nuclear power and weapons, balanced the budget in most years and allowed an increase of less than $150 billion in the federal debt in a period of more than twenty years, and kept inflation within a range of 2 percent to 3 percent annually—a rate increase generally favored, even by conservative economists.

All of this was done with the powerful House Rules Committee in place, with the seniority rules generally operative, and with members returning to their districts and states when Congress was out of session, some to work in law offices (risking conflict of interest) or to work on their farms or in their businesses. These members of Congress ran in campaigns in which there were no limits on expenditures or personal contributions, with little or no regulation beyond requirements that contributions and expenditures be reported.

Scandals were few, limited largely to personal misconduct, and none seriously prejudiced or affected the operations of the House or the Senate.

Throughout these two decades the traditional efforts of the Senate to have more power over appropriations (mostly to increase them) continued, but those efforts were largely rejected.

Between 1952 and 1967, bills to create a joint budget committee, composed of members of both the House and the Senate, were passed eight times in the Senate but were never accepted in the House. The issue came to a head in 1962, when the House Appropriations Committee refused to go to the Senate wing of the Capitol for a conference.

The primary responsibility for taxes, constitutionally assigned to the House of Representatives, was also recognized and honored. All revenue bills originated in the House. In practice, the claims of the House went further than the right to originate bills. Tax bills in the House were offered to the membership under very strict rules. The revenue bills passed in these decades by the House were essentially what the Ways and Means Committee offered. The Senate, especially under the Finance Committee chairmanship of Sen. Harry Byrd Sr., honored this distinction and seldom attempted any major modification of the tax bills sent to it by the House of Representatives.

The separation of power and of responsibility between the House and the Senate on foreign policy was not as clearly maintained as was that on taxes and appropriation. Encroachment in this case was not from the Senate but from the House of Representatives.

Before, during, and in the years immediately following World War

II, foreign-policy responsibilities were largely restricted to the Senate and to the executive branch, with little interference from the House of Representatives. When foreign-policy programs, following the war, required authorization and appropriation of money, the House inevitably became involved. For example, whereas the United Nations Charter was approved by the Senate only in 1948, the United Nations Participation Act of the same year was passed and approved by both the Senate and the House. The Greek-Turkish aid program was passed by a vote of 67 to 23 in the Senate and by a vote of 287 to 108 in the House. Similarly, both the House and the Senate participated in formulating and approving the European Recovery Act, thus setting a precedent (with the exception of the approval of treaties) for participation of the House in foreign policy matters on a basis roughly equivalent to that of the Senate.

The growing use of joint resolutions by the House and by the Senate on foreign-policy issues further blurred the lines distinguishing the powers of the House and of the Senate on foreign-policy matters. The most significant example of such resolutions was, again, the Near East Resolution passed during the Eisenhower administration, which did two things: It gave the House equal standing with the Senate in foreign-policy determinations and made the resolutions, because the House participated, a kind of declaration of war, as did the joint actions on the Tonkin Gulf Resolution in 1964, as later interpreted by the Johnson and Nixon administrations.

Once involved in foreign-policy decisions, the House had to take responsibility for them. The House was under pressure to prove itself right within the allotted two years of a House term, while senators have a range of six years before being called to account. It is almost impossible to conduct foreign policy, or even to understand it, on a two-year cycle.

The principal instrument for House meddling in foreign policy was the rider attached to appropriations and other bills, such as the one carrying the name of Rep. Edward Boland of Massachusetts. This prohibited aid to anyone seeking to overthrow the government of Nicaragua.

In recent years, Congress—both the House of Representatives and the Senate—has attempted to micromanage foreign policy. Both houses, with greater and greater frequency, have attempted to give detailed directions and to impose restrictions and to require reporting on foreign assistance and other legislation relating to foreign policy. A quantitative indicator of the extent of such interference is the great increase of reporting requirements on such programs: from 200 in 1973 to more than 700 by 1988.

A more formal action on the part of Congress to further control executive power in international affairs was the passage of the War Powers Act in 1973 (a kind of closing-the-barn-door-after-the-horse-has-fled action by members of Congress who had supported the Vietnam War). The act probably involved an unconstitutional concession of power over foreign policy not only from the president to Congress but also one within Congress, from the Senate to the House of Representatives.

While the House was taking on foreign policies that structurally and functionally it was not constituted to carry out, it was subjected to attacks by reformers strongly supported, if not led, by Common Cause, with help from the League of Women Voters and most of the press. This made it difficult for the House not only to carry out its new responsibilities but also to accomplish its traditional and constitutional responsibilities.

The principal result of the reforms of the '70s was that power and responsibility, which had been exercised and accepted by the Speaker of the House, by the Rules Committee, by committee chairmen, and by ranking members of various committees, was widely dispersed among a growing number of committees and subcommittees and caucuses. Committee staff members were increased. By the end of the '70s, the Democratic leaders of the House acknowledged that their position of leadership had been seriously eroded. Each congressional office had become a separate political party.

In 1974 the House took responsibility for making committee assignments away from the Ways and Means Committee. During the same year, Congress approved the Congressional Budget and Impoundment Control Act, which largely repeated what was acknowledged to be a mistake in the 1946 Reorganization Act. The 1974 act established a joint budget committee and a complicated process for comprehensive treatment of spending and tax policies, a process that eroded the House of Representatives' basic and primary responsibility for expenditures.

In 1975, supported by a large number of new members, the junior members of the House attacked seniority as a basis for picking chairmen.

In 1977 the House adopted a code of ethics, which limited outside earned income and required elaborate reports on gifts, honoraria, and so forth. No limits were imposed on unearned income. The limitation on earned income has been cited as the reason for the bookselling devices that brought Speaker of the House James Wright and Sen. David Durenberger so much trouble, leading to the resignation of Wright from the House of Representatives and the censure of Durenberger by the Senate.

Having failed to bring about good, effective, pure, and Platonic government through reorganizations, budget reform, or codes of ethics, the reformers turned to the electoral process as the source of the trouble, and money as the source beyond the source. Common Cause did, and does still, cite money as the root of all political evil, unmindful or indifferent to the fact that the Bible holds that there are two temptations of a higher order, and both more dangerous. One is the desire for power and the other is pride. In politics pride is expressed by trying to make one's mark on history.

•

The 1970 campaign finance reforms, culminating in the revised (under Supreme Court orders) 1976 act, changed the way in which House members, in particular, financed their campaigns. The revised legislation limited individual contributions, allowed people of great wealth to spend as much of their own money as they wished (as in the Perot presidential campaigns), and made members increasingly dependent on funding of their campaigns by political action committees, especially those organized by corporations.

During the years in which these changes in legislative and policy responsibilities were effected, burdening individual House members with more and more responsibilities, the length or number of days that Congress is in session annually increased dramatically. Once again, we see that Congress is now essentially in continuous session, which is bad for Congress and bad for the country. This leaves members with fewer days to spend with their constituents, forcing them to spend more money on impersonal communications, much of it concentrated during campaigns, and leaving them more and more dependent on the mass media, which in turn sends them back to the PACs for funding treatment.

Members of the House are less and less representative of the nation as a whole and of their particular constituencies. There is less time and opportunity for the *process* of representation. And the House has little of the democratic and populist nature that the Founders intended.

The House also has suffered from the great increase in the number of constituents in each district. The Founding Fathers worried that districts of 30,000 might be too large. When I ran for Congress in 1948, the average district size was about 340,000—about the number Lewis Mumford said was the maximum for a manageable political unit. The average congressional district size today is about 600,000—twenty times greater than that held to be reasonable by the Founding Fathers and twice what Mumford believed was a workable political unit. And the size of House districts is growing every day.

What should happen is a return to smaller districts. The objection is that this would make the House too large. But this might not be so bad. Today, Germany's Bundestag has 662 members, the British House of Commons has 651 members, the National Assembly of France has 577 members, and the Diet of Japan has 512 members.

Yet in Japan the ratio of constituents to each representative is approximately 238,000 to one, in Germany 120,000 to one, in France 96,000 to one, and in Britain 87,000 to one. With all of the responsibilities a member of the House carries for domestic programs, added foreign-policy chores, casework service to more than a half-million people, getting re-elected every two years, giving some attention to private and family matters, and so on, it is not surprising that what was called a House banking service (it was not; it was really a check-cashing service) might have been abused a few years back.

What should be done to make the House a respected and effective legislative body once again?

1. The House of Representatives should be "disorganized" or reorganized to about what it was in the 1950s.

2. The full power of the Speaker, of the Rules Committee, and of

the Ways and Means Committee should be restored, along with the seniority system and the strong-chairman tradition.

3. The budget process now in effect should be abolished, and the process followed under Chairman Clarence Cannon in the '50s be restored.

4. Sessions of Congress should be shortened so that members of the House can spend more time with their constituents, thus freeing themselves in some measure from the need to spend large amounts of money to communicate with these constituents both during sessions and in campaigns.

5. The House of Representatives should reassert its dominance over appropriations, and the Ways and Means Committee should assert its authority over taxes. The House should yield to the Senate primary responsibility over foreign policy relative to the House and not participate in joint foreign-policy resolutions. The House should stop or control the offering of riders on legislation affecting foreign policy.

6. The federal election laws should be either repealed or significantly modified by removing the limitations of individual contributions and outlawing contributions from both labor and corporate political action committees as now constituted.

7. House members should retain their parking privileges at the airport in Washington and their gyms. It's good for the country to try to keep sane as many members of Congress as possible.

8. The number of staff members should be reduced by at least 50 percent.

9. The number of citizens in each district should be reduced by 50 percent and House membership doubled.

10. The code of ethics should be revised to require reporting of income, but set no limits on outside earned income. A person

should be able to run for office and serve in office without being continuously in danger of acting illegally.

A SPEAKER IS NOT A PRIME MINISTER

When I came to the House in 1949, Sam Rayburn was chosen to be Speaker. He was the dominant and controlling force in the House until his death in the early 1960s. His strength was not his legislative achievements, his program, his partisanship, or his personal magnetism. Rather, his power was institutional.

Under Rayburn, the House of Representatives operated according to his conception of what the constitutional and traditional role of the Speaker and the House of Representatives should be.

Even during the Eisenhower presidency, when the Democratic Party was casting about for a spokesman, Rayburn refused to be cast as the head of the party. He left that role to Adlai Stevenson, the defeated presidential nominee, and, in a limited way, to Lyndon Johnson, as Democratic leader of the Senate.

Rayburn felt that the Speaker, as first-ranking member of Congress and third in the line of succession, was a *constitutional* officer. He seldom left the Speaker's chair to address the House of Representatives, and then only when he thought the matter under debate was of compelling national importance, or when he thought that the House of Representatives was about to do something so foolish that it might reflect negatively on the integrity of that body.

He was so true to the rules of the House and to its traditions that I cannot recall a member accusing him of unfairness or partisanship. The Republican leaders of the House were left in the frustration of respect.

There was structure and hierarchy in the Rayburn House. The

lines of authority, power, and responsibility within the House were clear, as were the distinctions in the roles of the House and the Senate, the courts, and the executive branch of the government. Rayburn is reported to have leaned down from his Speaker's chair in the House chamber just before President Truman gave his first State of the Union Address and said, "Remember, Harry, you are also still Harry Truman."

He supported House chairmen and committees in conflict with the Senate or the executive branch. When Clarence Cannon, a chairman of the House Appropriations Committee, refused to go over to the Senate side of the Capitol for a conference on an appropriations bill, Rayburn stood by Cannon on the grounds that appropriations were a primary responsibility of the House. This responsibility, Rayburn said, should in no way be compromised, even by a concession as to place of meeting with the Senate.

A second clear rule under Rayburn was that no games could be played with the Ways and Means Committee on tax measures. Not long after Rayburn was gone and the House had a different Speaker, the Rayburn rule was broken by his former protégé, Lyndon Johnson. Early in his administration, Johnson sent a tax bill to the Senate as a kind of dove sent out from the ark to see whether spring had come. Finding little response, the president then held the bill in abeyance, thus weakening the traditional role of the House.

This erosion of House responsibility continued through subsequent speakerships and presidencies until, in the first Reagan administration, a tax bill was passed in the Senate before it was enacted in the House. That would not have been tolerated in the Rayburn years.

The change in the conception of the role of the Speaker began in the time that John McCormack held the office. McCormack had been an able majority leader under Rayburn, but the qualities that make a good leader in the House do not necessarily qualify that person for the speakership.

The Rayburn traditional and constitutional approaches to the speakership became further confused under Carl Albert. But the real distortion of the office occurred under the speakership of Tip O'Neill. O'Neill let himself be cast as Democratic Party spokesman and leader rather than, as had been the case with Rayburn, the leader and agent of the House of Representatives. I believe Rayburn's concept was intended by the Constitution.

That concept was drawn from the British Parliament, in which the Speaker is elected by the majority but then required to resign from his seat in the Parliament to ensure greater objectivity and detachment from party politics in his office.

Rayburn also had the dignity befitting his concept of the speakership. It is difficult to imagine that Rayburn, had he lived beyond his speakership, would have appeared in television advertisements for luggage or beer.

Rep. Tom Foley's conception of the Speaker's office seems to have been closer to that of Rayburn, but in the office Foley, for a variety of reasons, was not able to restore it to what it had been under Rayburn.

The Newt Gingrich view of the role of the Speaker (with curious support from the press, comparable to what it showed for Rep. Jim Wright in his short time in the office) goes beyond even the O'Neill conception. When he came to office, Gingrich seemed to think of himself as a kind of prime minister, chosen by the House of Representatives. To him, the speakership is a partisan job and a quasi-executive job.

Since, under the Constitution, Gingrich cannot bring down the government, he was in 1994 ready to act instead as head of a kind of "countergovernment." Through control of appropriations, this

Gingrich-style parliamentary government can operate as an effective check on the executive branch and seize direction of the executive branch from a hapless executive. Though he first appeared stunned by the Democratic rout and by the rise of Gingrich, President Clinton was anything but hapless.

The Gingrich concept, implicitly, was of a new, extra- or trans-constitutional government, with power divided between the president, elected by the people, and the Speaker as premier, elected by the politicians—rather like France.

As it turned out, the country did not much care for Gingrich or his premiership.

The country was right. The Gingrich model showed a consistent attitude of disregard and disrespect for the Constitution. For in our system, Congress does not execute and the Speaker of the House does not direct his party or the federal bureaucracy. Gingrich's overreaching was constitutional overreaching as well as personal overreaching. He proposed balanced budgets, with or without constitutional approval; three-fifths congressional majority requirements on issues such as prayer in public schools; and possibly congressional veto power over Supreme Court rulings.

President Clinton was certainly sensitive to the balance of power, but there is no evidence that he was sensitive to Gingrich's attempt at constitutional usurpation.

More recently, Gingrich has supposedly been humbled, but there can be little doubt that he would try again to act as a prime minister from the Speaker's chair if he had another chance, perhaps under a Republican president.

Thomas More, in the play *A Man for All Seasons,* warns his son-in-law, Will Roper, that it is dangerous to cut down the law to achieve even desirable ends. Gingrich says he has learned his lesson. But has he learned that it is not well to ignore constitutional deference, habit, and tradition?

OLD ADVICE FOR NEW MEMBERS OF CONGRESS

Between the time they are elected and the date of their swearing in, new members of Congress live precariously—in a condition not very different from that of newly hatched green turtles on the shores of Tortuga as they make their run for the safety of the sea. The young turtles are beset by attackers from the air, by land animals, and even by fish waiting for them in the shallow waters offshore.

Waiting for new members of Congress is a variety of predators: various committees of their own parties, numerous foundations, think tanks, "public interest" groups, and special interests. Some of these are concerned about policy, some about procedures. Some are concerned about morals and deep ethical concerns. Lobbyists lurk in the shadows or hover in the air.

The press, especially the columnists, gives advice—solicited or unsolicited.

The John F. Kennedy School of Harvard—somewhat in the way of Mohammad inviting the mountain—hosts and instructs new members, telling new congressmen how to be congressmen.

The Brookings Institution stands ready, not so much to advise as to pronounce. Note that Brookings is an institution, not an institute, like the Carnegie. Members of Brookings do not say that they are with or from the organization but of it, just as members of separate choirs of angels do not say they are with or from the cherubim but of it.

The Heritage Foundation will be waiting for conservatives in need of help. Common Cause will be present, insisting that it is, possibly, the only pure, uncontaminated public interest lobby. The Americans for Democratic Action, which originated in order to protect liberals from communist influence and now includes as one of its purposes protecting little liberals from toys that are dangerous, physically or psychologically, is still around. (The ADA is strong on maintaining attendance records of members of Congress.)

Newly elected members, of whatever class, will be asked by one or more of these organizations or people to support reorganizations or reforms of various kinds. They will be told that it is essential to their success to have a dedicated, hardworking staff; that it is vital that they know the rules of procedure of the body to which they have been elected; that they should maintain a near-perfect, if not perfect, attendance record; that national politics is very complicated, or that it is simple, if one only follows the principles of the organization applying the pressure.

Some of these counselors will condemn the seniority system.

Party spokesmen will emphasize the importance of party loyalty. Democratic Party spokesmen undoubtedly will quote remarks long attributed to Speaker Sam Rayburn that "those who go along get along." Others will praise "the middle way," the vital center, and the art of compromise. A few will explain how important it is to have good relationships with the press.

Most of this advice is questionable. Some of it is very bad. Every two years, I offer a set of ten countercommandments, which, if observed by members of Congress, will save them much time and save them from making many mistakes.

1. Do not have a perfect or near-perfect attendance record.

Watch ADA on this. If a new member has an attendance record that is better than 80 percent, there is reason to believe that he or she has been wasting time. (See the first chapter of this book.) A member who has been in office for several terms should work his attendance record down to 65 percent to 75 percent.

Note that this will not be well understood by the press.

2. Do not worry too much about rules of procedure or spend too much time trying to learn them. The Senate rules are simple enough to learn, but they are seldom honored in practice. House rules are too complicated. Use the parliamentarian. (My own rule in the House of Representatives was not to trust a member who quoted the Bible, chapter and verse; the Internal Revenue Code, section and subsection; or the Rules of the House.)

3. Beware of a staff that is too efficient. My old administrative assistant, Jerome Eller, advised that a member of Congress should never trust a staffer who regularly got to the office before the member did. Or who stayed later.

4. Don't worry too much about understanding the issues or being a "policy wonk." Remember that politics is much like professional football. Those who are most successful are, as the dean of my college said, smart enough to understand the game but not smart enough to lose interest.

5. Don't knock seniority. You may have it sooner than you anticipate.

And remember what Gilbert Chesterton said: that it makes no sense to have the oldest son of a king succeed his father, but it saves a lot of trouble. (Alexis de Tocqueville held that in a democracy, seniority is a last defense against anarchy.)

6. Unless the issue is of overwhelming importance, don't be the only one or one of a few who are right. It is difficult to say to one's colleagues in Congress, "I am sorry I was right. Please

forgive me." They won't. It is easier to say, "I was wrong." Forgiveness is almost immediate.

7. Remember that the worst accidents occur in or near the middle of the road. Bipartisanship and balance are usually stressed by the League of Women Voters. Be wary of all three.

8. Do not respond to the appeal of "party loyalty." This can be the last defense of rascals.

9. Abide by the advice given to young members of Congress forty years ago by a leftover New Dealer (see Part I again): "Vote against anything introduced that begins with the syllable *re.*" Reorganizations, recodifications, reform, and especially resolutions. The puritans really do slay St. George and feed the dragon.

10. Perhaps most important: the advice of Ed Leahy, noted reporter for the *Chicago Daily News*—"Never trust the press."

13

The Rules of Chaos: Democrats, the Two-Party "System," Perot

*T*he reform commission that remade the Democratic Party in 1972 was chaired by George McGovern, the eventual party nominee.

Since 1972 the *rules* of the Democratic Party, rather than issues or personalities, have determined who would be the party's nominee for the presidency. But whereas the rule changes for the 1972 and 1976 campaigns were formulated by the national party, the rules and procedures for the elections to follow (in 1980, 1984, 1988, and 1992) showed a progressive increase in the power of state parties, state legislatures, and governors over operations of the national party. There has been a decline especially in the influence of senators, representatives, and what once was the national party.

Candidates for the Democratic Party presidential nomination, following the two Stevenson defeats by Eisenhower, were drawn from the Senate: Kennedy-Johnson in 1960, Johnson-Humphrey in 1964, Humphrey-Muskie in 1968, and McGovern-Eagleton (until Eagleton was replaced by Sargent Shriver) in 1972.

Following the defeat of the McGovern ticket in 1972, state influence became progressively stronger. The committee in charge of rules for the 1976 nominating process and convention included Jimmy Carter. The rules adopted served the Carter presidential effort admirably. They eliminated the winner-take-all primaries, always the contests in which nationally known senators did well. The change assured Carter a share of primary delegates and left him free within the rules to garner delegates from nonprimary states, where state politicians had basic control. Carter won the nomination and picked a senator, Walter Mondale, as the vice presidential candidate, after looking over a list of applications from senators, including Edmund Muskie, Frank Church, Adlai Stevenson III, and others.

Mondale had made an early bid for support as a possible presidential candidate two years earlier, but had abandoned the effort. Again in 1980, Carter, after turning back a challenge from Sen. Edward Kennedy, picked Mondale for the nomination. Mondale picked not a senator but a House member, Geraldine Ferraro, for vice president.

After that one interlude, the dominance of governors returned. Control or influence of governors and state legislatures, which had been growing following the adoption of the 1976 rules, was further strengthened by the organization in 1984 of the Democratic Leadership Council. The council's declared purpose, as stated by one of its founders, Sen. Sam Nunn of Georgia, was "to do everything we can to move the Democratic Party back into the mainstream of American political life." The council's initial membership of forty-two included eighteen House members, fourteen senators, and ten governors. It was dominated by Southern and Western office holders. Among the governors were Bruce Babbitt of Arizona, Bill Clinton of Arkansas, and Richard Riley of South Carolina.

In 1988 the dominance of governors was restored with the nomination of Gov. Michael Dukakis of Massachusetts. Again there was a nod to the Senate in the choice of Sen. Lloyd Bentsen, also a member of the Leadership Council, as the vice presidential candidate.

By 1992, through the work of the Democratic Leadership Council and others, the power of the state leaders and self-defined moderates was further enhanced, especially by changes in primary dates and laws. States moved to set primary dates early and to advance the dates of caucuses so as to get early attention for both political and financial reasons. Iowa and New Hampshire competed to be the first test.

New Hampshire, several times, has threatened to have its primary ahead of any other state, even if it meant setting the date in the year preceding the election. (New Hampshire in this competition made the mistake of moving its primary date to mid-February rather than having it in mid-March, its traditional date. March is a much better time for decision in New Hampshire. Frost heaves, reflecting thawing, have begun to show on the roads. The sap is rising in the maple trees. The Ides of March and the spring equinox approach.)

More effective and serious in its effect on the nominating process was the establishment, largely with support of the Democratic Leadership Council, of the Super Tuesday primaries, on March 10, 1988. On that day primaries were held in eleven states: Delaware, Florida, Hawaii, Louisiana, Massachusetts, Missouri, Mississippi, Oklahoma, Rhode Island, Tennessee, and Texas.

The early date and the number of primaries on that date, as well as the states in which they were held, gave special advantages to the candidates favored by the Democratic Leadership Council, which in 1992 favored Bill Clinton. Senators who ran in 1992 were pretty much on the outside looking in.

The "bonding" of governors is closer than that of senators. They may even have a slight inferiority complex relative to senators. Carter and Clinton both ran against Washington, including the record of Democratic Congresses.

More important, it is easier for incumbent governors to run and organize: to qualify for matching funds and to campaign without being subject to continuous charges that they are missing votes. It is easier for governors to run against Washington, even against Congresses controlled by their own party, than it is for senators and House members to do so. (Robert Dole tried running as Citizen Dole, after thirty years inside Washington, with virtually no success.)

Well, Bill Clinton was nominated in 1992, and Al Gore, who had as a senator made an unsuccessful bid for the presidential nomination in 1988, was chosen as Clinton's running mate, in a repeat of the 1976 procedure in which Carter, a governor, chose Senator Mondale as his running mate.

And the Democratic Leadership Council has or has had strong representation in the Clinton administration. Both Gore and Clinton were among the forty-two original members, as were Babbitt, subsequently secretary of the interior; Bensen, later secretary of the Treasury; Riley, secretary of education; Tim Wirth, former senator from Colorado, now in the State Department; and Leon Panetta, former congressman, later White House chief of staff.

And since 1992 additional states have further altered their selection procedures, dates of primaries, and so on. This was, as a rule, done not to open up the political process but rather to give the respective states real or imagined advantages over other states in the process of selecting the presidential candidate. Arizona challenged New Hampshire with proposals for an earlier primary, as did Louisiana.

•

What has been the net effect of these two influences—the Democratic Leadership Council and state and local politicians—upon the Democratic Party? They are almost obvious. By embracing a vaguely Republican form of moderate-ism, the party has been able, at least in the short run, to co-opt the Republican national ticket (aided, it must be said, by aging and inarticulate ticket leaders who themselves were quite vague). But the sacrifice the party has made has been the loss of its soul.

The party can no longer articulate what principles it stands for; it cannot hold together congressional coalitions because it no longer has the principles with which to do this; it can no longer inspire the young; it can no longer lead the people toward ends that require self-ishness and sacrifice. To co-opt or outmanuever is different than to lead.

The Democratic Party no longer stands for work, social justice, an enlightened foreign policy. It is the party of lesser tax cuts, of lesser balanced budgets, of big government, but smaller, more efficient big government.

The Democratic Party is no longer a progressive party. And the nation needs a progressive party, just as it needs a conservative party.

It is fine to be in touch with "the mainstream" of the American people, but it is the special mission of the Democratic Party to be in touch with the people who are *not* a part of the bond markets, not members of PACs, not even members of labor unions—the millions of Americans who are frozen out of the politics and the economy of the nation. In some cases, they *are* the mainstream, or the silent majority.

A Democratic Party that can win but forgets the disenfranchised people of the country is a hollow party that wins hollow victories.

The impact of state legislators and governors has been to make the party more parochial and more narrow in vision. State government is largely administrative, and Bill Clinton, as governor of the United States, approaches the presidency as a series of administrative tasks and compromises.

State politicians also are more likely to be dominated by special interests—lobbyists, unions, special pleaders, local fixers, and the large corporations. Clinton brought to the White House the Little Rock mentality on fund-raising and presidential access to special interests.

What he did not bring was knowledge of Congress and the executive branch, which a governor does not get through his basically subservient dealings with the federal bureaucracy. The president, of course, now has that experience. But this is expensive on-the-job training, and the people who staffed the Clinton White House in the first term were also largely inexperienced in federal government. They too got experience, but *they* have now left the White House. Moreover, the Clinton staff has all along been largely based on the gubernatorial model—political and administrative personnel, but few Washington veterans who could be called wise men or long-range thinkers.

In the Clinton presidency, the dominance of governors and of so-called centrists in the Democratic Party is now firmly established. But this has made the party less clearly defined and less Democratic, while it has made the first popular Democratic presidency since Roosevelt and Truman more confused and less Democratic.

ELEANOR ROOSEVELT

On college campuses these days, I am often asked who my heroes are, or role models, or persons I respect. I am not sure about heroes, but Franklin Roosevelt was certainly the decisive political figure of my generation. And, as I have said, people with whom I served in Congress, like Sam Rayburn and Wayne Morse, Paul Douglas and Phil Hart, were people I respected.

Some of my teachers at St. John University had a great impact on me, as did the life and legend of Thomas More and his book *Utopia*.

But there are two people who, it seems to me, personalize what the Democratic Party ought to be and once was. One is Eleanor Roosevelt; the other is Adlai Stevenson.

Eleanor Roosevelt entered the marketplace of action and controversy unwillingly. She never left it. She was also a commentator. Yet she always saw her accepted role as not to judge the world but to improve it. Mrs. Roosevelt had the qualities of tolerance and forgiveness, for she knew the capacity of men for confusion and misunderstanding. She never allowed her interest in humanity to distract her from interest in individual men and women.

Although she believed that the movement of history was toward a better life, she never allowed hopes or dreams of a better future to interfere with dedicated action and attention to the present. *Tomorrow Is Now* was the title of her last book.

Eleanor Roosevelt was a realist, ready to accept compromise, but only when principle was recognized and given the greater weight on the scales. She was prepared—when she could not be sure—to make mistakes in public policy on the side of trust rather than on the side of mistrust and suspicion, to err on the side of liberality and hope rather than on the side of narrow self-concern and fear. She was blessed, as were all who knew her, in that as she grew in age, she also grew in spiritual strength and wisdom.

In the 1950s, when truth was being driven from the field, when doubt was expanded, when suspicion and accusation held the high ground, when younger persons fled in fear, Eleanor Roosevelt stood firm.

One writer described her as "fine, precise, hand-worked like ivory." And like a figure carved in ivory, she became more beautiful with age. Eleanor Roosevelt reached that high state of serenity in which she moved and spoke and acted freely, without fear and without concern for the judgment of biographers or any judgment of the world.

ADLAI STEVENSON

When Adlai Stevenson died, we lost the purest politician of our time.

Stevenson's approach to politics was marked by three principal characteristics:

1. A decent respect for the opinions of mankind in world affairs.
2. A willingness to accept the judgment of the majority in domestic politics and in general elections.
3. The unselfish surrender of his own personal reputation and image for the good of the common effort if, in his judgment, that surrender would advance the cause of justice and order and civility.

Adlai Stevenson did not grow in honor and in reputation through the organizations he served, but rather they grew by virtue of his service.

He demonstrated early in his career, and throughout his public life, the highest degree of political humility in his indifference to what historians and biographers might say about him.

Stevenson was not ahead of his time or outside of his time, as some of his critics said. He was a true contemporary, passing judgment on his own day, expressing that judgment in words that proved his deep concern for the integrity of the language, and finally committing himself to the consequences of his judgment.

I would feel better about the future of the Democratic Party if I felt it was drawing its inspiration from the life and work of Adlai Stevenson, rather than from the playbook of Dick Morris.

In the words of Chaucer, Adlai Stevenson was a worthy knight who from the time he first rode forth "loved chivalry, truth and honor, generosity and courtesy."

THE TWO-PARTY SYSTEM: FORMULA FOR DISASTER

John Adams, as previously cited, in a commentary on the politics that might follow the adoption of the Constitution of the United States, stated his opinion that the worst possible development would be politics controlled by two strong factions.

We now have the very condition that Adams warned against. Today free and effective participation in the process of choosing a government, especially the president of the United States, is limited and controlled by two parties: the Republicans and the Democrats. Not only is effective participation in the political process denied to new parties and independent candidates, but recent restrictive laws and practices have had the effect of suppressing limited movements of protest or division within the two major parties.

The moves to control politics in the interest of the Republican and Democratic parties did not begin until early in this century. When the Republican Party was born in 1854 as a party of protest against the extension of slavery into territories, it combined various dissident Whigs, Free-Soilers, Anti-Slavery Democrats, and fringe groups, including Know-Nothings and Barnburners. In this century, following the success of Teddy Roosevelt and his Bull Moose Party in the 1912 campaign (in which Teddy ran ahead of the official Republican nominee), Republican Party initiatives were undertaken to restrict third-party activities.

In some states, laws were passed to limit the effectiveness of movements such as those of Populists, Progressives, and various socialistic, possibly communist, parties. The limited successes of Henry Wallace and of George Wallace in more recent elections resulted in the imposition of additional state restraints on any political action outside the two established parties.

Prior to the passage of the amendments to the Federal Election Campaign Act in 1975—amendments that, for the first time in our history, gave federal preferential status to the two established parties— laws protecting, advancing, and securing the two parties were largely actions of state legislatures, sustained by state, and occasionally federal, courts. The one exception was a federal law passed in the 1950s that outlawed the Communist Party in the United States, a law subsequently declared unconstitutional by the U.S. Supreme Court.

Republicans and Democrats usually found common ground in supporting legislation to give either or both protected status. The "two-party system" came to be accepted, not only as a condition to effective government in the United States but also as an article of public faith, accepted by politicians, professors, and the press.

Gerald Ford stated his faith, saying, "I believe in the two-party system." Marshall Field, a prominent newspaper publisher, expressed the faith of the press in a 1976 statement, declaring, "This is a two-party country," much as an editor of *Pravda* might have declared of the former Soviet Union: This is a one-party country. One might just as well say: This is a two-religion country. Freedom of religion would mean that the citizens could choose one established church or the other.

As a result of these laws, media support and propagation, and popular belief, third-party or new-party or independent candidacies have had little success in the United States in this century. The ultimate barrier to significant independent or third-party success is the generally prevailing rule of practice of the winner-take-all state electoral votes. Only Strom Thurmond and George Wallace, using the race issue as the basis of their campaigns, have won electoral votes as independent candidates. Ross Perot, although he received almost 20 percent of the popular vote in the 1992 presidential election, got no votes in the electoral college. He did come close to winning one electoral vote in the state of Maine, which allocates electoral votes on the basis of congressional districts combined with statewide results.

The state-imposed limitations on any independent or non-Democratic or non-Republican presidential candidate have been challenged with very little success in the past two decades. Any successes came largely as a result of court actions. Court decisions usually occur after the election is over and the damage has been done, as in the case involving Dr. Benjamin Spock and the People's Party. A court held that Spock had been wrongfully excluded from the presidential ballot in Hawaii.

In 1976 I ran as an independent candidate, principally to establish a basis for a second Supreme Court challenge to the constitutionality of the 1975–76 amendment to the federal election law, and also to challenge the exclusionary and discriminatory state laws and practice.

Our effort had little effect upon the federal law, but as a result of the campaign, election laws in eighteen states were altered or struck down by both state and federal courts. Three cases reached the Supreme Court. When we abandoned our ballot placement effort, my name was on the ballot in only thirty states. However, when John Anderson ran as an independent candidate for president in 1980, building on our '76 effort, he was able to get on the ballot in about thirty-five states.

In 1992 Perot made the ballot in fifty states. He was helped by changes that had been forced on the states in earlier years and also by the fact that he spent, according to reports, more than $70 million of his own fortune on his campaign.

•

State and federal election laws are not the only obstacles independent and third-party candidates face. Of a different origin, but just as serious as exclusion from the ballot, is the exclusion from coverage by the media, especially from television. The media's position against third- or outside-party candidates has been shown also in dealing with candidates of the two major parties if they show signs of weakness.

Shortly before the election of November 1964, President Johnson announced that he was going to give a major address. In fact, it was not much of an address, and the television networks gave some thought to covering it simply as a news story. When Johnson learned this, he let it be known that he was unhappy. He wanted the speech broadcast live. The networks carried the speech live. Sen. Barry Goldwater and the Republicans asked for equal time, but their request was turned down by the courts, including the Supreme Court.

Twelve years later, in 1976, shortly before the election of that year, President Ford announced a news conference. Most broadcasters treated the Ford appearance as an unimportant event. None carried it live. News polls at the time indicated that Carter was likely to win. The media were not eager to give time to a candidate who was likely to lose. This was called the "nearness doctrine" by one network spokesman who thought defeat was near for Ford. Better nearness than fairness.

In the 1992 campaign, the Republican Party's nominating process rendered ineffective the David Duke effort to be included among that party's candidates, but Pat Buchanan was admitted, after proposals to exclude him by legal action were abandoned.

In 1992 the Democratic Party excluded from party notice all but five candidates. Only the chosen five were included in party-sponsored debates, and the exclusion was honored by the television networks, including Public Broadcasting. The combined thrust of the legal and other actions taken by the two major parties—and supported by the Federal Communications Commission, and the media, generally, and especially those elements of it that profit from having television and radio licenses—is that there shall be only two parties, and also that within those two parties, dissent shall be discouraged.

Candidates planning to become involved, as either independent or third-party candidates, or even as modest dissenters in either of the two established parties, would do well to look to the record of the two parties' officials, of the Federal Elections Commission, of the Federal Communications Commission, of the courts, and of the media.

THE PEROT PHENOMENON
("FROM AARDVARK TO AMWAY")

Through 1997, the ongoing Perot campaign might have become a "movement." If it has, it runs quietly, either deep or shallow. Some pundits say it is dormant but will revive as the 2000 campaign comes on, and that when it does, it will be directed against President Clinton, Al Gore, and their administration, as in 1996. Others say it will be directed against Republicans. Most pundits say the Perot campaigns hurt George Bush and Bob Dole more than they hurt Clinton. Perhaps so.

Totem animals are the Democrats' donkey and the Republicans' elephant. The Perot movement, if it has become one and is searching for an animal symbol, might best choose the aardvark. The aardvark, according to naturalists, did not evolve from any other animal or previous state of being, and it is not evolving into something different. It is both genus and species. It is like the pig in some respects, like the anteater in others, although the aardvark eats only termites because it has no gizzard. It is somewhat like a rabbit and like a kangaroo. It is like a donkey, like an elephant, etc. But no animal is like the aardvark unless it is an aardvark.

As was the Perot movement of 1992, the aardvark is a kind of existential experience, not continuing anything from the past or moving or changing to become something different in the future.

Perot supporters or, better, followers in 1992 numbered about 20 million people. They were not a single-issue group, nor were they fanatics or "kooks" (with the usual exceptions). Their conventions and meetings had the look of Amway or Tupperware conventions. Overall they appeared to be better balanced than people one sees at Republican and Democratic conventions. Many of them are from a recently identified sociological group, the exurbanities: people living beyond the suburbs and beyond coherent legal and political structures. Perotistas apparently live beyond the reach of public transportation, water systems, and sewage, having their own wells and their own septic tanks (the ultimate symbol of independence) and served by volunteer fire departments and county police.

What they have in common is the belief that the country is not being well governed by the Republican and Democratic politics. They are willing to cast votes that can, at most, communicate disaffection and the desire for some small measure of nobility in politics.

Given recent history, Perot has had easy pickings for his critical observations, and it appears that the second Clinton administration will not leave him without targets.

The Perot campaigns have shown that on occasion a person of wealth is willing to spend a good part of his fortune (in the spirit of which Jefferson wrote the Declaration pledge of "lives, fortunes, and sacred honor") for the common good. Perot's willingness to put his fortune on the line has been a positive thing. The campaigns also have shown how ridiculous the campaign laws of the country are. Most important, the two Perot drives have given vent to voter frustration and reinvolved millions of citizens who had given up on politics.

The Perot movement may encourage citizens not only to examine the substance of government but also to examine the election laws and procedures, so that effective political challenges can be made not only by outsiders of great wealth but also by ordinary citizens and citizens' groups. That is what the rights to free speech and assembly in the Bill of Rights are really all about—the right to take part, especially for the dispossessed.

As Perot would say, "It's as simple as that."

RETURN TO CHICAGO

The choice of Chicago as the site of the 1996 Democratic Party convention was a surprising one, unless the president and leaders of the party, for reasons as yet not evident, felt the need for the kind of protective security that only an experienced Chicago police force and the Illinois National Guard could provide.

In the past half century, the Democratic Party has faced two important moral-political challenges. The first was that of civil rights, the focus of the 1948 convention in Philadelphia. At that time, the party acknowledged its responsibility to take political action following the example of the Supreme Court in 1944, first because of the importance of the matter, but also because the Democratic Party, especially in its southern components, had, with some aid from Republicans, exploited racial differences and divisions.

For the Democrats to raise civil rights was high risk. The choice promised to be divisive, if not disastrous. But the party took the moral high road.

The results were divisive but not disastrous. The convention approved a civil rights plank. The Dixiecrats walked out and ran their own candidate. Truman was nominated and then elected in the November election of 1948.

In 1968 the Democratic Party faced a comparable political and moral challenge: the Vietnam War.

The issue was not as deeply divisive as the civil rights issue of 1948, nor did it promise to be disastrous to the party if the antiwar position carried the day. The heart of the conflict in Chicago was over whether the party would ratify a war to which the country had been committed in its enlarged state by the Johnson administration; this, despite what seemed to be a pledge to avoid such a commitment made by candidate Johnson in the 1964 campaign for the presidency. Johnson had promised not to expand the war.

The Johnson administration was firmly set on having the party accept, and thus share, guilt for the war. In the most controlled, violent, and undemocratic convention in the history of the country, the prowar position was endorsed.

Those of us who opposed the war expected that delegates we had won, or deserved to have won by every reasonable standard, would be accepted; that a reasonable debate would be conducted; and that a plank reflecting the differences existing among the delegates would be accepted. It was not to be so.

The unit rule, under which a majority of a state delegation or a state party was allowed to control the entire delegation, was supposed to be abolished in 1968. It was not. Those in control of the convention put off that change until 1972. Delegates who had been chosen two to four years before the convention, long before the Vietnam War had even become an issue, were seated and did the administration's bidding. Their credentials were challenged but without success.

The administration and the party officials controlling the convention did not limit their defenses and offenses to party rules and procedures. The approaches to the convention hall were protected by coils of barbed wire. The Chicago police were present in great numbers. The police were joined by the state National Guard, courtesy of then

Gov. Otto Kerner. They were equipped with guns and a "crowd container," consisting of a frame of barbed wire mounted on the front of a jeep or other military vehicle.

We learned after the convention that there had been a third line of offense: the U.S. Army Reserves. They had been put on partial alert to move into action if the Chicago police and the Illinois National Guard proved inadequate.

The surveillance and control preparations went beyond these more or less open demonstrations of force.

When I moved into my suite of rooms in the Hilton Hotel, the Secret Service, which proved itself wholly loyal to its code of professionalism and honor, told me that I had their word that my rooms were not bugged and that we could speak freely within those confines, but they warned that they could not say the same for the telephones, which they said were tapped. They warned us not to say anything on the telephones that we wished to keep private.

In later congressional hearings, it was acknowledged that army intelligence, indeed, had tapped our phone lines.

The saddest and most incredible occurrence of the convention was that of the evening of August 28, following the vote nominating Hubert Humphrey. One would have expected that with the pro-administration position sustained and their candidate nominated, the Johnson forces would have been somewhat satisfied. Not so. Beatings of students and others among my supporters took place on the sidewalks and streets outside the Hilton Hotel and in Grant Park, across Michigan Avenue. Dr. William Davidson and my brother Austin, also a surgeon, set up an emergency hospital on the fifteenth floor of the Hilton Hotel.

This was not the last act of violence perpetrated by the police. We spent Thursday cleaning up our campaign headquarters and preparing to leave on Friday. Sometime between 3 and 4 A.M., as nearly as we could mark, the police, aided by hotel employees, raided our rooms and working space on the fifteenth floor. Some fifteen or twenty police officers burst out of the elevators into the fifteenth-floor lobby. They proceeded to round up people in the lobby and then to open bedroom doors, get people out of bed, force them to join others in the lobby, and then to conduct all of them downstairs into the main lobby, where, ringed by police, they were forced to sit on the floor like prisoners of war.

One girl, near hysteria, told me that she had been playing bridge, and holding a 21-point hand, when the police broke up the game.

When, having learned of the raid, I reached the lobby, I asked who was in charge. No one stepped forward. I directed the captives to rise and return to their rooms on the fifteenth floor. The police left the hotel.

My last warning from the Secret Service was that as soon as I left Chicago, planned for Friday, the Daley police intended to arrest anyone found in the city having any identification with my campaign. I delayed my departure to Saturday after advising—actually warning— all supporters to leave Chicago or at least to find some space, such as the airport, which was beyond Mayor Daley's jurisdiction. As our chartered American Airlines plane flew out of Midway Airport, the pilot came on the public address system and said, "We are now leaving Prague."

Years later, I was sent an album put together by someone who had been at the convention, showing, on opposite pages, scenes from Prague and from Chicago, 1968. The differences were marginal: military uniforms rather than those of police, tanks instead of crowd containers, gun smoke instead of tear gas.

Apparently, these events were supposed to be wiped from memory, or from consideration, by the Democrats returning to the Chicago scene in 1996, and sealed or supplemented by having the current mayor of Chicago, a son of the Richard Daley of 1968, and Tom Hayden, a protester in Chicago (but not a campaign worker), plant a tree.

If the Democrats were seeking a former convention site that would remind the party of past acts of political courage and credit, they should have gone to Philadelphia and recalled the work of that convention, rather than to Chicago, the scene of the quasi-fascist convention of 1968.

14

The Press on the Press

*T*homas Babington Macaulay, nineteenth-century English statesman, historian, and essayist, observed that there was nothing so ridiculous as the English people engaged in one of their periodic bouts of self-criticism, remorse, and moral reform. Macaulay never lived to see the American press engaged in similar acts of self-examination, apology, or defense.

The media are especially prone to such inquiry in campaign years.

In 1988 the self-examination centered on the question of whether the press and other media had gone too far in searching out and reporting moral faults and failings on the part of presidential candidates, especially Gary Hart. Their conclusion was that they had not gone too far, but that events, facts, realities, and the candidate had forced the media to provide coverage.

In 1992 the question was, Did the press cover the issues well enough? The answer, after much agonizing, was, No, but the press is better for the self-analysis.

In 1996 the question became, Did the press overdo emphasis on the horse race and on constant, instant polling? The answer, regretfully, was yes. But just asking the question shows how much the press cares and that it is self-aware, even if it can't promise to do better next time.

The quadrennial defenses of the press are comparable to those made by a former editor of *The Washington Post,* who attempted to explain and excuse the press for its part in sustaining the anti-communist fervor of the 1950s. The editor acknowledged that within a month after Sen. Joseph McCarthy's famous Wheeling, West Virginia, speech in February 1950, it was clear that McCarthy was using fraudulent material. So why did the press act as it did? Because, said the editor, McCarthy's charges appeared to be of the most profound national security significance and might be true.

Then, the editor said, the Senate panicked and held hearings. "For the press to have ignored the most newsworthy event in Congress (however phony the thing was beginning to look), the focus of congressional and, almost at once, national attention, is preposterous." But it was *press* coverage that made the charges the matter of national attention. And it was the press coverage of the Senate hearings that made those hearings significant. Once the press had examined McCarthy and his charges and knew both to be hollow, why did it persist in fanning the flame?

Again, the press failed miserably in covering the Vietnam War. Long after there was massive evidence that members of the administration, especially Dean Rusk and Robert McNamara, did not know what they were talking about in stating military needs, in describing events in Vietnam, and in projecting victory, the press dutifully headlined their every statement, and printed "facts" from administration handouts, almost without challenge or question. Most newspapers and the other media generally continued to support the war well into 1969, despite abundant information (from their correspondents on the scene) as to what the situation was and what was happening in Vietnam.

The most telling evidence of this failure was *The New York Times*'s publication of the events at the My Lai No. 4 hamlet, Song My village, in March 1968, where, according to the *Times,* "American troops caught a North Vietnamese force in a pincer movement on the central coastal plain yesterday, killing 128 enemy soldiers in day-long fighting. . . .

"While the two companies of United States Marines moved in on the enemy force from opposite sides, heavy artillery barrages and armed helicopters were called in to pound the North Vietnamese soldiers." This dramatic operation, it was later determined, was, in fact, the My Lai massacre.

The media's behavior during the Vietnam War, as in the McCarthy period, proved the observation that the press, or at least its chieftains and stars, acts like blackbirds in the fall: A bunch of them settle on a telephone wire. When one flies away, all fly away. When one returns, all return.

Most of the media appeared not to have discovered the truth about the Vietnam War until after publication of the Pentagon Papers, which was widely called a heroic act, performed in the name of "freedom of the press" by the press. But there was little that was surprising in the papers. To discover that people in the Pentagon had actually talked about the war and raised questions about operations, tactics, even purposes, should not have been surprising. That there were plans to stifle criticism and that the whole truth was not being told to Congress, the press, or the American people was not news to anyone who followed that war closely.

The media will occasionally question their own methods and their substantive reporting, but one can be certain that they will not find themselves seriously deficient or wanting. The media are demonstrating the truth of an observation by Oswald Spengler that there are never but two estates operating in a society: the civil and the religious.

When one formerly recognized loses power, that power is picked up by the other, in some form.

Whereas churches today often question the infallibility of church spokesmen and leaders, editors may not (safely) question fellow members of the press. They claim power and authority that can be traced to unsigned editorials (some go back to Moses, who came down from the mountain with the first unsigned editorial). Columnists, TV commentators, and anchormen stop just short of claiming ancient clerical powers once covered and sustained by "grace of office": the power of absolution (which has been handed down by Barbara Walters) and the seal of the confessional (now called "confidentiality of sources").

More limited but still essentially clerical powers also have been picked up by the press. The press has its own index, determining what the public should read or hear or see. The ultimate expression of this power is in *The New York Times*'s masthead, which asserts that the *Times* prints "All the news that's fit to print." One can fairly ask, By whose determination?

The media run a kind of beatification and canonization procedure and also determine who is to be forgotten, forgiven, censored, and condemned.

Beyond protecting one's sources, there is secular variation of infallibility. For example, the faults and failures of members of the news media are not to be exposed on the grounds that such exposure might reduce public confidence in a free press.

These principles were applied by *The New York Times* some years ago in its report of a marijuana party given by a man who was then President Jimmy Carter's drug adviser. A report that the party had occurred was carried in the *Times*. The paper stated its source as two *Times* employees who attended the party as invited guests. The story was not reported by either or both, but by another *Times* reporter to whom they told the story. The reporter who wrote the story refused to reveal his source, protecting those who had confessed. The *Times* subsequently defended its suppression of the names of the sources and participants in the party by saying it would not publish information that might reflect adversely on "the press."

The process of press self-examination can do little harm and very little good. The inevitable conclusion will always be that the press, under difficult circumstances, has done as well as could have been expected. The situation is similar to what happens when monkeys at the zoo get involved with examining each other. The work is serious. There is a great deal of scratching and scrutiny. Something is usually found, or appears to be found. Sometimes it is merely tasted; sometimes it is eaten after careful consideration; sometimes it is shared with the others. In the end, the monkeys appear to be deeply satisfied. Life in the zoo goes on as before.

NEWS AND POLITICS ABSORBED BY "MEDIA"

The best period for political information and education in America in this century was, I believe, the time between the coming of radio and the time when television became a major medium for political communication; that is, from the early 1930s to the 1950s. This period was marked by Franklin Roosevelt's dominating use of radio.

The effect of radio was manifest in two major ways. First, it countered the monopoly power of the writing press. Ideas other than those of publishers and editors like Hearst and McCormick could be transmitted to the people. Second, radio provided a medium through which the politician, candidate, or officeholder could speak directly to citizens and voters and do so without significant distractions.

The new era of television politics began modestly with the

Kennedy-Nixon debate of 1960. Many of the experts who analyzed that debate concluded that the televised debate could well have been the cause of Nixon's defeat. Kennedy was judged to have shown maturity, a quality, they said, that he had not previously demonstrated. He also demonstrated mastery of what has since come to be called "the numbers." Kennedy showed good humor, and, most important of all, he looked good on the black-and-white screen. Nixon looked pale and showed the shadow of a beard. Some of these same experts concluded that if the debate had been conducted on radio, Nixon would have been declared the winner and might have been elected. They may or may not have been right, but one certain result of that debate was that makeup people subsequently became almost as important in political campaigns as speechwriters.

The impact of television on politics was compounded with the coming of color television, with its gestalt of sonics, graphics, special lighting, and other props first developed and applied in commercial advertising and then transferred to political campaigns. Nicholas Johnson, a commissioner of the Federal Communications Commission when television was just beyond its innocence, said that as a means of communication, television was suitable only for dictatorships or totalitarian governments. Marshall McLuhan went beyond that. In his judgment only minimal personal responsibility survives television society and we are into the range of the nonrational—in which "media becomes the message." As noted by Umberto Eco in *Travels in Hyperreality*, television, an instrument for "merchandising," has now become the merchandise itself. "The mass media do not transmit ideologies," he adds. "They are themselves an ideology."

Thus, what the news-producing units of television had failed to do through hybridization of the news (mixing reporting and opinion), homogenization of the news, or making the news was achieved through advertisements interspersed among news stories; something Van Gordon Sauter, a former head of CBS News, first dubbed "infotainment."

In the half hour of evening network news, approximately twenty-two minutes are given to news and eight minutes to advertising. So when Walter Cronkite delivered the evening news, coming on at the time of day that in the Age of Faith was reserved for vespers (later established by Longfellow as "The Children's Hour"), the possible shock of crises being reported was eased by advertisements for Tums; Poli-Grip, mint-flavored; creams for removing brown spots from hands, face, and neck; iron tablets (promoted by the image of a "mature" man running after a young woman on a beach); and finally, just before Walter said, "That's the way it is," an ad for Ex-lax.

After Dan Rather took over for Cronkite, I anticipated that psychic and emotional relief might become the material of the advertisements and that products like Sominex and Nytol would be advertised. I was not quite right. The ads interspersed in the Rather news programs more commonly include products promising relief from slightly more sophisticated or culturally induced disorders than those of the subject matter of ads on the Cronkite program, but they are not yet at the highest level of anxiety.

Rather is doing his best. I was especially struck one evening by his expression of great compassion for victims of an earthquake in Mexico. He ended the news program with a deeply spiritual reflection on the meaning of life and death. His reflection had been preceded by an advertisement for hemorrhoidal relief, and was followed immediately by an advertisement featuring a man in a Roman collar, presumably a priest, proclaiming the virtues of Polident for cleaning and whitening dentures—apparently a kind of dental absolution.

Various proposals are now being made as to how television should be used or controlled relative to politics. One proposal is that free time should be given to candidates and political party spokesmen— free but limited as to duration.

It is also proposed that only candidates themselves be required to make political presentations. They would be required to speak without props—no American flag in the background, no bust of Abraham Lincoln on the desk, no wife or children in attendance, and especially no dog.

It has been suggested that a political television advertisement should last at least five minutes.

These are all compromise proposals, unlikely to be accepted; unlikely to be effective in changing the medium very much, even if accepted.

There are two ways of effectively dealing with the problems of television, news, advertising, and politics. One is a sort of guerrilla solution suggested by Umberto Eco. He argues that the battle for the survival of man as a responsible, rational being in the communications era is not to be won, or cannot be won, where the communication originates, but only where it arrives. *The audience must control the message.*

To accomplish this, Eco says, the first chair in front of every TV set must be occupied by *the group leader.* I suggest that remote controls should go with every television set—not just one, but enough to supply everyone in the watching group, thus giving every person a veto over what is on the screen. The potential for effective guerrilla action is enhanced by such technological aids as VCRs, cable television, continuous news and commentary stations, HBO, and other choices, which allow the messages to be multiplied, fragmented, or distorted. This is a cultural equivalent of the military techniques of jamming radio and television communications in war.

The second, more direct and more practical, method would be to ban television political advertisements as we now ban cigarette and liquor advertisements. Religious advertisements and religious promotion on television should also be banned. Thus we would protect people from threats to their well-being at both ends of the spectrum of human concern: drugs (nicotine and alcohol) at one end, the lower end, and religion and politics at the higher level. This would leave the middle range of human needs, interests, and vices (detergents, deodorants, and automobiles, for example) to television.

Along with the ban, there should be rigorous enforcement of the equal time provisions of the federal communication law (giving or selling equal time to all candidates), and of the fairness doctrine, requiring the presentation of conflicting views. If such enforcement drove television stations to refuse political advertisements, and to all but abandon political newscasting, leaving that communication to word of mouth, to the print media, and marginally to radio, the republic would be well served.

OF TIME AND TELEVISION

Time is not easy to handle. It has baffled philosophers. Aristotle's best effort was to say that time is "not itself movement but neither does time exist without change. Time is neither movement, nor independent of movement." Moreover, although he held that a continuous quantity is divisible, time, "past, present, and future, forms a continuous whole." Time, he said, seems to be an "indivisible instant."

Theologians have been less troubled by time than have philosophers. Theologians accept time essentially on faith, holding that since God created the world, He must have created time, or that time came with creation, and therefore was concomitant to the act. "There is no time before the world," asserted St. Augustine, writing as a theologian, not a philosopher. He said that what we call the present has "no extent or duration, and that only past or future time can be long or short. Past and future have duration," he held. But then he asked, "In what sense can that which does not exist be long or short? The past no longer is; the future is not yet." This theory was challenged by George Allen, the longtime coach of the Washington Redskins, who in his player selection and game strategy followed the principle "the future is now" (*vide* Eleanor Roosevelt—see chap. 13).

Theologians seem less interested in the beginning of time than are philosophers, and are more concerned about the manner and the time of its ending and with what comes after that. St. Thomas Aquinas held that time existed in God or with Him, although time was not particularly important until after the creation of the world and the division of the work into seven days, or periods. St. Thomas tried to sort out time by defining two "nows": the "eternal now" and the "first, or beginning, now," from which our time begins.

Politicians, especially in presidential elections, play fast and loose with concepts of time. In the 1996 campaign, for example, there were assertions that one party would build a bridge to the twenty-first century, which is obviously not yet a place or a time. One candidate for Congress in 1996 even promised to "reshape our future." Ronald Reagan, in his time, imagined the past and remembered the future.

In any case, God, insofar as the record can be traced, did not meddle much with time once it began. He did stop the sun in the heavens, a kind of first daylight saving time, to help Joshua finish the Battle of Jericho, but He did not lengthen the day, only the time of light. Politicians have done the same with modern daylight saving time, although some critics have charged them with meddling with God's time, and dairy farmers have protested that the change has affected the flow of milk from their cows.

Poets have actually been less passive and reflective in dealing with time than have the theologians and philosophers. They have resented it, denounced it, challenged it, ignored it, or made the best of it.

Shakespeare, the master, played the whole range of relationships. He surrendered to it in one sonnet:

> *Ruin hath taught me thus to ruminate*
> *That time will come and take my love away.*

In another sonnet, he struck back in challenge:

> *Yet do thy worst, old Time: despite thy wrong,*
> *My love shall in my verse ever live young.*

John Milton seemed to be afraid to challenge time, asserting that he would, in eternity, get even:

> *And glut thyself with what thy womb devours,*
> *Which is no more than what is false and vain,*
> *And merely mortal dross;*
> *So little is our loss*
> *So little is thy gain.*
> *For when as each thing bad thou has entomb'd,*
> *And last of all thy greedy self consum'd,*
> *Then long Eternity shall greet our bliss*
> *With an individual kiss . . .*
> *Then all this earthly grossness quit,*
> *Attir'd with stars, we shall for ever sit,*
> *Triumphing over Death, and Chance, and thee,*
> *O Time*

Lesser poets have been more ready to compromise, suggesting that we make the best, or most, of time. One* wrote:

Be a gleaner of time
Claim what runs through the hour glass
When no one watches
What is counted by clocks, ticking
When no one listens
Save remnants
From the cutting room of day
End pieces from the loom of night
Brand and hold
Unmarked, maverick minutes
Salvage time left derelict
By those who despair of light
Yet fear the dark
Steal only from sleep
And from eternity
Of which time no one dares ask
What? or Where?

The general historical record is that most people have been and are rather accepting of time, not attempting to either understand or control it. They try to get along with it, occasionally hanging an adjective on it in passing, or subjecting it to a verb of some usefulness. Most of the adjectives are uncomplimentary: devouring bloody, avenging, threatening, demanding, deceiving, relentless, greedy; or more obvious, like past and present, early and late, good and bad. The verbs

* Eugene McCarthy.

applied have been quite direct. Thus, time is wasted and saved; it is lost and found; it has been released and regained; it is served. Time is occasionally taken out, and then declared in again; there is free time and borrowed time.

Time measurers have taken a wholly different approach. They abandoned hope of understanding time and undertook to measure and control it. "Try anything" was their theory, so they tried drops of water, sand in an hourglass, notched wheels with weights moved by springs, electric impulses, ions. The appearance, if not the reality, of controlling time was found marketable in every society.

In today's backward societies, along with an English bicycle or an American ballpoint pen, a watch—preferably Swiss, though Japanese will do—is a sure mark of status, even of upward mobility. As in more advanced civilizations, the wearer can at least appear to have some mastery over time. He can set his watch backward or forward. He can look at the dial as though he were supposed to be where he is, or possibly to indicate he should be somewhere else, or must go there soon.

Immediacy became a factor with the introduction of the wristwatch, eliminating the delay that went with the use of the pocket watch, especially the kind that had a protective cover. In early modern civilization, roughly 1950 to 1975, watchmakers attacked time most subtly. They introduced the self-winding watch to free the busy man or woman from the primitive task of winding. Newer watches drew their power from more mysterious, scientific, nonhuman sources. Ions were "in."

At the same time as the power sources of watches were changing, so was the face of the watch. The poorer classes and less important persons might have a watch with hours, minutes, and even seconds indicated, but the movers and shakers, and those aspiring to such status, budgeted their time in larger lots. The second hand was the first to go.

Numerals began to disappear, until in some cases only four markers divided the day and the night into quarters. Then followed watches with no numerals or markers. Finally, the in thing for super, super executives was to wear no watch at all, thus defying time itself and possibly even death along with it. In so doing, they give a partial response to philosophers, as though to say, "I will measure the now by my changing, and my changing by the now," and to the theologians, "I shall measure as I am measured."

With radio and television came a new treatment of time. Time was offered for sale and, as a result, necessarily graded. Old categories were cast aside; time was rated as "prime," "choice," and "good"—the same grade designations, incidentally, used in the evaluation of beef, with three additional classes at the lower level of quality.

Treatment of time on radio and television is not limited to commercial application. These same media have attacked the philosophical and theological conceptions of time as well. Whereas most philosophers hold, or have held, that no moment of time is like any other moment, radio and television mavens say that there is such a thing as "equal time." And radio and television do say, without concern for contradiction, that there is "unique time," not equal to or like any other time. But this time is defined by what it is attached to; it does not stand alone. Thus, *60 Minutes* time, Dan Rather's time, or David Letterman's time is marked forever as a distinctive commercial entity.

Radio and television have also introduced other conceptions of time, such as "shared time," "pooled time," and "time slots."

The media have asserted control over time that had been denied to God by theologians—at least until the world ends. Thus television interviewers, without apology to the diety or the saints, regularly say, "We (or you) are out of time."

15

People and the Press

"I f you don't get it, you don't get it." That's *The Washington Post*'s advertising slogan. So I was somewhat surprised, a couple of years ago, to be invited to a reception given by Katharine Graham, the publisher of the *Post*, for Robert McNamara on the publication of his book *In Retrospect*—McNamara's apology for his conduct during the Vietnam War.

I didn't get it. In twenty years, I had not been invited to the residence of the publisher. I had never been on social or friendly or good political terms with the author.

I was out of town on the day of the reception, but would not have gone had I been in Washington. I had no very clear reason for not going, other than a vague sense that the event was to be a kind of rite of reconciliation, a return of a prodigal son. I was not prepared to participate.

If one were to apply to Robert McNamara one sobriquet, in the manner of Lincoln's The Great Emancipator, or Reagan's The Great Communicator, it would best be "The Great Vindicator."

The early response to the publication of *In Retrospect* was anger, if not rage, on the part of those who had been against the war, those who had fought it, those who had been for it from afar, and those who had managed it and promoted it. The later attitude of most of all of the above was that what they had learned from McNamara's book had vindicated them.

President Clinton said his opposition to, and avoidance of, service in the war was justified by McNamara's confession; that he had been vindicated. Admirals and generals claimed a kind of vindication for not having prosecuted the war successfully, evidently because McNamara had not believed in it strongly enough.

Officers—some retired, some still in service—felt vindicated for having accepted and made fraudulent reports of body counts and of military progress, reports supporting McNamara's false and misleading public statements.

Leading newspapers that had supported the war and supported McNamara when he was nominated to be secretary of defense and during his service in that office—especially *The New York Times*—attacked him, but still accepted him as their vindicator. The *Times* did not need full vindication from McNamara, though, as it had granted itself partial vindication with the publication of the Pentagon Papers in 1971.

McNamara should not be allowed to claim too much guilt or power. For example, to claim that his resignation in protest, at one or the other critical point in the escalation of the war, would have made much difference is probably false and self-aggrandizing. It might have saved McNamara from his personal anguish.

And it would have been a small help to the antiwar movement. "One would have wished," wrote Daniel Berrigan in 1971, "when Robert McNamara . . . stepped off the scene, for some *public* utterance."

High-ranking military and naval officers, now retired, say they were convinced that the war could not be won under the political restraints being imposed upon it. But not one of them resigned in protest. Gen. Douglas MacArthur in the Korean War did not resign, but he challenged political policy and got himself fired. This is a better way to act than to serve silently and wait for vindication.

The accretion of McNamara's self-confidence began before he became secretary of defense. It was amplified as he took over that office.

McNamara was a former whiz kid, a Harvard Business School graduate. He came from Ford Motors, at a time when it was gospel that American automobile companies could make no mistakes, at least no small ones.

A power personally attributed to the prospective secretary of defense was "a steel-trap mind." And he was coming into the Pentagon, which at that time believed it, too, was above failure.

I began to have doubts about McNamara's judgment and accuracy in the Kennedy years, with his part in the Bay of Pigs. Then came his "have the boys home by Christmas" claim and his "two wars like Vietnam" in the early Johnson tenure. I was moved to question his reliability when on November 30, 1965, on his return from Vietnam, he said, "The most vital impression that I bring back is that we have stopped losing the war."

I would not be numbered among those vindicated or said to be vindicated by McNamara. In retrospect, I would rather credit my vindication to the voters of New Hampshire in March 1968. Or to the soldier in uniform who appeared at an early rally in New Hampshire and gave me a small package, which I thought contained a book. When I opened the package later in the evening, I found it to be a small case. The case contained a Medal of Honor, given to the soldier for his service in Vietnam, and a note saying that he was ashamed of what the United States was doing in Vietnam.

The veterans of the war, of course, are an exception. They have spoken not of having been vindicated but of having been betrayed.

SARAH McCLENDON

I do not wish to suggest that everything about the American press today is negative, or that all journalism is practiced in the manner of the *Post*. Over the last fifty years, I have found many people to admire in journalism.

Sarah McClendon has been my friend through four and a half decades and through nine and a half presidential administrations. As a consequence of this long association, I have come to a better understanding of the biblical statement "Before Abraham was, I am" than I otherwise would have. As I apply the word of the Lord, it comes out in this way: "Before I am, Sarah was."

Sarah and I first met during the Truman presidency. That was a good beginning, a basic one. President Truman never claimed that he had chosen for any position either the best or the brightest people. He would say that he had chosen a good person. And if he wished to add distinction, a "damn" good, or even a "g-damn good person." On the negative side, he had three degrees of judgment: "no good," "no damn good," and "no g-damn good."

Consequently, he never had a problem in replacing anyone who had been declared "the best," with a "second" or "lesser best." In similar manner, he hesitated to appoint "blue ribbon committees or commissions." His committees were more like "brown ribbon" committees. A brown ribbon, I believe, is what one gets merely for bringing a dog to the show.

My first political involvement with Sarah McClendon was on issues affecting her constituency of readers in central Texas—places like

Odessa, Tyler, and Midland. These were not easy readers. If you have ever been to Midland, Texas, you know it is well named.

One of the first issues we were involved in was that of migrant workers. We conspired as to how to inform her constituency that the Emancipation Proclamation and the antislavery amendments to the Constitution applied to rented slaves, as well as to fully owned ones.

In the broader field of journalism, Sarah was never a fixture, but always a moving force. She, like noted journalist Doris Fleeson, spurned White House and other government backgrounders. As a counterforce, Sarah introduced the "foregrounder," the secret of which was to anticipate presidential and other government news by asking questions that were not anticipated, and to ask them before the "spin doctors" had done their work.

Sarah seemed to proceed on the theory that it was impossible, or nearly impossible, to make a dishonest person honest, but that with a little luck and with courage, one might make a dishonest person truthful, at least for a short while.

It was not enough in dealing with Sarah just to vote right or to "be right." She insisted that you be right for the right reason. Thus, Sarah affirmed T. S. Eliot's judgment that "the last temptation is the greatest treason: to do the right thing for the wrong reason."

Sarah, to add a contemporary note, did not have to wait for Robert McNamara's book for vindication. Her judgment was formed early, I believe, when as one with a record of service in World War II, she realized that Kilroy—whose name was everywhere in World War II and good on every IOU, even in Korea—had either been mustered out of Vietnam or had gone absent without leave.

Sarah approached most presidents whom she observed, possibly all of them, in the spirit of Aunt Mabel in a William Stafford poem.

After listening to a senator speak, Aunt Mabel said: "He's a brilliant man, but we didn't elect him that much."

WILLIAM F. BUCKLEY JR.

I have known William F. Buckley Jr. for thirty years. We have debated several times. I have appeared on *Firing Line* a number of times. Once we shared a platform on the subject of J. S. Bach, and Bill had the last word—he played.

Only once have we fully agreed politically. In 1980 Bill and I both thought Ronald Reagan was the best candidate for president.

In 1980 there were three visible candidates for the presidency: Ronald Reagan, Jimmy Carter, and John Anderson, an independent.

Since the political issues were unclear, I decided to subject the three candidates to three fundamental tests, all of which, I think, Bill Buckley approved. The three tests were (1) general philosophy, (2) intellectual discipline, principally reading and study methodology, and (3) religion.

The philosophical dividing line was belief in creationism as opposed to evolution. Anderson said he believed in both, an expected liberal Republican position. Carter said he believed in evolution (and he could do it, as in his statement that he would "evolve" a foreign policy and "consummate it, openly and publicly"). Reagan said that he believed in creationism.

I scored Reagan as the winner. First, because nothing evolves significantly in four years, or even in eight, and, as a belief, creationism gives a president an out. When a president says "I believe in evolution, not in revolution," he is in trouble. If the idea of evolution had been accepted by Jefferson, we would probably still be subject to the Crown.

Distinguishing among the candidates on the basis of their reading habits was slightly more difficult. Jimmy Carter said he was a speed reader and that his retention rate had improved by 50 percent. That worried me. Fifty percent of what? And which 50 percent did he retain?

Anderson said he was a voracious reader. He did not say what he read voraciously. But I watched his vocabulary and found it marked by relatively unusual words (though not for Bill Buckley), and often slightly out-of-context words: words like denigrate, perpetrate, catastrophic, and voracious. I concluded that Anderson was heavy into the Reader's Digest Word Study program.

Reagan said that he didn't read very much. Again I thought he scored best.

The third test—religion—was difficult to administer. All three candidates said they were "reborn." The difficulty of scoring arises from several sources. First, there is no historical base, and there are no real witnesses, since the act of being reborn is essentially personal. There is no history or theological tradition that one can use as a point of reference.

Carter said that he had been reborn while walking in the woods with his sister, after he had lost an election for lieutenant governor of Georgia to Lester Maddox.

Anderson said that he had been reborn when he was quite young, on hearing the story of Salome's dance and the beheading of John the Baptist. He did not explain whether it was the shedding of the veils or the beheading that had moved him, but apparently it was a "catastrophic" experience. Reagan said that he had been reborn, but that he didn't quite know when it had happened or what it had done to him. Again Reagan scored first, by my standards.

Bill Buckley did not disagree with any of this evaluation.

My first knowledge of Buckley came on my reading his report of seeking God at Yale. I think God has been hiding or running from Bill ever since, afraid of getting caught on *Firing Line* and being asked, "Why did you let that ape stand up in the Miocene epoch?"

What could God say? anticipating Bill's assertion that "That's when it all began to come apart. Why didn't you keep him on all fours? There was no need for such a radical step."

Bill hasn't caught God yet, and he hasn't quite caught the liberals. He *has* forced them to abandon their name, or at least load it with qualifying adjectives, so as to make the word quite useless.

Bill Buckley has never been dull, never been bored, never been humorless, nor has he ever despaired. He has been a friend to God *and* man, the latter being the harder duty.

IN PRAISE OF CROSSNESS

In a conversation among people who approved the works and character of the late I. F. Stone, one participant nonetheless observed that Izzy had been a "cross" person. It is an interesting term. I went back through the decades, searching my memory for my first encounter with crossness, until I got to one of my grandmothers, the Irish one. She, I recalled, had a reputation for crossness. Her grandchildren and other people were admonished not to cross her, or to provoke her. There were other cross people in her day, most notably a parish priest and several nuns who taught in the parochial school.

It was never explained to me, in those years, just what constituted crossness. One was, it seems, expected to recognize it in contact, or to accept on faith that like many other things never fully explained to children, one would come to understand later in life what crossness was.

After reflecting on crossness, that of my grandmother and of Izzy Stone and of other people whom I now identify as cross, I have concluded that I now understand crossness and, beyond that, that crossness is not a bad character trait. Cross people generally have had a good influence in society, and we might be better off today if more attention were paid to contemporary cross people.

It should be noted that there are variations among cross people reflecting personality differences, professional associations, and general cultural and historical conditions, but that there are also recurring, definable, identifiable marks that distinguish cross people from angry, cynical, bitter, cantankerous, and other markedly, or even marginally, unpleasant people.

The following are among the dominant, distinguishing qualities of cross people:

They are resigned, reluctant though their resignation is, to folly in thought and in action.

They do not become cross or provoked because of malicious actions or random foolishness, but by behavior that my grandmother would have labeled as "uncalled for," with the clear implication that the person who had crossed her had been taught better, told better, or simply should have known better.

Cross people are not only resigned but are also restrained. They do not denounce folly. Neither do they praise it in the manner of Erasmus, who just missed being cross by being too forgiving and kindly.

The protests of cross people are not raucous, loud, or aggressive. Most often their disapproval is shown through silence, when something might have been expected to have been said.

Their spoken and written criticism may be moderately satirical, moving to the border of denunciation or of condemnation but never crossing the line, leaving it to the person who has merited or attracted the cross notice to acknowledge or at least realize his or her fault.

Cross people do not stare other people down. They are more likely to look away, out of modesty or unbelief. They do not, as a rule, say things like "I told you so," but are more likely to repeat, with some emphasis, what they have already said or written.

Cross people cannot be said to be patient. They are not. But their impatience is controlled, moderated by two special virtues, little known or practiced in our time. These virtues are long-suffering and benignity, both recognized as operative virtues in the Age of Faith and as special gifts of the Holy Ghost.

Cross people are not pessimistic but optimistic in the way I. F. Stone said he was—that is, in the manner of Gilbert K. Chesterton. Chesterton said pessimists are people who see how bad the state of the world is and despair, whereas optimists see how bad things are and do not despair.

Cross people are evenhanded. They do not play favorites. The prototype of cross people, undoubtedly, is the prophet Isaiah, who found it difficult to understand and tolerate the ways either of man or of God.

Among the great essayists in the English language, two stand out above all others as near perfect examples of cross people: Jonathan Swift and Samuel Johnson. In the American literary record, Ambrose Bierce, of *The Devil's Dictionary* fame, and H. L. Mencken are close.

Although many poets show signs of crossness, two deserve special credits for consistency. Robert Frost is reported to have been offended not only if a critic challenged his writings but also even if one attempted to praise his works. Frost, in a cross mood, distinguished himself from his contemporary poet Carl Sandburg by noting, "Carl says, 'The People, Yes,' and I say, 'The People, Yes and No.' "

The second exemplary example of a cross poet is William Butler Yeats, who demonstrated his crossness most clearly in his poem that asks the question: "Why should old men not be mad?" in which he recalls "a likely lad with a sound fly-fisher's wrist" who turns into a "drunken journalist." Finally, after noting that old books tell that nothing better may be had, Yeats concludes that old men must be mad. He might have added as a footnote, "or at least cross."

Among recent journalists and commentators, Doris Fleeson was outstanding in her crossness. She was cross especially with members of her own profession. She spurned background briefings and special dinners for the press. She was cross with presidents and with nearly all other politicians.

Among more contemporary journalists and commentators, several have achieved clear status as cross people: the late Henry Fairlie of *The New Republic;* Richard Harwood, an ombudsman for *The Washington Post;* Andy Rooney of *60 Minutes;* and Leon Wieseltier of *The New Republic.* Pressing for recognition are Meg Greenfield, David Brinkley, Mary McGrory, Russell Baker, and James J. Kilpatrick.

Finally, almost certain to make the goodly company of cross people as its outstanding political member was the late Sen. William Fulbright.

MEMORIES OF NED KENWORTHY

For those who knew Ned Kenworthy, the news of his death in 1993, even though he had retired as a *Times* reporter in 1977, fell, as the Irish poet Forgael wrote of the death of Columcille, "like a wound on the land." Ned was memorable for many reasons: his professional integrity, his dedication and competence as a writer, his good spirit, generosity, and kindness.

I first met him when he reported on Congress. Ned was serious, thorough, always in a hurry—bustling might be a better word—with a handful of papers, and papers stuffed in pockets. He was singular among reporters, as one of whom it was regularly said, "You know, before he became a reporter, he was a teacher of English." There may have been other reporters who had a similar background. If so, they either concealed it or never let it show in their writing. Ned neither denied his teaching background nor concealed it.

My closest association with Ned Kenworthy was during the campaign for the Democratic Party's presidential nomination in 1968. Later, the *Times*'s report of his death, written by David Rosenbaum, stated that his work in that campaign "may have been the tour de force of his career." I do not challenge Rosenbaum's judgment.

It was not quite clear whether, in the early days of that campaign, Ned was there by assignment or by his own request, possibly even insistence. He was one of three reporters covering the 1968 campaign who understood, as reflected in their writing, both the substance of the effort and the method. The other two were Mary McGrory and Shana Alexander.

Coming upon a Kenworthy story was like coming out of dark and confusion into light and certainty. His writing was pure, and I suspect that if asked about his prose, he might have said, as did Robert Lowell in defense of his poetry, that he had thought about every word.

Ned was the favorite of the young people in 1968—their counselor and confidant. When I talked to him by telephone a few days before his death, he inquired about several of them by name: Had I seen them? Did I know what they were doing—Parker, Cindy, Ann, and others?

In New Hampshire while campaigning in a notions shop (there were many of them), Tom Wicker, who had joined the press bus and who at that time was on a number of talk shows, was being recognized. Ned was being left out. We assigned people to recognize Ned. He seemed puzzled yet pleased at first, but soon began to cast about to see who was putting him on.

Ned applauded a town meeting at which the local sponsors had decided to have grade-school children ask the questions. The first questioner asked a most involved question, and was asked by the candidate if he reported for *The New York Times.*

Ned was a grammarian and a student of literature. When he was in the press corps, covering a speech or a conference, one was more free to use literary references but less free to be careless about one's grammar. He and I had a cause that was never fully realized: namely, the restoration of the ablative absolute to political use. It might have ended many debates, possibly wars, as in Sen. George Aiken's suggestion that the Vietnam War could be ended by the use of that construction. The president only had to say, "The Vietnam War having been won, we will now return to a victory celebration."

Ned was stung by what may have been the worst pun in American political history, prompted by Robert Kennedy's use of a quotation from Aeschylus. I told Ned the quotation was an "Aeschylation of the campaign."

Ned was as distressed as I was when a reference to Willa Cather and her novel of Nebraska *O Pioneers!* elicited no response from an audience in a high school in North Bend, Nebraska, the heart of Cather country, or at a speech at Creighton University in Omaha.

Nebraska was a strange interlude in the 1968 campaign. Rose Kennedy came to help her son Robert campaign by visiting Father Flanagan's Boys Town on Mother's Day. We were to learn later that, at the time of her visit, there were few, if any, boys at the home.

Ned may have been too kind to me along the way. In an article he wrote for the *Times,* summing up the 1968 campaign, he said that my approach to political problems was "moral and religious" (I thought it was moral and pragmatic). And he wrote in the same article that I did not ask the administration and the Democratic Party for repentance but only for confession, which, he added, "may be good for the soul, but politicians have never believed it is good for the party." Ned knew the difference between confession and repentance, amnesty and pardon.

He was a great journalist and a good man.

16

Three Issues for What's Left of the 1990s

*P*resident Bill Clinton likes to talk about the future, almost as much as Ronald Reagan liked to talk about the past. We have all heard that Clinton wants to build "a bridge to the twenty-first century." Reagan wanted to restore the "shining city on a hill." But it seems to me that there is work enough to be done in the present.

This is not a book about issues; it is not a tract or a political platform, but some issues simply cry out for attention and for good sense. They ought to be clarified *before* the next century, for we have been kicking them around in American politics for twenty years or more.

These three issues, cited earlier, are social and political equality; economic opportunity, specifically the chance to work a job, perhaps even a decent job; and freedom of political expression, specifically the right to protest.

All three issues have been shrouded by cant and nonsense, and all three get at the heart of what the country should be and how it has lost its bearings.

•

The first issue is *the new equality*. This is a drive for an equality of result or condition—an equality of conformity. It is not the traditional American desire for equal opportunity allotted to separate individuals.

Alexis de Tocqueville, in *Democracy in America,* wrote of the powerful appeal and danger of the idea of equality in a democratic society. He wrote of its potential for demagoguery.

I would be less concerned about the rise to popularity of the word and the idea if I thought it the result of conscious intention to elicit political support—that is, if those who made the appeal knew that they were being demagogic. I fear, however, that the use of the word is not intentionally demagogic. It seems to approach the automatic "It is good" justification feared by George Orwell.

In his inaugural address in 1980, President Jimmy Carter said, "We have already found a high degree of personal liberty, and we are now struggling to enhance equality of opportunity."

One may well question the president's language. Liberty was a goal of the American Revolution. We have it in this country, not because we "found" it but rather as a result of our having declared it a political and social goal and then having achieved it in some measure. As to the president's second point, that "we are now struggling to enhance equality of opportunity," such language does not clearly describe the concept of equality as it is applied today. Economic, educational, political, and cultural equality—and *not* equality of opportunity, enhanced or otherwise—is the goal in the new application.

Economic equality, in this new conception, is to be achieved primarily through equalizing income. Equalization of wealth—that is, of wealth already accumulated—may come later. Economic equality is conceived not as a base upon which differences may then build, but as an average. One former governor used to ask occasionally if it might be better if people doing unpleasant work were paid more than those whose work is culturally and physically preferable.

Political economists have developed the notion of a negative income tax as the basis for tax reform. Essentially, the idea is this: Everyone should have enough income to pay taxes at the beginning or threshold rate, and if one does not have enough income to reach that level, something should be done to make up for the deficiency. Where the idea came from or how the taxable level of income was chosen as the standard for judgment and adjustments is not clear.

It seems that the tax base is to be accepted as a first principle upon which we are to build. It is an axiom, rather like "I think, therefore I am." One could as well assert that, for the good of the commonwealth, everyone should pay $1,000 in income taxes, and then proceed through measures of redistribution to raise all incomes to the level at which everyone would have to pay $1,000 in taxes.

The idea of a negative income tax is appealing. Professors of political economics can diagram its operation. Ideas that can be diagrammed, especially in economics and in political science, are very popular. It is easier to teach with a diagram or a chart. A diagram conveys an impression of certainty. Thus, the business-cycle theory of economics was popular because the charting of the cycle gave the appearance of scientific order in a confused discipline. Prosperity was followed by recession, and that, in turn, by depression, after which the cycle swung up through recovery back to prosperity. The theory seemed to have the certainty of the seasons or of the phases of the moon—until the economic moon went down in 1929 and did not come up.

The second area in which the new concept of equality is being applied is in politics and government. The principle of "one person, one vote" was formally recognized in a Supreme Court ruling affecting defined political jurisdictions. The court did not in its ruling extend the principle to relationships among jurisdictions. The ruling simply said that within given units of government, each vote should be equal to every other vote. Thus, since the Constitution provides for direct election of the House of Representatives on the basis of population, the rule requires that each congressional district have roughly the same number of people.

The Constitution also provides that each state, no matter what its size, shall have two senators. Thus, the citizen of a small state gets proportionally more of a vote in the Senate than the resident of a large state. The Constitution further provides that the president shall be elected through the electoral college, on a state-by-state basis, thus weighting the votes of smaller states favorably as against those cast in larger states. The drive now is to eliminate that weighting by abolishing the electoral college and instituting direct popular election of the president. No proposal has yet been made to reduce senatorial representation to a strict population base.

The principle of equality is also applied through the Federal Election Campaign Act, which attempts to equalize the nonvoting influence of citizens on candidates for political office. The current law limits the size of contributions to a political candidate in any one campaign to $1,000 per contributor. This limitation is considered a transitional phase to a time when all campaigns will be publicly financed. The argument for the limitation is that the larger the contribution, the greater the influence a contributor has on the officeholder and the more time he gets to spend with the officeholder. Theoretically, with public financing, every taxpayer will have made an equal contribution and will be entitled to as much time with the officeholder as any other taxpayer. What time nontaxpayers will get has not yet been determined by the reformers.

Despite the $1,000 limit on contributions in the last national elections, and the fact that the fall presidential campaigns were financed principally through federal grants, within a few days of the elections, President Clinton was vacationing in Australia and the Far East and in South Carolina for another Renaissance Weekend. Around this time his press secretary said the president would continue to lend out the Lincoln bedroom to major contributors to his campaign and the Democratic Party because such people were "his friends."

It does not take much imagination to foresee a time when citizens might go to court, charging that they were discriminated against because their calls were not taken in presidential telethons and transmitted to the president for his attention. A full practical application of this principle would argue for an equal right to speak or otherwise communicate with all officeholders, even removing the personal screening of Jim Lehrer and the commission on debates.

The objective of equalizing communications and influence on officeholders is also sought in efforts to control lobbyists. Proposals generally recommend more thorough regulation of lobbyists, limits on their expenditures, and public disclosure not only of expenditures but also of meetings and communications with officeholders.

It will not be surprising if someone suggests having lobbyists provided at government expense, so as to insulate officeholders from the undue influence of their principles, in somewhat the same way that officeholders are to be insulated from their constituencies. Under this arrangement, anyone who had a case to make to the government would apply for a lobbyist, who would be assigned from a pool in the way that public defenders are assigned by the courts. There could be classes of lobbyists (No. 1, No. 2, and so on) who would be assigned by a commission according to the seriousness or difficulty of the case to be made to the government. This procedure would establish a second level of purity and of detachment. A third and a fourth level might be added in pursuit of that absolute certainty and safety sought by the animal in Franz Kafka's story "The Burrow."

The new concept of equality also is applied in government and government-influenced employment practices, in what has been labeled the "quota system." The rationale of the quota system is that, since not every person can be hired, we should have within each employed group a representation or sampling of the total employable workforce. Selection currently is on the basis of physiological characteristics of age, sex, and race. There are some obvious historical reasons as to why these standards are being tried. There also are some obvious difficulties in their application, especially if one attempts to extend the principle—as will surely be done—to other racial and ethnic groups or to groups defined more in terms of psychological differences than racial and cultural differences—such as manic-depressives or battered husbands.

The drive to realize the new idea of equality has saturated education in recent years. The standardized curriculum, national standards, quota admissions, open admissions, and free college education are all manifestations of this drive. Full application of the principle could lead to compulsory college education, with the level of education so reduced that all who enter do so with the assurance of successful graduation. With no possible abandonment of hope at any point, they could look forward to something like the judgment of the Dodo after the caucus race in *Alice in Wonderland:* "Everyone has won, and all must have prizes."

What are the dangers in this drive to a newly conceived equality?

I see a danger first in the inevitable weakening of those institutions that are expected to give form and direction to society, such as professional and educational institutions, and that have traditionally been treated as having an identity separate from political control.

I also see the new equality significantly affecting the individual American's conception of his place in society. Most people cannot stand either physical or cultural isolation and will seek certainty in a community of people or a culture. The cultural security of Americans traditionally has been found in a society of some tension, but a society in which a balance could be achieved between individual freedom and liberty on the one side and the social good on the other. The alternative now offered, the security of equalization, is depersonalizing. It is a deceptively angelistic conception of man in society. It is one that cannot be sustained. It will in all likelihood move people in search of security, if not identity, to accept greater and greater socialization of their lives.

•

The second issue is economic opportunity—the chance to work as well as the chance to enjoy leisure and other benefits of work.

Samuel Gompers, the great leader of the early American labor movement, declared that if one person in America is out of work, we should redistribute existing work so that this person might be employed. Yet, in the course of the last presidential campaign, with 7 million potential workers unemployed and another estimated 7 million underemployed, organized labor ran advertisements advocating the eight-hour day, five days a week of work, and overtime.

A recent Harvard study reports that people in the United States who are employed are working more hours a year than ever before in modern time—on average 160 hours a year more today than in 1969, or the equivalent in hours of a full month of work.

A Brookings Institution report estimates that if the overtime being worked in the United States were distributed, it could give work to approximately 3 million of the unemployed. The average overtime being worked per week is approximately three and a half hours a week, or about 8 percent to 10 percent above the basic legal-hours level. If the current trend continues, the average American will be working sixty hours a week by the year 2020.

Overwork is not just the mark of overachievers, workaholics, and hyperconsumers, according to the Harvard study, but of almost everybody: those in high-income groups, middle-income classes, poorer classes, and the working poor. Two-income families are becoming the norm rather than the exception. Women are entering the workforce and are present in it in unprecedented numbers. Latchkey children have vastly increased in number, and the demand for preschools, kindergartens, and post-school care has increased.

The Japanese, now working an eight-hour-day, six-day week, are considering shortening working time to five days a week, which would leave their workers laboring about 150 fewer hours a year than U.S. workers. Germany, where economic productivity per working person is the highest in the world, has shortened working time to the point where German workers work 300 fewer hours a year than their U.S. counterparts.

In other countries—Australia, the Netherlands, and France, for example—movements to lower average working time below forty hours a week have been successful.

Yet, despite all this evidence that it makes economic and social sense, the shortening of working time is opposed by both management and labor in the United States, by the government, and by most labor economists.

Corporate executives, in a survey conducted by Dr. Juliet Schorr of Harvard, expressed almost unanimous agreement that working hours must be increased even more in American industry if we are to be competitive in the "global market." Their arguments are comparable to those made by business and industry against Henry Ford's $5-a-day-for-eight-hours reform—introduced in 1914.

Ford held that workers not only had to be paid enough so that they could buy what they were producing but also that they had to be given enough time, in the case of the car, to at least drive to and from work. In 1926 Ford went to the five-day week, thus giving workers more time to drive, both during the week and on weekends.

Labor union leaders who denounce state right-to-work laws conversely defend the right of their own members to work overtime.

And the government has shown little interest in the issue, except on the negative side. The most memorable labor policy of recent years was that of the Reagan administration in 1981, when it suppressed action of the Air Traffic Controllers Association. The organization sought to gain a thirty-two-hour workweek for its members. The air traffic controllers received scarcely any support from organized labor, even when President Reagan fired the striking members.

Politicians, especially Democrats, in the face of organized labor's opposition, have been slow to act in any positive way on unemployment. In 1979 a bill to shorten working time was introduced to the House of Representatives. It had only thirteen sponsors and was never acted upon. A companion bill was never introduced in the Senate. A similar bill introduced in Congress in 1985 received even less attention than that which had been given to the 1979 measure.

The Clinton administration, early on, in what was referred to as a "stimulus package," proposed to provide jobs for 500,000 workers through expenditures of $30 billion. That would leave approximately 6.5 million workers without attention.

Moreover, public works expenditures make little sense in our current economy. Public works can stimulate our economy where jobs and dollars are scarce. But such spending will not work in an economy already burdened with excessive waste. And waste is the mark of the U.S. economy.

We continue to overproduce and overconsume automobiles that

are oversized and overpowered. We have produced and continue to produce unnecessary and obsolete defense materials and services. We carry on a space program without cost control or benefit measurement and carry an obligation to pay interest in the amount of more than $200 billion a year on the public debt. More pork-barrel spending hardly seems the solution.

Historically, the principal means of dealing with the general fiscal and economic disorders in the country has been unemployment supported by underemployment and overwork. This approach is costly, outmoded, and inhumane. The United States should be providing an example for the industrialized world. Instead it has become an economic and social backwater, standing still or falling behind while newer ideas, or old unused ones, reflecting changes in production and in social institutions, are adopted in other countries like Germany.

The Democratic administration and the Republican Congress are missing a unique opportunity to redistribute work. This is a far more equitable approach to economic stagnation than keeping some employees working full-time and overtime while others are dismissed. The government should reduce the working time of retained employees and spread work among those who would otherwise be dismissed. It should begin by doing this with its own workforce when cutbacks are necessary. It should require contractors and others doing business with the government, especially in military equipment and supplies, to do the same.

When mobilizing for war, we can act with dispatch and reasonable efficiency to make necessary change possible. Yet we resist mobilizing the economy for the purposes of productivity and social justice.

Adjustments to economic reckoning following the borrowing binge of the '80s have left us floundering and confused. But we can manage our economy to benefit people. And that means redistributing work.

Here is a simple principle of social decency and minimal justice: Employ the maximum number of people rather than a minimum of people working maximum hours.

Will this cost? Yes, it will. Some of the overtime pay that already-employed workers would have to give up to employ the unemployed might be returned to them in tax credits or breaks (and offset by more progressive taxation). And some lost income, frankly, would be lost. But what is the social cost of permanent unemployment and a permanent, or an expanded, welfare class?

And what is the social cost if the few who keep their jobs must work continually to keep them? Or if they must use more and more of their income to consume goods that serve (unsatisfactorily) as substitutes for free time with their families and genuine leisure? It's a question of what kind of society we want.

It has been half a century since Congress, with the federal Wages and Hours Act, adopted the forty-hour workweek and fifty-week working year. Add to that all of the progress in technology, automation, computers, and so on, yet the rule accepted by politicians and labor leaders remains the same: Those lucky enough to have a job must work forty hours—plus overtime. It is time to change the rule.

•

The third issue that deserves a full airing in the 1990s is civil liberties.

The country needs to face new threats to privacy posed by technology, new threats to civil association posed by technology and reform laws, and especially new threats to free speech. In part, this involves the attempt to regulate the Internet in a way that would destroy it. But the threat to free speech today primarily comes from politics and government.

Whereas the threat to free speech and association in the 1950s came from Joe McCarthy and anticommunism (a sort of ism or counter-ism in its own right), the threat in the 1990s has been from political correctness, left and right (sometimes a convergence of the two). The threat today is from a less aggressive but just as pernicious form of political conformity. Today, Americans are even told how to be patriotic.

Several times in the 1990s, the House of Representatives and the Senate have considered a constitutional amendment to outlaw flag burning. The amendment, no doubt, will be back. Forty-nine state legislatures already have taken action indicating their willingness to approve such an amendment when Congress sends it to them. The only thing that has stood in the way has been a few votes in the Senate. And that barricade may now be gone.

The movement to "defend the flag" by prohibiting protest speech follows two Supreme Court rulings (one in 1989 and another in 1990) that protected flag burning as a form of political expression— the one form of speech most clearly intended to be protected by the First Amendment in the Bill of Rights.

Rallying to the flag (as well as to religion) at the expense of what is symbolized is not a new phenomenon. In the 1950s the cross and the flag were used as props in the anticommunist movement.

A "god" float was included in the first Eisenhower inaugural parade. The president-elect composed and read his own prayer for the occasion (Billy Graham was not yet, fully, Billy Graham). In the same period the words "under God" were included in the Pledge of Allegiance to the flag.

Constitutional amendments were proposed in that era to declare the United States to be "a Christian nation." One amendment provided that non-Christians, such as Jews and others, be required to take an oath that was different in form and content, and presumably directed to a different deity, from that to be taken by Christians.

Dennis Chavez, senator from New Mexico at the time, was moved to challenge the abusive use of religion: He spoke on the Senate floor, defending both his Spanish forebears and his religion, declaring, "My ancestors brought the cross to America and you have made a club of it."

George Bush invoked both flag and God in his campaign of 1988. While George was asking the people to "read my lips," his wife reported that she and George knelt each night and prayed out loud—a clear discrimination between people and deity.

But when Bush made an issue of Michael Dukakis's action as governor on a "pledge of allegiance" issue, no rhetorical response comparable to that of Senator Chavez's was elicited. It should have been challenged, at least, by the simple observation that the persons who seemed most ready to show the flag were automobile dealers (especially those selling Japanese cars); people running roadside stands, who in the South generally also display the Confederate flag; and people who have two or more homes, with the flag usually shown at the country or ocean or lakeside establishment. One seldom sees the flag flying Barbara Fritchie–like out of the windows of apartments on Fifth Avenue in New York, but they are everywhere in evidence in places like Southampton, Cape Cod, and other watering holes.

The flag "defenders" should be reminded that both flags and oaths are and have been respected and treated seriously in Western culture.

The traditional sanction of the oath was the deity. This, in times when taking the name of the Lord in vain was looked upon as a grievous fault.

The taking of an oath, to flag or deity, should be limited to important decisions and commitments and should be a matter of dignity and solemn affirmation. Children should not be conditioned to take an oath casually, nor should it be used as a device to establish order at the beginning of a school day.

It has been the tyrannies, the absolute monarchies, the totalitarian states, and the governments of those civilizations that are uncertain of themselves, and that exist in fear of collapse, that have made oath taking and recognition of signs and symbols a regular, rigid, and universal requirement. For example, in the Nazi period in Germany, each time a citizen met another on the street, he took an oath of allegiance, or declared his allegiance to Hilter and Nazism, with a sign and the words "Heil Hitler."

Respect for oath taking was strongly held by the Founding Fathers. The conservative Alexander Hamilton, for example, opposed the expurgator oath designed to root out the Tories in New York State. The oath, he said, "was to excite the scruples in the honest and conscientious and to hold out a bribe to perjury." "Nothing," he said, "can be more repugnant to the true genius of the common law than such inquisition into the conscience of men."

The members of the current Congress, in the tradition of Joe McCarthy, George Bush, and others, are again exploiting patriotism and loyalty, a matter far more serious than frivolous and unreflective oath taking. It is an action that does more than just erode the First Amendment. It is a frontal attack, running in the face of Tocqueville's assertion, and Jefferson's and George Mason's belief, that freedom of speech and of expression is the first and fundamental condition for establishing and maintaining a free society.

If one were to reach for rhetoric, approaching that used by Dennis Chavez in his defense of a religious symbol, the cross, one would charge that the advocates of this amendment are prepared to take the flag—the symbol of American freedom and specifically freedom of speech—and make a gag of it.

17

Inalienable Duties

*T*he Declaration of Independence makes clear reference to the "inalienable rights" of all men. Among those rights, it declares, are three of particular political significance: life, liberty, and the pursuit of happiness.

The *duties* of citizenship, essential to securing and sustaining these inalienable rights, are not mentioned directly in the Declaration of Independence or in the Constitution, but their necessity and reality were implicit in the very conception of self-government. What are the fundamental responsibilities, or inalienable duties, of the citizen? They are (1) to defend the country, (2) to pay taxes to meet the costs of government, and (3) to participate in the political actions that are essential to self-government.

I

There was no searching inquiry into defense and into war making at the Constitutional Convention, but providing for the common defense is listed as one of the fundamental purposes of the new government. The inclusion of the right to bear arms in the Bill of

Rights was related to the need for national as well as personal self-defense. It was not included to protect the rights of squirrel or people hunters.

As early as 1785, well before he became president, Thomas Jefferson recognized the need for military and naval operations when he wrote to John Jay from Paris: "Our people are decided in the opinion that it is necessary for us to take a share in the occupation of the ocean, and their established habits induce them to require that the sea be kept open to them. . . . Therefore," he continued, "we should in every instance (even at the cost of war) preserve an equality of right to them in the transportation of commodities, in the right of fishing and in the other uses of the sea."

As president, Jefferson took action against the Barbary pirates. His later experience with the embargo of American goods and his observation of the War of 1812 moved him to an even stronger military position. Although he did not go so far as to support Alexander Hamilton, who wanted a standing army, he came to believe that serious thought must be given to the maintenance of a military establishment, which he thought should be, in a democracy, based upon universal military service or liability for such service. He wrote to James Monroe in 1813: "It is more a subject of joy that we have so few of the desperate characters which compose modern regular armies. But it proves more forcibly the necessity of obliging every citizen to be a soldier. This was the case with Greeks and Romans and must be that of every free state. . . . We must train and classify the whole of our male citizens and make military instruction a regular part of collegiate education. We cannot be safe till this is done." The safety he was concerned with related to two threats: outside military action against the United States and the internal danger of a mercenary, nonrepresentative army.

At the outbreak of World War I, the United States had a navy of limited readiness and an army numbering about 200,000 officers and men, which included 67,000 National Guardsmen. A draft registration act was passed on June 3, 1916, and another in 1918. Overall, 24.2 million men registered, of whom 2.2 million were actually inducted.

In 1940 a draft act again was passed as preliminary to full involvement in World War II. In 1951 that act was extended for twenty years, to meet the needs of the Korean War, and it was then allowed to expire during the Nixon administration. This era, 1941–1971, was the only prolonged period during which the United States, in effect, did have a universal military service program. Not all males of eligible age were called up, but all were formally subject to the draft.

Before the act was allowed to die, it had been—first in the Johnson administration and then in the Nixon administration—thoroughly corrupted through the granting of many exemptions, especially to students of almost every kind, in an effort to insulate the war from Americans who might be most likely to criticize it if they or their children were forced into it. Since the Johnson administration believed that the Vietnam War would end quickly, it did not anticipate having to answer for its exemptions. But the war did not end quickly, and the Nixon administration followed a similar policy of exemptions, with the addition of a new device under which a potential draftee could decide within a range of three or four years when he would be subject to the draft.

As the war was winding down in the early 1970s, the draft law expired. No attempt to extend it was made in the Nixon administration, and the drive to establish a large "volunteer" army was initiated. This proposal was supported by militarists, based on their belief that only militarily minded people, either by their nature or by their commitment, would make up the military forces. Consequently, the United States, they believed, would have a ready and uncritical military force.

Antimilitarists in general and anti–Vietnam War activists in particular accepted and supported the volunteer proposal because they thought that their consciences, and the consciences of others in the future, would be eased if they would not have to perform military service.

The volunteer army idea has not worked well. The Department of Defense has not been able to attract enough capable and qualified persons to the armed services. Our armed forces are far from a cross section of the U.S. population; our military is unrepresentative of the nation. Standards of admission have been lowered; financial and other benefits have been increased; cash bonuses for enlisting have been offered.

The volunteer army has been a designation for what is essentially a mercenary army. Alexis de Tocqueville and others have warned that such a military is the most dangerous and undesirable type for a democratic state. This is especially true when a major function of our military is to act as an army of occupation, or as a presence—as ours is in Europe, in Japan, in Korea, and in other parts of the world.

II

The second inalienable duty recognized in the Constitution is the responsibility of citizens to pay taxes. The revolutionary slogan "Taxation without representation is tyranny" is credited to James Otis. Otis did not say, "Taxation with representation is tyranny" or that taxation in itself is tyrannical, or that, in the ideal state, citizens would pay few or no taxes. The Sixteenth Amendment, the so-called income-tax amendment, was the last formal acknowledgment on the part of the people of the United States of their willingness to pay taxes "to pay the debts and provide for the common defense and general welfare of the United States," as stated in Article 1 of the Constitution.

Recent U.S. presidents and presidential candidates seem to have a different attitude toward taxes. Candidate Jimmy Carter said that the federal tax code "was a disgrace to the human race." As candidate, and as president, Ronald Reagan generally opposed taxes, while annual federal deficits run to hundreds of billions and the federal debt is well into its third trillion. Reagan's slogan, in the Otis manner, might well be a declaration in favor of representation without taxation, which, in its consequences, may well be as tyrannous as the colonial taxation without representation.

Opposition to paying taxes is not limited to presidential and other candidates and officeholders. Antitaxation programs are sustained by individuals, by their representatives, by lobbyists, by foundations, by corporations. The drive to eliminate tax paying, to avoid payment, or to be exempted is manifest at all levels of tax paying and directed against nearly every form of taxation, but it is especially evident at the higher and lower levels of income-tax liabilities.

The reasons given for exempting citizens from tax obligations are multiple. Such words as fairness and equity are invoked regularly. Concern is voiced for the poor and for people in low-income brackets. Efficiency in the administration of tax law, simplification of the code, stimulation of business, encouragement of capital formation and savings—all are among the reasons or justifications offered. Lobbyists and various representatives—individual and institutional—are quick to take credit for eliminating high-level income-tax obligations or for reducing them. Politicians generally—Republicans and Democrats, liberals and conservatives—claim credit for reduction or elimination of tax obligations at the lower end of the income scale.

But paying taxes, like voting, is a basic, if minimal, act of citizenship.

There are roughly 131 million potential "taxable units" in the United States. Of these, it is projected that about 108 million will file tax returns. Some 20 million people, or taxable units, will not file because of income insufficiency. Of the 108 million filers, about 17 million will pay no taxes this year; 23.7 million will pay no taxes when the most recent tax reform bill is operative.

When the 1986 tax bill was under consideration, Democrats and Republicans boasted of the number of people who would be excluded from paying the basic federal taxes.

Approximately 50 million of 130 million potential taxpayers (or approximately 38 percent) will pay no taxes (that is, basic income and capital gains taxes to the federal government), thus creating two classes of citizens—one paying basic taxes and the other exempted for varying reasons from fulfilling, even in a minimal way, this obligation of citizenship.

John Wesley is supposed to have said that, even in the church, some small financial contribution should be expected, if not extracted. Certainly the same would seem to be true of support for civil government, even though the rate is very low. Tocqueville reported that in 1831, during his visit to the United States, fifteen of the existing twenty-four states required property ownership, military service, or tax payment as a prerequisite to voting.

III

I have described what has happened to two of the inalienable duties of citizenship—military service and paying taxes. The third is participation in political action and decisions.

Jefferson warned that if the people became indifferent to politics and to government, the magistrates (an early version of the bureaucrats) would take over. Although there were serious restrictions on suffrage in the early decades of our national existence, those who had the right to vote evidently took their responsibility seriously.

Tocqueville was greatly impressed by what he saw or was told, for he wrote in *Democracy in America* in 1831: "To take a hand in the government of society and to talk about it is his [the American citizen's] most important business and, so to say, the only pleasure he knows." He continued, "If an American should be reduced to occupying himself with his own affairs, at that moment, half his existence would be snatched from him; he would feel it as a vast void in his life and would become incredibly unhappy."

In each succeeding election, the percentage of eligible American voters who cast their ballots drops to its lowest level ever. Between 50 percent and 70 percent of qualified American voters regularly decline to vote—the higher number occurring in off election years. In 1996, 260 million people, or 78 percent, did *not* vote for Bill Clinton.

Undoubtedly many voters have been kept from participating by unreasonable registration and residence requirements; by state laws giving special preference to the Republican and the Democratic parties; by laws making it difficult for third- or independent-party candidates to get on the ballot; by machine voting, which makes write-in campaigns practically impossible; and by restrictive party rules.

Some analysts attribute declining and low voter turnouts, in part, to such factors as the high mobility of the American population, disenchantment with the conduct of politics, and the deadening and distracting effect of television.

But are these adequate explanations?

After every campaign, politicians and press deplore low voter turnout. Thus, as each campaign approaches or begins, they encourage political participation and support "get out the vote" drives. At the same time that the drives for voter participation go on, legislative and political actions of various kinds discourage citizens from full participation in politics. Whereas the poll tax has been outlawed as an impediment to participation in political action, in its place, public records and reports of financial contributions, even minimal ones, are now required in many states. Complicated reports are required in many jurisdictions.

But more significant than all of these local and state controls and interferences with basic and fundamental participation in politics is the Federal Election Campaign Act as amended in 1975–76. The law not only sets severe limitations on financial contributions to campaigns but also provides for government financing of political action with operating control centered in the Federal Election Commission.

Not only does the 1975–76 law limit and discourage individual contributions and commitment, but it encourages and strengthens intermediary organizations (the political action committees) to further depersonalize politics and come between citizen and politics and government. Whereas individual contributions to a campaign are effectively limited, the same amount contributed through a PAC is multiplied in power, but only at the sacrifice of the independent judgment of the contributing citizen.

•

And so we find ourselves, almost at the start of a new millennium, an American republic lacking in republican virtues. The three inalienable duties of citizenship have been seriously compromised. First, we have compromised military service with the initiation of the volunteer (mercenary) army; second, we have exempted many of our citizens from responsibility for supporting the government by paying taxes; and third, we have transferred fundamental responsibility for political action from citizens and voluntary associations to the government and governmentally approved political units, the PACs.

The renewal of citizenship—the sort of public happiness the Founders knew, celebrated, and expected—is already twenty-five years overdue.

18

The View from Eighty

EDITOR'S NOTE: We end this book with five looks backward that are biographical in nature. Two are from interviews, one is an intellectual biography—in sketch form—in Gene McCarthy's own words, and the last two are poems.

From *Chronicles* magazine, July 1996.
Bill Kauffman is the interviewer.

Q: What happened to the good old Midwestern Progressive/Populist tradition? From Bob LaFollette to Richard Gephardt is a mighty long fall.

A: You see it in Minnesota, where some of the old Farmer-Laborites strongly opposed the fusion of the Democrats and Farmer-Laborites back in 1944. They said they would lose the spirit of Ignatius Donnelly and the old Progressives and the Non-Partisan League. I think the conservative force in Minnesota was actually the labor movement. They became pretty much establishment; it came to a head in the 1968 campaign.

The party lost its bearings in '68 on the issue of the war in Vietnam. If [Hubert] Humphrey hadn't been the candidate, the Democratic Farmer-Labor Party would've been the most anti-war party of any state in the union because they had the double tradition: the isolationism of the Farmer-Laborites, some of them opposed even to our involvement in World War II, and the internationalist Jeffersonian strain that had come from some of the old Democrats. But with Humphrey as the candidate advocating the war, why, the traditional position was rejected and the party became simply an instrument of the national party.

Q: Isn't it odd that in 1968 the most prominent antiwar figures in politics and music were both Minnesota poets, Eugene McCarthy and Bob Dylan?

A: Well, I wasn't recognized as a poet. Dylan came out of the northern part of Minnesota, which was pretty radical: the most radical labor faction in the state was the Iron Range. Bob didn't do much in Minnesota politics. . . .

What happened to the party is that it accepted the Great Society, which was really quite foreign to the tradition of the Non-Partisan League and the Farmer-Laborites. They also were not a welfare-directed political movement. It was more like the New Deal: They were going to change the structure and let welfare disappear because people didn't need it. [Lyndon] Johnson supposedly thought he was completing the New Deal, but actually the Great Society was an abandoning of the New Deal, whose main thrust was to provide work and a decent income. The emphasis in the Great Society was we're going to have more food stamps and more help for the poor and more rent subsidies and more Medicaid provided by the government; I think that's where they lost it.

Q: As far as I can tell, no major American politician writes his own speeches, let alone his own books, anymore. Should this concern us?

A: I think it's a serious matter. I can see where presidents need help, because they're writing for history. I never thought [John F.] Kennedy's speechwriters were well chosen . . . When Biden's [Sen. Joe Biden of Delaware] plagiarism was exposed, I was critical of him because he didn't plagiarize anything from me: the ultimate insult! He had a quotation from Bobby Kennedy, and Adam Walinsky went public and said Biden had plagiarized Kennedy, who'd plagiarized Adam. It's like a surrogate mother: If the kid turns out well, she says "it's mine!" For scholars of the future, it'll be like reading T. S. Eliot and asking, "Where did he get this? Who was the ghostwriter?"

Q: You've run for president both within and without the two-party system. Where do you prefer to be?

A: John Adams said the worst thing we could have under our Constitution was politics controlled by two strong factions. There are three or four things on which the Progressives ought to be committed, but they seem indifferent. One is abolition of the federal election law, which they should have opposed in 1974–75 because it actually legalized the two-party system. You force politics into two parties, then you force it into confrontation, especially when you have an administration that can't be overthrown except every four years. The federal election law denied political freedom and set up the process by which the corporations and corporate PACs have become the dominant force in American politics.

Q: How do we break the two-party stranglehold?

A: I don't think we can get Congress to do it. Jim Buckley and I and a few others took the federal election law all the way to the Supreme Court. The New York ACLU joined us, but the liberal Democrats didn't support us.

Q: Newspapers and television and radio stations are owned today by chains and faceless conglomerates. How do we break up these concentrations?

A: Newspapers are privately owned—you run into freedom of speech but there's nothing to keep us from limiting the owner-ship of television and radio licenses. Newspapers probably shouldn't be allowed to own a television station, or at least not more than one, because then the TV stations are dependent on the government.

Q: The Washington press corps never tires of boasting how fear-less and independent they are. Did you find them so?

A: *The Washington Post* is practically a house organ for any admin-istration, and it's big into telecommunications. The only way you can have freedom of speech is to have more people speak-ing, and I suppose that is the most serious threat to personal and political liberty in the country: the concentrated control over television and telecommunications.

And there are other things we ought to be concerned about in a free and open democratic society: the redistribution of eco-nomic power. The way I see it, the way to progress is to go to a six-hour workday.

Q: How do you do that without massive intervention by the federal government?

A: We did it in 1938, when we went to the eight-hour day, five-day week, and retirement at 65. What you've got now is a modern-day enclosure movement. Every time AT&T lays off 10,000 people, the market goes up. It's like Adam Smith: Throw the serfs off the land and you'll be more productive. Old Sam Gom-pers in 1893 said if one man is out of work, you ought to have a redistribution of work until he's absorbed. Now we say, who cares? Put 'em on welfare.

It's unrelated, but we've come to accept the protection of in-come which comes from capital rather than income produced by labor. So we have to pay for government out of taxes on income and on wages, while we've progressively exempted capital. The old Progressives, the Henry George people, said the only things you should tax are land and capital gains.

We ought to have a capital levy on accumulated wealth. It's a better plan than taxing the next generation and the one after that—let's tax the two that are gone. Paul Mellon, in a recent book, said he didn't know how much wealth he had; he didn't even know how much was accumulated every year. We ought to call people like Paul Mellon and say, "Paul, we worry about you. You don't know how much wealth you've got; you might not have any. So what we're going to do is start taking it away from you until it gets down to where you recognize it. When you can count your money, Paul, raise your hand and we'll stop taking it away."

Q: You spoke in 1968 of the "militarization of American life." How have we been changed by our fifty-year experience with what George Washington warned against: an "overgrown military establishment"?

A: Alexis de Tocqueville warned about democracies creating a military establishment that was bigger than needed, for it becomes a republic within a republic. And that's what we have now.

Q: To some extent, isn't this the result of defense commitments made by Democrats in the 1940s?

A: I went to Congress in 1949, and we cut the defense budget before the Korean War to, I think, $16 billion a year. Then the war came on, and it went up and never came down again. The military-industrial complex was not in place in 1950, it was only after the Korean War that they put their marbles in a row. . . .

You could see the military-industrial complex developing though in the 1947 Defense Reorganization Act and in the changing of the War Department into the Department of Defense. I called the Pentagon and asked, How did this happen? There must have been a meeting where somebody said, Look, we're gonna change the name of this damn thing, because if we call it the War Department people are gonna say, "Where's the war? And if there isn't one, where are you gonna have it?" And we don't want to answer that question. So let's call it the Department of Defense because defense is unlimited. And it's true: We never declare war anymore. We just declare national defense.

And then they did away with the draft. The volunteer army is really a mercenary army. The militarists said we want an army that is there because they want to fight. They're under contract and will fight any kind of war. The liberals said, we want an army in which we don't have to fight if we don't want to; you can stay out of a war you don't like. In Desert Storm, some of the soldiers said they signed up, they have a contract, and so they gotta fight. And some of the people who might have been critical of the war said, "They signed up; they gotta fight." So it insulated a military action from any kind of social or moral judgment.

Q: You've written of "our loss of control over our foreign and military policy." What do you mean by that?

A: There was really no decision on Desert Storm; it was kind of a happening. I suppose it started, linguistically, when [Richard] Nixon called the Cambodian action an "incursion." It was the first incursion in history. You wonder where they get a word like that. There's no verb for incursion. You can't incurse. In an invasion, you invade; an incursion, on the other hand, is an existential happening. Who, me? Who decided? It just happened.

They started to call Grenada an incursion, but it worked too well so they called it an invasion.

Now that communism is gone, they're building up the real danger: Islamic fundamentalism! Allah is coming. I thought we'd done in Allah in Desert Storm. It's crazy. Bhutto argued that Pakistan should have a nuclear bomb, that Islam was the only major religion that didn't have the bomb. The Christians got their God and they got their bombs. The atheists have lots of bombs but no God. The Israelis got the bomb to go along with Yahweh, but he was never very reliable, he just had tricks: Blow the trumpet and the walls will fall, stop the sun in the sky. In Islam, all they had was Allah, and Allah really needed some support.

Q: You have bemoaned the "personalization" of the presidency. What do you mean by that?

A: Harry Truman was the last really constitutional president. He knew when he was president and when he was Harry Truman. He had respect for the Senate in foreign policy. He knew what the House of Representatives was. He respected the role of the courts. When he attempted to take over the steel companies and was overruled by the court, he backed down, but he went to the court for a test. On the other hand, when Kennedy had trouble with the steel companies, he had the FBI and IRS call the people up and say, We're going to look at your reports. Johnson brought them into the White House, and said: If you fix prices in my presence, it's all right; if you do it in Pittsburgh when I'm not there, you're violating the antitrust laws.

Q: This strange notion of the presidency as a "bully pulpit" from which to sound off about dirty movies, national malaise, etc.—is this one aspect of personalization?

A: It is. Nixon said, "I'm the moral leader of the country." Well, who the hell said so? Who ever said the president was supposed to be the moral leader?

Q: So if you had been elected in 1968, you wouldn't have used your office to campaign against free verse?

A: No, I'd concentrate on the real range of presidential responsibility. When Arthur Schlesinger defected to Bobby Kennedy from my campaign, he said I didn't have a conception of the strong presidency. He said I'd have been a president like [James] Buchanan. That was a hell of a thing to say, because nobody knows what Buchanan was like. If he'd said I'd be like [Ulysses S.] Grant, why, it means I'd have been a drunk, but you say Buchanan and everybody imagines the worst.

Q: Political reporters were befuddled by your habit of quoting [G. K.] Chesterton. Would you describe your politics as distributist?

A: Part of it is distributist. I used him in opposition to the federal election law and the reform of Congress. He said that the Puritans always kill St. George but keep the dragon; that's Common Cause. The distributism of [Hilaire] Belloc and Chesterton is not quite pertinent today. They had an idea of small shops and plots of land; we need distribution now in communications, politics, work.

Q: What do you make of the restoration of Richard Nixon's reputation?

A: I say just let him rest. I've always thought the worst thing he did was not Watergate; it was the enemies list. To use the power of the FBI and IRS to persecute people, to "teach them a lesson," was essentially fascist.

Q: In the 1960s the Democrats had men—you, Sen. William Fulbright, Sen. Richard Russell—who understood that there were limits to power, both at home and abroad. Do you see any current Democrats in that same tradition?

A: Sam Nunn seemed to have some idea of what to do with the military-industrial complex, but most of it was supportive. He was like Henry Jackson: a force, but not for good. They moved in when Jackson died. They had to have another "if you knew what I knew" guy. I don't think Nunn quite proved out. . . .

Q: My guess is that you're the only presidential candidate in recent years who would repeal several constitutional amendments.

A: I'm pretty skeptical of every amendment adopted after the anti-slavery amendments.

Q: What about the direct election of senators?

A: You have to have direct election because there's hardly any relationship between the way state legislators think now and the way senators ought to be thinking. Part of the problem is that party politics has been taken over by governors. They change the dates of the primaries not to provide for a more open politics but to get more control. For example, moving the New Hampshire primary up to mid-February. I had made the case that the time for it was March 15, when the sap was rising in the maple trees and the New Hampshire people were awake. February is the month in which human life is at its lowest ebb. The mind slows down and the body slows down—there's been no good results since 1968.

II

**From *Believing*, by Eugene Kennedy, Doubleday, 1974.
Kennedy is the interviewer.**

I turn the question to politics and to McCarthy's own conception of his role in 1968, asking whether or not he perceived it as possessing religious significance. He does not answer right away, but with the voice of a man who has thought a lot about these questions, he goes on.

"Well, I thought we did have something going, a real movement. I think we had a constituency of conscience. Then we were saying to the country that we had problems that were serious and that we had to approach and deal with. Now I think George McGovern was almost a pure Methodist preacher in the way he approached the American people. He didn't have that context of meaning I think is important. He was asking the people to be against something, to make a moral judgment on somebody else. The country didn't respond and the reason was simple. They didn't want to make judgments on themselves.

"In 1968 we didn't want to make judgments on Lyndon [Johnson]; we were not interested in imputing moral fault to him. That wasn't the issue. When people get into these positions of power the conditions that affect them make them see the world very differently. It's like ITT. Those people live in another country, and once in a while they come out and see the way the rest of us have to live. You can't be believable without the right context. I think that is really what George didn't have.

"I met a young man in an airport in 1972. It was almost like something out of the Old Testament. He said to me, and this was before the election, 'Nixon will win. The people won't vote against their own guilt.' You know, that was a remarkable statement. I almost expected to see the young man depart in a chariot into the skies, as though his life had been justified by that insight.

"McGovern didn't offer the people any salvation, just condemnation. But Nixon said something like, 'I'm okay. You're okay. We're guilty together.' But he never moved beyond that. While he was saying that, McGovern kept telling the people they were all guilty. Nobody in that campaign offered pardon or any clear and decent way of salvation. I think the people could have been moved; they could have been helped to understand the issues such as those on poverty or individual liberties or the other things that are really at the heart of life. I think that is what we tried to offer, a context that gave us a clear way of dealing with our problems, admitting them, and of finding some kind of real salvation through changing ourselves."

He does not seem harsh or bitter, but it is clear that he feels he did something purposeful and honest, something he believed in and something he feels made him a believable candidate.

"We're all defining our meaning all the time. We're engaged, as some philosopher said, in a revolt against the unbelievable and against irrelevance. But somehow we've got to get these issues into perspective so that people can recognize them as genuinely religious. We have to work it down where it reaches the people who don't go to church anymore. . . .

"I think the young people do have an idea about a priesthood of service, that they want to do something to help the rest of the world. They're really looking for leadership, for somebody to show them how to do that effectively. The young sense that they don't know what they want to happen; the tragedy is that they don't feel they could make it happen even if they did know. They don't have any representation, and they feel that there are forces they cannot influence that are directing their lives. We need somebody to represent this kind of impulse. It's not the same kind of thing that George Wallace said, although he came closest, I suppose, to trying to speak for the average man. He said, in effect, that he really didn't represent people but that he would take care of them. He said, 'I won't let them bother you; I won't let them bust your children, tax your house, or send your boys to war.' "

McCarthy pauses again, thinking of what? He shrugs and goes on, "I think we need somebody to represent our deeper aspirations in a clearer and less selfish way. I think that Moltmann in his *Theology of Hope* said it up to the point we are now, to the point where it had to be said. We're really the ones who have to carry it on."

He turns back to his own political vision for a moment. "We tried to offer a way of redeeming society, to let America admit that it had been wrong and that we have to pay more attention to the poor and that we have to care about individual liberty. I think that it is a religious thing, that is the kind of thing that gives hope. I just don't think you can divide these things. . . ."

The subject shifts to prayer, and after being interrupted by a brief phone call, McCarthy goes on. "I don't know how you define prayer. I suppose it is saying, 'Here I am,' and letting yourself have a chance to reflect on life and on God. I always thought vespers was a pretty good thing for that. There was incense and there was a pretty good mood to it; it was at the right time of day—in the evening with no pressure connected with it. Every other religious service had to have some other special intention and vespers just wasn't loaded down with this. It had something of the freedom of the dance in it, especially at solemn vespers." The poet is obviously speaking again, with prayerful times remembered that can no longer be found in a crowded and noisy world. "And, of course, you don't have vespers anywhere anymore."

I ask him whether being a poet did not make a person stand on the front lines as some kind of a man of prayer at this time in history. He picks up the book of poetry from which he had read before and, smiling gently at a thought that he likes but would have hesitated to say for himself, he says, "I wrote a preface for this book that may have something to say about what we've been talking about. It goes like this:

> The ancient map makers used the term terra terribilia to identify what was beyond their knowledge of the earth. A notion on one of these maps describes the terra terribilia in these words:

> *All beyond is nothing*
> *but dry and desert sands,*
> *inhabited only by wild creatures*
> *or dark impassable bogs,*
> *of Scythian cold*
> *or frozen sea,*
> *beyond which there is nothing*
> *but monstrous and tragical fiction.*
> *There the poets*
> *and inventors of fables dwell.*
> —From the preface to *Other Things and the Aardvark.*

"I wrote that book as a tribute to American poets, for men like Robert Lowell, William Stafford, Reed Whittemore, James Dickey, Philip Booth, and the many others who have written of this country and of its people. These poets have gone beyond the 'known' and the 'certain' into the terra terribilia in the search for truth."

That is where McCarthy stands, a believer who, in his own way, will always be trying to find the path into the dark forest that surrounds the modern world.

III

From *Once a Catholic,* by Peter Occhiogrosso, Houghton Mifflin Co., 1987. (This version is edited and adapted from the original.)

I was born in Watkins, Minnesota, which was, like so many other towns in the Midwest, a place of no visible distinction. The town had two doctors, one Catholic and one Protestant, and two hospitals with maybe four rooms apiece. My [maternal] grandparents had married in Germany and had come here as part of the emigration that followed the Revolution of 1848. My father's father, who was Irish, died shortly before I was born. I'm told that he was something of a scholar and historian. He was particularly learned about the British treatment of the Irish over the years. My maternal grandfather, Chris Baden, founded a mill and became a blacksmith because there wasn't one in town. His appeared to be the only German family in a sea of Irish.

My mother was a pillar of tolerance and strength, security, and gentleness. Her life was not one of "quiet desperation" but rather of quiet hope. My father died in 1973 at the age of ninety-eight. His life span, one-twentieth of the time since Christ, covered the period of the greatest technological change the world has ever known. He was born in 1875 on a 160-acre farm in central Minnesota. He bought cattle in Minnesota, North Dakota, South Dakota, and Montana for shipment to the South St. Paul Stockyards. He also worked as the postmaster in Watkins until he was ousted by the Democrats after Woodrow Wilson won the 1912 election. That turned him against the Democrats, but after he wasn't reappointed by the Republicans following their return to power in 1920, he had even less regard for the GOP.

The Irish in Minnesota were strongly influenced by Archbishop John Ireland, a Republican who banned the Jesuits from the state. My father was tolerant of priests, doubtful of all politicians, generally suspicious of doctors, and slow to take pride in sons or daughters. He was wary of seed dealers and farm organizers. "Watch out for farmers," he would say, "who put signs at their gates or let people paint ads on their barns that read, 'Member of Farmers' Organization,' or 'De Laval Cream Separator Used Here.' The next sign you'll see there will be 'Farm for Sale.'" As we drove through the countryside, he observed, "You can tell a German's farm from an Irishman's. The Germans start with a big barn and a small house. The big house comes later. The Irish start with a large house and a small barn. Neither is ever changed."

The core of culture in Watkins and the adjacent country was the church or, rather, religion. Our church was named St. Anthony's—not after St. Anthony of Padua, who was known for his power to help people find lost objects, but for another St. Anthony. Our St. Anthony was one of the desert fathers best known for having resisted the temptations of the devil, who appeared at his desert hut in the form of a pig. Just what the temptation was, and how it was presented through the pig, was never made clear. In any case, the pig's appearance before St. Anthony and his rejection of same were represented in four stained glass windows set above the confessional on the south side of the church. I was especially attracted to these windows because, as was clearly indicated in the glass, they had been donated by my father, M. J. McCarthy, in memory of his father.

The pig in the window was small and rather attractive. In repelling it, St. Anthony had a staff in hand, and there it was, above the confessional most used by the parish priest, on the side of the church where the afternoon sun lit up the stained glass and made the confessions less threatening. The confessionals on the darker, north side of the church were used by visiting missionaries who probably attracted people who either had more serious sins to confess or who had not gone to confession for a long time. Fallen away from the church, they were now returning in the shadows.

The parish priests were, in order of succession, Fathers Willman, Roemer, and Bozja. They all spoke German and English, which was necessary in that parish, and they gave sermons in both languages at the same Mass. The rosary, which was said on Wednesday nights in May, was recited in German, but Stations of the Cross were in English. High Mass was sung in a mixture of Latin and German, but children's Masses were in English, as I recall. We used to say that sins were committed in English, confessed in German, and pardoned in Latin. Vespers were in English, but the hymns were in high Latin, particularly "Salve Regina" and "Tantum Ergo." But the hymn that we used to wrap up the more serious devotions, such as forty hours or High Mass, "Holy God, We Praise Thy Name," was sung in German.

Religious instructions were the province of the Benedictine nuns who ran the school. They placed an adequate emphasis on guilt, but not enough to develop in us the neurotic hang-ups that have been duly reported in those ubiquitous memoirs—or possibly imaginations—of Catholic childhood. That sort of thing was simply not as prominent in the Midwest as it may have been in other parts of the country. Sins were classified, of course, into mortal and venial and, above all, the sacrilege, which left an indelible mark on the soul. That was a particularly meaningful phrase at a time when we still used indelible pencils, the kind that when dipped in water or moistened with saliva would leave a mark on your tongue or hand like a tattoo, lasting for weeks.

The only sacrilege we could remember ever having occurred took place after a couple of boys shooting marbles in the church basement (which was allowed in winter months) came to blows. Sister Lucretta, who had the reputation of being the toughest nun in the school, stepped in to break things up when one of the boys, apparently swinging away while still on his knees in shooting position, struck her accidentally below the belt—or in her case, below the rosary.

Sister Lucretta immediately announced that a sacrilege had been committed—the consecrated body of a bride of Christ had been struck.

As young amateur moralists, we held that since it had been an accident, no true sacrilege had been perpetrated. Nonetheless, we watched the kid closely for the next few months to see if any physical change might afflict him, maybe a withering of the hand.

Other than that event, sins were basically broken down into the areas of obedience: fighting, stealing, and lying. And of course, there were the sins against the Sixth Commandment. Swimming naked in Clear Water Creek, for example, was considered a matter for confession, although that was really a seasonal sin. Skating with girls was suspect, depending on how you held them—crossed arms behind the back was banned.

But if there was guilt, there was also plenty of forgiveness available and easy atonement. In addition, we had more than our share of protective and supplemental prayer practices: plenary and partial indulgences, making the nine First Fridays—to which we added the nine First Saturdays—forty-hour devotions, and missions. There were a few girls who fainted regularly during the First Friday ceremonies, including my sister. The fainting was considered a sign of piety, and the possible effect of fasting from midnight was discounted as an explanation.

Watkins was about twenty miles from Collegeville, home of St. John's Abbey. After I finished high school at St. John's Prep, I went on to college there. In my first year in college I decided that ideas were important and that I wanted to pursue an academic career. The only two professions recognized at the time were law and medicine, and neither one attracted me.

The school itself grew out of a Benedictine base that was established in 1856, when a Benedictine priest, two clerics, and two brothers arrived in Minnesota Territory under the auspices of Bishop Cretin of St. Paul. At the time, "Yankees"—German and Irish Protestants from New England—were moving to the area in expectation of statehood being granted. Between 1854 and 1857, the population of the territory grew from 32,000 to 150,000.

The prime mover behind all this was a Benedictine monk and future abbot named Boniface Wimmer, who obtained a grant from Ludwig, king of Bavaria, to provide clergy for Minnesota's 20,000 German Catholics to prevent their seduction by the Methodists. Over a hundred years later, the Methodist threat may still be palpable, since all the best Catholic basketball players prefer to go to Hamline University, a Methodist institution, instead of the Benedictine St. John's.

By the 1930s the college had begun to take on a distinctive character, largely through the direction of one of the monks, Dom Virgil Michel. Father Virgil was a man of broad, almost universal interests who, before his death in 1938, had set in motion or promoted three significant programs. One was the liturgical movement, a sophisticated and historically advanced application of the Benedictine commitment to work and prayer as the essence of the creative and re-creative role of man. The second area was social action—he moved the school and the monastery to a deep and continuing concern for social justice, which was the Catholic emphasis in the 1930s.

Finally, the school supported rural cooperatives, agricultural economies, and the Catholic Rural Life Movement. The leader here, Monsignor Ligutti, had worked to integrate the coal-mining industry, if it could be called that, of Granger, Iowa, with agriculture. He moved from that to leadership in international agricultural policy and programs and, eventually, as adviser to popes, to a house on the Appian Way. The last time I saw him, at the Rome airport, I said, "Monsignor, it's a long way from Granger, Iowa, to the Appian Way, isn't it?" He answered, "No," and raised his eyebrows.

"Distributive justice" was the controlling and directing intellectual concept of the day, as opposed to our current words like equality— which was never mentioned in either the Declaration of Independence or the Constitution—or fairness, which has neither historical nor philosophical bearing. At St. John's Abbey, I met Dorothy Day and Peter Maurin of the Catholic Worker movement, the apostles of the poor. They denounced the "gospel to the rich," and they did not distinguish between the deserving and the undeserving poor.

I remember Dorothy for many things, but most fondly for a remark attributed to her at the time when, during extremely cold weather in New York, the Mott Street quarters were heated minimally by turning on the gas oven and opening the oven door. When someone observed that this was a rather expensive and inefficient way to heat an apartment, Dorothy supposedly said, "The poor are never economical."

I also met the Baroness de Heuck, who later married a man named Eddie Dougherty, who led another group concerned about the poor, especially blacks, in an organization called Friendship House. The baroness startled the monks in one of her lectures—it may have been the last she ever gave on campus—when she said the coming revolution would include monks hanging like dead crows from the telephone poles along the twelve-mile highway from the monastery to the city of St. Cloud.

I finished my college course at St. John's in three years, mainly to relieve my parents of the cost of another year's education, and tried to make a living. But after applying for several teaching appointments and receiving none, I decided to go on to graduate school in September 1935. I tried to borrow enough money from my hometown bank to finance one quarter at the University of Minnesota grad school—about $200, including room and board. But I was refused for lack of collateral, and ever since I've favored government loans for college students, which didn't exist at the time.

Eventually I got a teaching job and for the next four years taught high school English and coached basketball and baseball at various times. Those years were memorable mostly for testing my patience and endurance. The one clear breakout from boredom, near despair, was graduation exercises, because I could really sense the joy of the students. Most graduates weren't going on to college and had been educated beyond their parents' level. And for the parents, the graduation was the realization of their own lost hopes. That visible joy and satisfaction made the long, boring months of the term seem pretty much worthwhile.

Since I'd obtained a master's degree while teaching, I returned to St. John's as a faculty member. The years there, and after World War II on the faculty of St. Thomas College in St. Paul, were considerably more stimulating. During those years the Catholic intellectual movement flourished. The core of the movement was medieval studies, especially a revived study of Thomistic philosophy and natural law. Jacques Maritain was the acknowledged leader and spokesman, but there were also Étienne Gilson, Ives Simon, Christopher Dawson, and others. The writings of G. K. Chesterton and Hilaire Belloc were included for spice and accent. Teilhard de Chardin gave scope to the cosmology of the time. Dom Verner Moore and Abbot Butler, with later contributions from German theologians such as Karl Rahner and Hans Kung, helped set the stage for the Vatican Council meetings to come. For artistic support we read the novels of Evelyn Waugh, Graham Greene, Léon Bloy, Georges Bernanos, Dorothy Parker, and J. F. Powers, and two poets, Allen Tate and Robert Lowell. Also active at the time were popular Catholic apologists, like Fulton Sheen, and converts, like Heywood Broun and Clare Boothe Luce.

The years from 1946 to 1948, when I was elected to the House, were good ones. In my courses on social problems, I used to emphasize the need for federal legislation in housing, medical care, education, economic security, and civil rights, and I argued for the need for political action to achieve that. But I still hadn't given any thought to direct participation. That came almost by accident or default.

There was a lot of political activity in Minnesota in 1946, which involved a professor on the St. Thomas campus who was interested in the reform of the Democratic Farmer-Labor party, an effort being led by the then mayor of Minneapolis, Hubert Humphrey. They nominated me as their party chairman in the spring of 1948, and by early summer I'd decided to run for Congress against an incumbent Republican. It was a good year for Democrats and, running with Harry Truman, I got elected.

In the House my main concerns were civil rights legislation, which had become a central plank in the Democratic Party platform, and political economy. The critical committee was the House Ways and Means Committee, with jurisdiction over taxes, social welfare including social security, and trade. Later, in the Senate, I served on the comparable Finance Committee. For sixteen of my twenty-two years in the Congress—four in the House and twelve in the Senate—I served on those two committees. They were good, productive years in which the general welfare was advanced further, I believe, than in any other sixteen years in the history of the country.

I think the Congress from 1945 to the passage of the civil rights legislation was a good time whether one was a personal success or not— just being a part of that Congress was an honor. As to particulars, I could list half a dozen things I am proud of. I consistently challenged that anticommunist zealotry of the '50s. I offered amendments to protect the job security and the privacy rights of government workers, which was not very popular; I debated Joe McCarthy in 1952 on national radio when nobody would debate him. I escorted a Catholic writer and layman, John Connally, up the aisle when he was being questioned by the House Un-American Activities Committee.

I made a speech against Joe McCarthy three months after his famous West Virginia speech to the Holy Name Society of Montgomery County. I had only been in Congress about two years. I said that Holy Name Societies really ought to take up more than God's name. I said, "God can pretty well take care of His name—what you ought to be concerned about is the abuse of the good names of some persons being attacked by Joe McCarthy."

I had a feeling that if others had stood up against McCarthy the whole fervor and paranoia of that period could've been blunted. A lot of the things that happened in the 1950s that destroyed people's lives and had a terrible impact on society could've been stopped if people of greater stature in Congress had stood up. They could not get anyone to debate Joe McCarthy; nobody in the Senate would take him on. I knew he was Irish. He was just kind of bullying people. He said to me before the radio program aired [live], "Gene, we don't want to have this be an Irish brawl, do we?"

Then there was the struggle over the Vietnam War, which really began, from my point of view, in the Senate and the Senate Foreign Relations Committee, led by William Fulbright. At a certain point, the arrogance of the administration was such that it became clear that we would have to take the issue to the country. And we did. The young people and the academic community were responsive. The Democratic Party and, at first, the Catholic Church were not.

In Vietnam, the Catholic population was concentrated in the south, so the church position was closely identified with them, even though eventually there were bishops who said, "Let's stop it, it's gone far enough." But in the beginning, to a large extent, Catholics supported the war because of the Catholic missionaries—and Protestant missionaries, too.

I do think the church could play an important role in American political life now, the way it did in the 1930s, but it needs to refocus on dignity, work, and social justice. . . .

Also, I am still hoping that Christians and humanists in America will find a way to challenge corporate power, which depersonalizes everyone in the corporation. The church is pretty dependent on corporate contributions, and the Catholic schools certainly are. But the whole area of individual liberty is more and more restrictive, and the church ought not just to speak in general principle but lay out four or five actual programs—jobs, education, health, and housing—as we had in the New Deal and press for economic security of some kind. Still in all, it does seem the church is running a little bit ahead of the Democratic Party.

When you ask me if the current government would qualify as a "Christian" government the way I outlined it in my book *Frontiers in American Democracy*, I'd have to say that, while it's relative, I don't think it's as Christian or as humane as one could have said the government was in the '30s or in the early postwar period. I say that on two counts. One is its belligerency or militarism of our foreign policy, which gets into a religious area. The other is the question of social justice. Even though in terms of poverty and so on, things are better than they were in the '30s, the human involvement and the playback from the economy to the person are less humane than they were then.

Lament of an Aging Politician

The Dream of Gerontion is
        my dream
and Lowell's self-salted
night sweat, wet, flannel,
        my morning's
shoulder shroud.

Now, far-sighted I see the distant
        danger.
Beyond the coffin confines of
        telephone booths,
my arms stretch to read, in vain.

Stubbornness and penicillin hold
the aged above me.
My metaphors grow cold and old,
My enemies, both young and bold.

I have left Act I, for involution
and Act II. There mired in
        complexity
I cannot write Act III.

Courage at Sixty

Now it is certain.
There is no magic stone,
No secret to be found.
One must go
With the mind's winnowed learning.
No more than the child's handhold
On the willows bending over the lake,
On the sumac roots at the cliff edge.
Ignorance is checked,
Betrayals scratched.
The coat has been hung on the peg,
The cigar laid on the table edge,
The cue chosen and chalked,
The balls set for the final break.
All cards drawn,
All bets called.
The dice, warm as blood in the hand,
Shaken for the last cast.
The glove has been thrown to the ground,
The last choice of weapons made.

A book for one thought.
A poem for one line.
A line for one word.

"Broken things are powerful."
Things about to break are stronger still.
The last shot from the brittle bow is truest.

Index